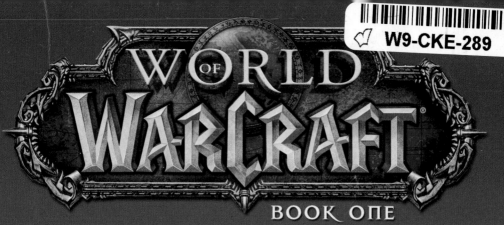

WORLD OF WARCRAFT

BOOK ONE

Writer: Walter Simonson
Penciler: Ludo Lullabi
Inker: Sandra Hope
with Richard Friend (#2)
with Philip Moy (#5&7)
Colors: Randy Mayor
with Carrie Strachan (#5&6)
Letters: Nick Napolitano (#1-2), Steve Wands (#3-7)

Collected Edition Cover and Original Series covers by Samwise Didier
Original Series covers by Jim Lee
Original Series Cover #7 by Ludo Lullabi and Sandra Hope
Special thanks to Jean Wacquet and Olivier Jalabert

For Blizzard Entertainment:

Chris Metzen, Senior VP—Creative Development
Shawn Carnes, Manager—Creative Development
Micky Neilson, Story Consultation and Development
Glenn Rane, Art Director
Cory Jones, Director—Global Business Development and Licensing
Jason Bischoff, Associate Licensing Manager

Additional Development:
Samwise Didier, Evelyn Fredericksen, Ben Brode, Sean Wang

Blizzard Special Thanks: Brian Hsieh, Gina Pippin

For DC Comics:

Jim Lee, Editorial Director
John Nee, Senior VP—Business Development
Hank Kanalz, VP—General Manager, WildStorm and Editor
Kristy Quinn, Assistant Editor
Ed Roeder, Art Director
Paul Levitz, President & Publisher
Georg Brewer, VP—Design & DC Direct Creative
Richard Bruning, Senior VP—Creative Director
Patrick Caldon, Executive VP—Finance & Operations
Chris Caramalis, VP—Finance
John Cunningham, VP—Marketing
Terri Cunningham, VP—Managing Editor
Alison Gill, VP—Manufacturing
David Hyde, VP—Publicity
Paula Lowitt, Senior VP—Business & Legal Affairs
MaryEllen McLaughlin, VP—Advertising & Custom Publishing
Gregory Noveck, Senior VP—Creative Affairs
Sue Pohja, VP—Book Trade Sales
Steve Rotterdam, Senior VP—Sales & Marketing
Cheryl Rubin, Senior VP—Brand Management
Jeff Trojan, VP—Business Development, DC Direct
Bob Wayne, VP—Sales

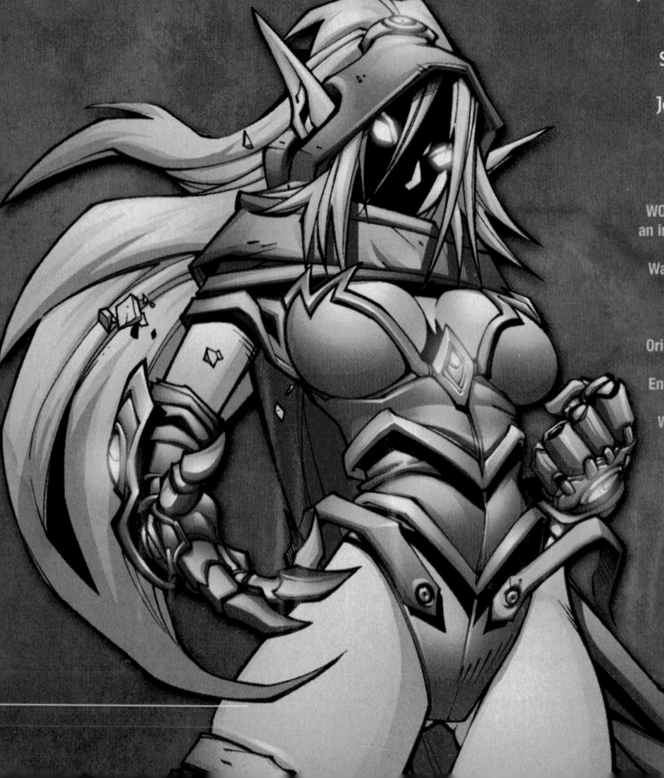

WORLD OF WARCRAFT Book One, published by WildStorm Productions, an imprint of DC Comics, 888 Prospect St, Suite 240, La Jolla, CA 92037.

Hardcover ISBN: 978-1-4012-1836-2
Softcover ISBN: 978-1-4012-2076-1

LICENSED BLIZZARD ENTERTAINMENT PRODUCT

INTERVIEW
With Walter Simonson and Ludo Lullabi

Gentlemen, let's talk about the genesis of the project—how did you "land" on WORLD OF WARCRAFT?

Ludo: I was interested in drawing a *Warcraft* adaptation even before the comic book series was created. I did some graphic samples, which were presented to Blizzard by my publisher in France (Jean Wacquet and Olivier Jalabert from Soleil). Blizzard liked the art style, and when WildStorm did their adaptation, I was hired!

Walter: WildStorm editor Scott Dunbier called me up out of the blue to ask me if I might be interested in writing a story based on the *World of Warcraft* online game. We talked about it a bit and it sounded like something I thought I'd enjoy doing. Simple as that.

Were you familiar with the Warcraft *universe and mythos?*

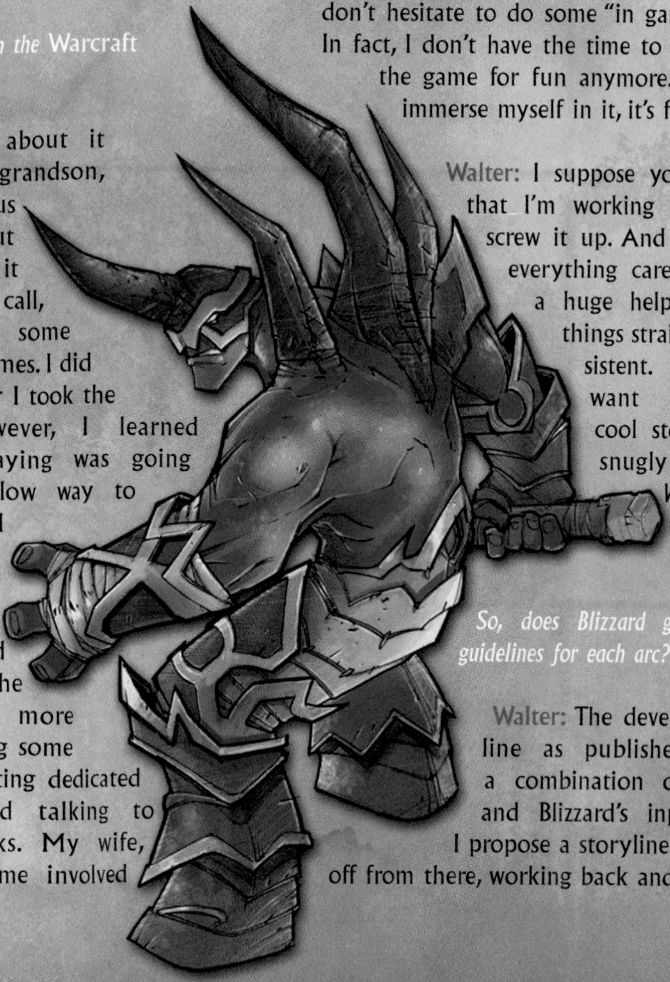

Walter: I knew about it because my grandson, Nikolai, is a serious *Warcraft* gamer—but I hadn't played it before I got the call, though I'd tried some console fantasy games. I did play for a bit after I took the assignment. However, I learned quickly that playing was going to be a very slow way to learn everything I needed to write a serious story set in the *Warcraft* universe. I could learn about the history much more quickly by reading some of the novels, visiting dedicated online sites, and talking to the Blizzard folks. My wife, Louise, also became involved in researching the Lore. There is so much of it that I needed all the help I could get! <g>

Ludo: I'm an avid player of the online game. Later on I started to play strategy games like *Warcraft III*, because they explore the mythology of *World of Warcraft* in more detail. The universe feels like home to me; its aesthetic is very close to my own graphic inclinations. My influences from American comics are Madureira, Ramos...that generation of artists born from video games and anime.

What is your approach to the mythos?

Ludo: I am trying to be as faithful as possible to the graphic guidelines of the game so that the players are not disappointed. If need be, I don't hesitate to do some "in game" research. In fact, I don't have the time to actually play the game for fun anymore. Each time I immerse myself in it, it's for work!

Walter: I suppose you could say that I'm working hard not to screw it up. And Blizzard vets everything carefully. They're a huge help in keeping things straight and consistent. Essentially, I want to tell a cool story that fits snugly into the *Warcraft* universe.

So, does Blizzard give you strict guidelines for each arc?

Walter: The developing storyline as published is really a combination of my work and Blizzard's input. Initially, I propose a storyline. We take off from there, working back and forth.

Ludo: I think Blizzard realized early on that my goal was to be very faithful to the look of the game. In that regard, as we shared the same objective, it became unnecessary for them to give me strict directions. They are still closely involved, making sure everything remains consistent and fits with the existing lore and themes of the setting.

Does the comic book version bring something new and / or different to the game itself?

Walter: I believe so. Taking my initial ideas for this first arc, Blizzard saw a storyline that could continue some narratives that hadn't been fully explored in the online game. So there's material in the comic based on the game but the comic also evolves beyond the game itself.

Great! What should we look forward to here?

Walter: Everything comic readers love: sex, death, betrayal! Some kick-ass fighting. And the beginning of the resolution of the fate of a character who disappeared from the *Warcraft* universe years ago. Just what you want to see in a *Warcraft* comic!

Are you going to be involved in subsequent arcs?

Walter: I am. Louise and I are going to be writing the next story arc in this ongoing WORLD OF WARCRAFT series.

Ludo: I just signed on for the third arc and am currently also working on WORLD OF WARCRAFT: ASHBRINGER with Tony Washington. For the rest, it will depend upon my super-busy schedule!

CHAPTER 0

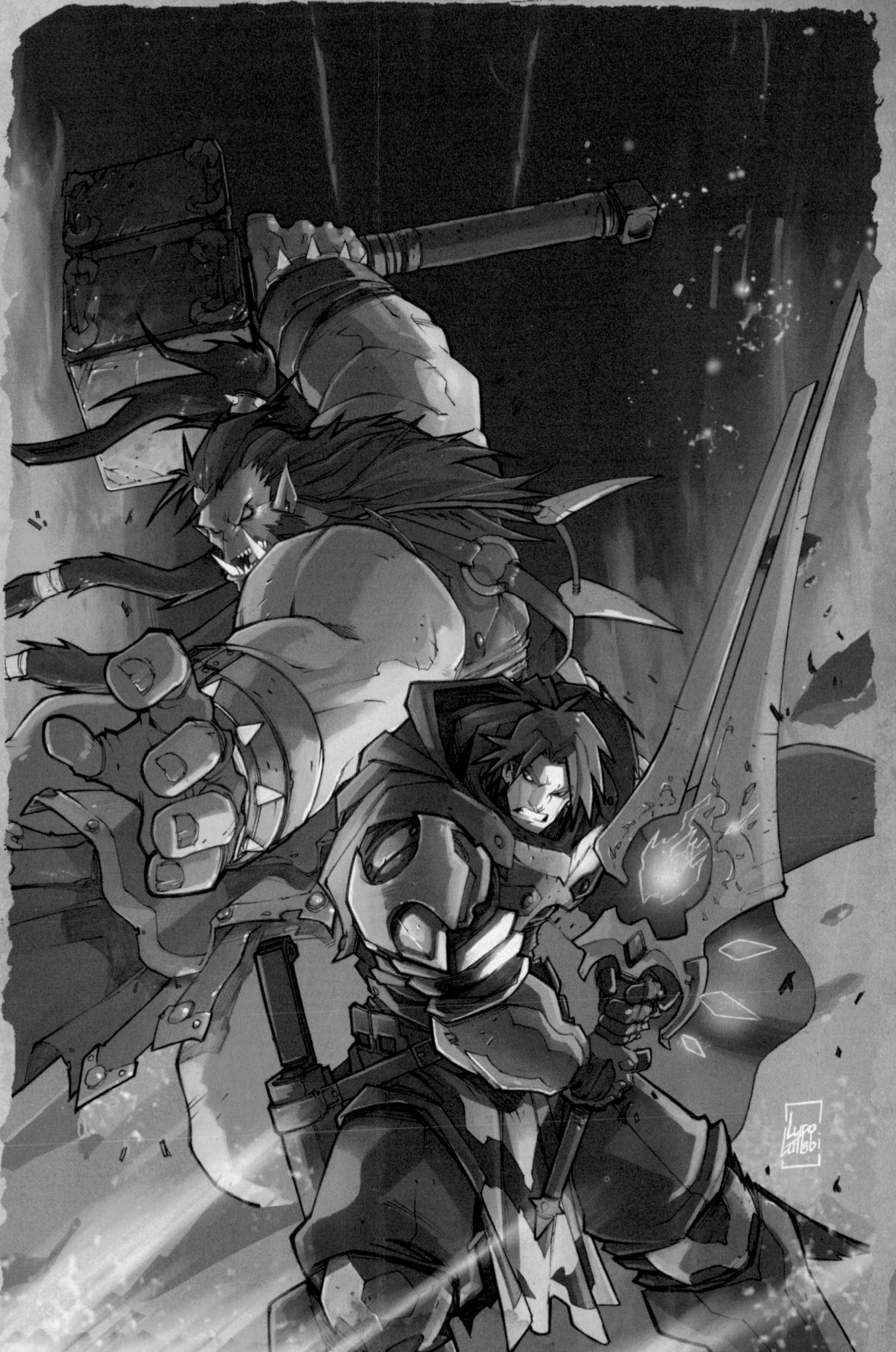

Ludo Lullabi

Blizzcon Exclusive Cover by Ludo Lullabi

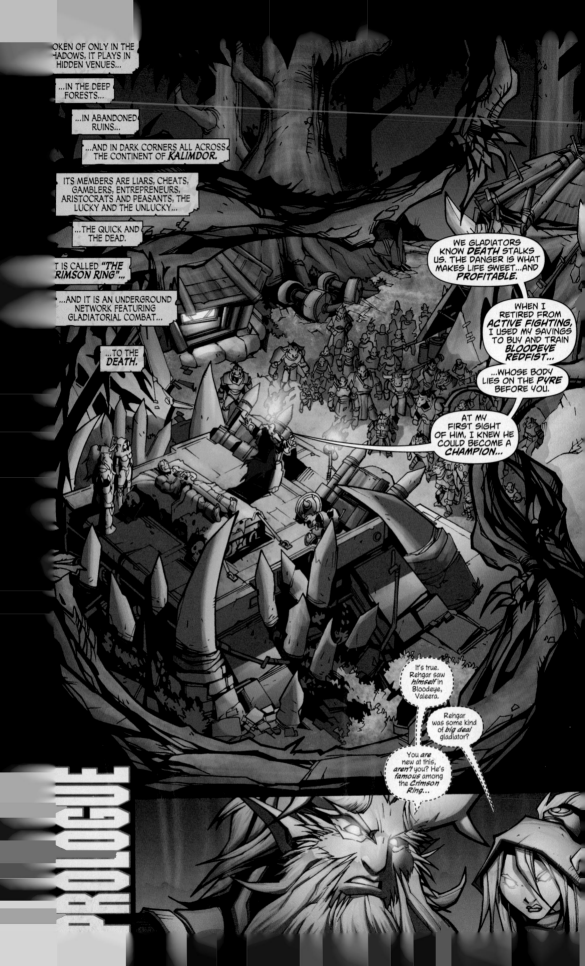

...OKEN OF ONLY IN THE
...HADOWS, IT PLAYS IN
HIDDEN VENUES...

...IN THE DEEP
FORESTS...

...IN ABANDONED
RUINS...

...AND IN DARK CORNERS ALL ACROSS
THE CONTINENT OF *KALIMDOR.*

ITS MEMBERS ARE LIARS, CHEATS,
GAMBLERS, ENTREPRENEURS,
ARISTOCRATS AND PEASANTS, THE
LUCKY AND THE UNLUCKY...

...THE QUICK AND
THE DEAD.

...T IS CALLED *"THE
...RIMSON RING"...*

...AND IT IS AN UNDERGROUND
NETWORK FEATURING
GLADIATORIAL COMBAT...

...TO THE
DEATH.

WE GLADIATORS
KNOW *DEATH* STALKS
US. THE DANGER IS WHAT
MAKES LIFE SWEET...AND
PROFITABLE.

WHEN I
RETIRED FROM
ACTIVE FIGHTING,
I USED MY SAVINGS
TO BUY AND TRAIN
*BLOODEYE
REDFIST...*

...WHOSE BODY
LIES ON THE *PYRE*
BEFORE YOU.

AT MY
FIRST SIGHT
OF HIM, I KNEW HE
COULD BECOME A
CHAMPION...

It's true.
Rehgar saw
himself in
Bloodeye,
Valeera.

Rehgar
was some kind
of *big deal*
gladiator?

You *are*
new at this,
aren't you? He's
famous among
the *Crimson
Ring...*

PROLOGUE

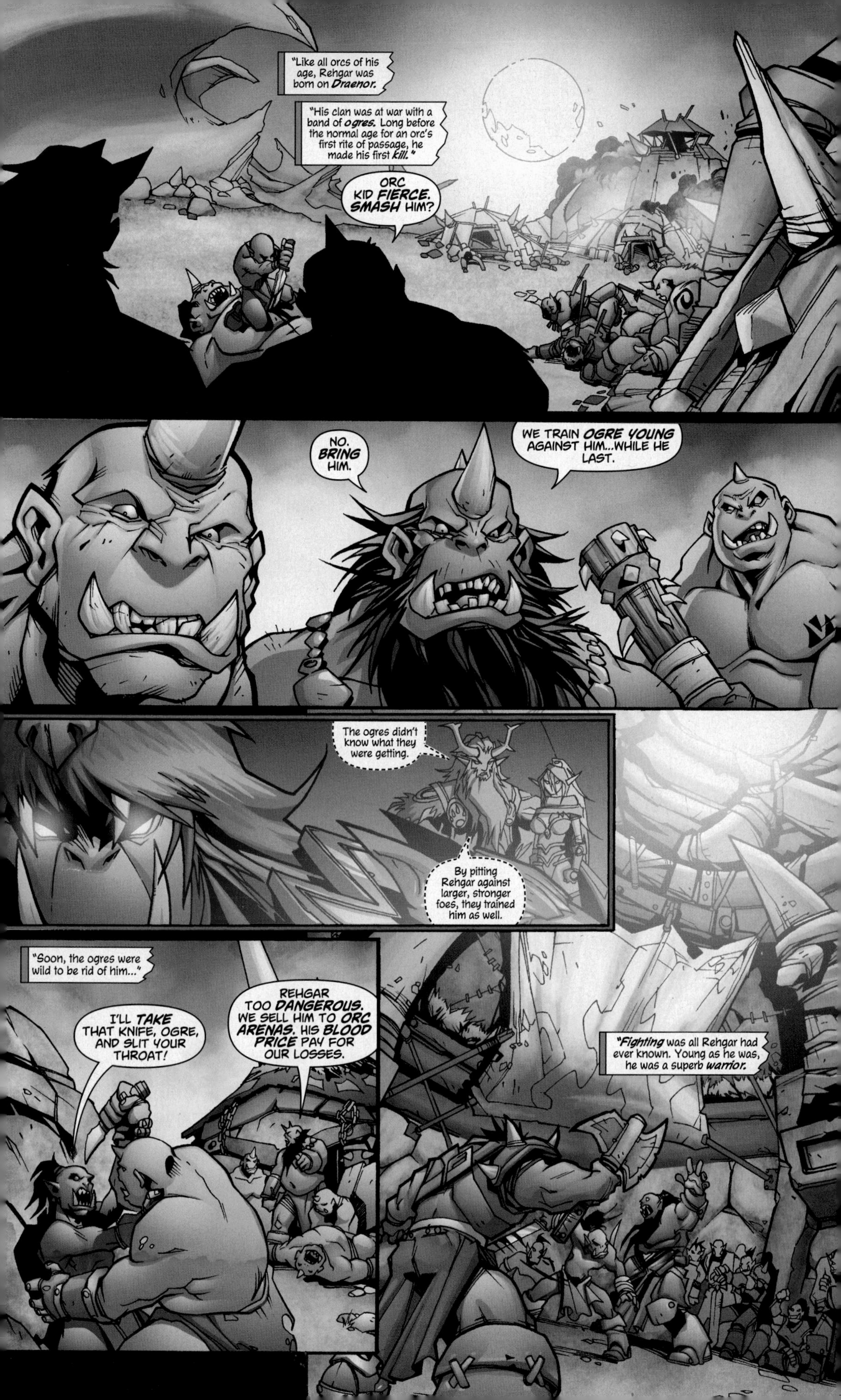
"Like all orcs of his age, Rehgar was born on Draenor.
"His clan was at war with a band of ogres. Long before the normal age for an orc's first rite of passage, he made his first kill."
ORC KID FIERCE. SMASH HIM?
NO. BRING HIM.
WE TRAIN OGRE YOUNG AGAINST HIM...WHILE HE LAST.
The ogres didn't know what they were getting.
By pitting Rehgar against larger, stronger foes, they trained him as well.
"Soon, the ogres were wild to be rid of him..."
I'LL TAKE THAT KNIFE, OGRE, AND SLIT YOUR THROAT!
REHGAR TOO DANGEROUS. WE SELL HIM TO ORC ARENAS. HIS BLOOD PRICE PAY FOR OUR LOSSES.
"Fighting was all Rehgar had ever known. Young as he was, he was a superb warrior.

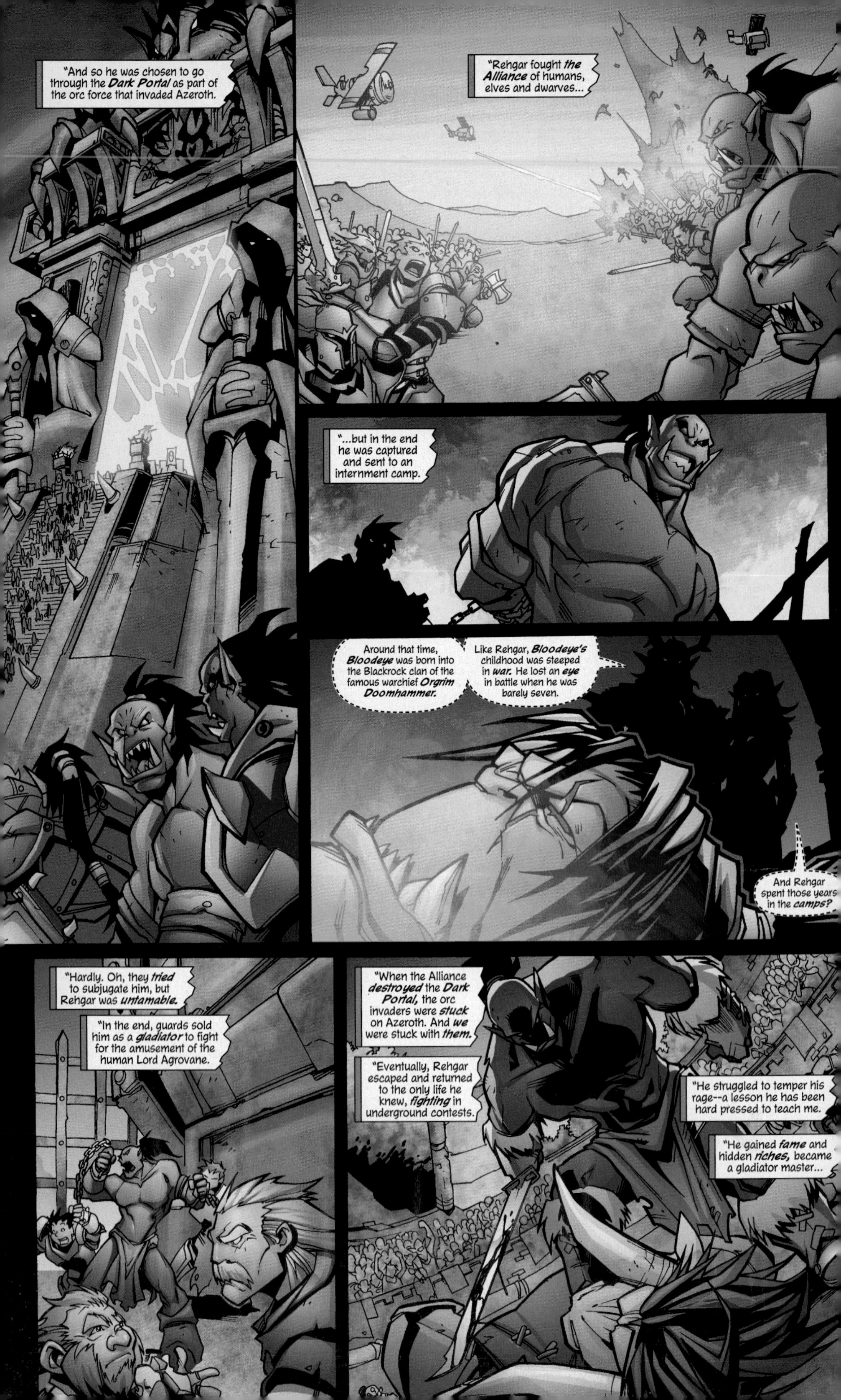
"And so he was chosen to go through the Dark Portal as part of the orc force that invaded Azeroth.
"Rehgar fought the Alliance of humans, elves and dwarves...
"...but in the end he was captured and sent to an internment camp.
Around that time, Bloodeye was born into the Blackrock clan of the famous warchief Orgrim Doomhammer.
Like Rehgar, Bloodeye's childhood was steeped in war. He lost an eye in battle when he was barely seven.
And Rehgar spent those years in the camps?
"Hardly. Oh, they tried to subjugate him, but Rehgar was untamable.
"In the end, guards sold him as a gladiator to fight for the amusement of the human Lord Agrovane.
"When the Alliance destroyed the Dark Portal, the orc invaders were stuck on Azeroth. And we were stuck with them.
"Eventually, Rehgar escaped and returned to the only life he knew, fighting in underground contests.
"He struggled to temper his rage--a lesson he has been hard pressed to teach me.
"He gained fame and hidden riches, became a gladiator master...

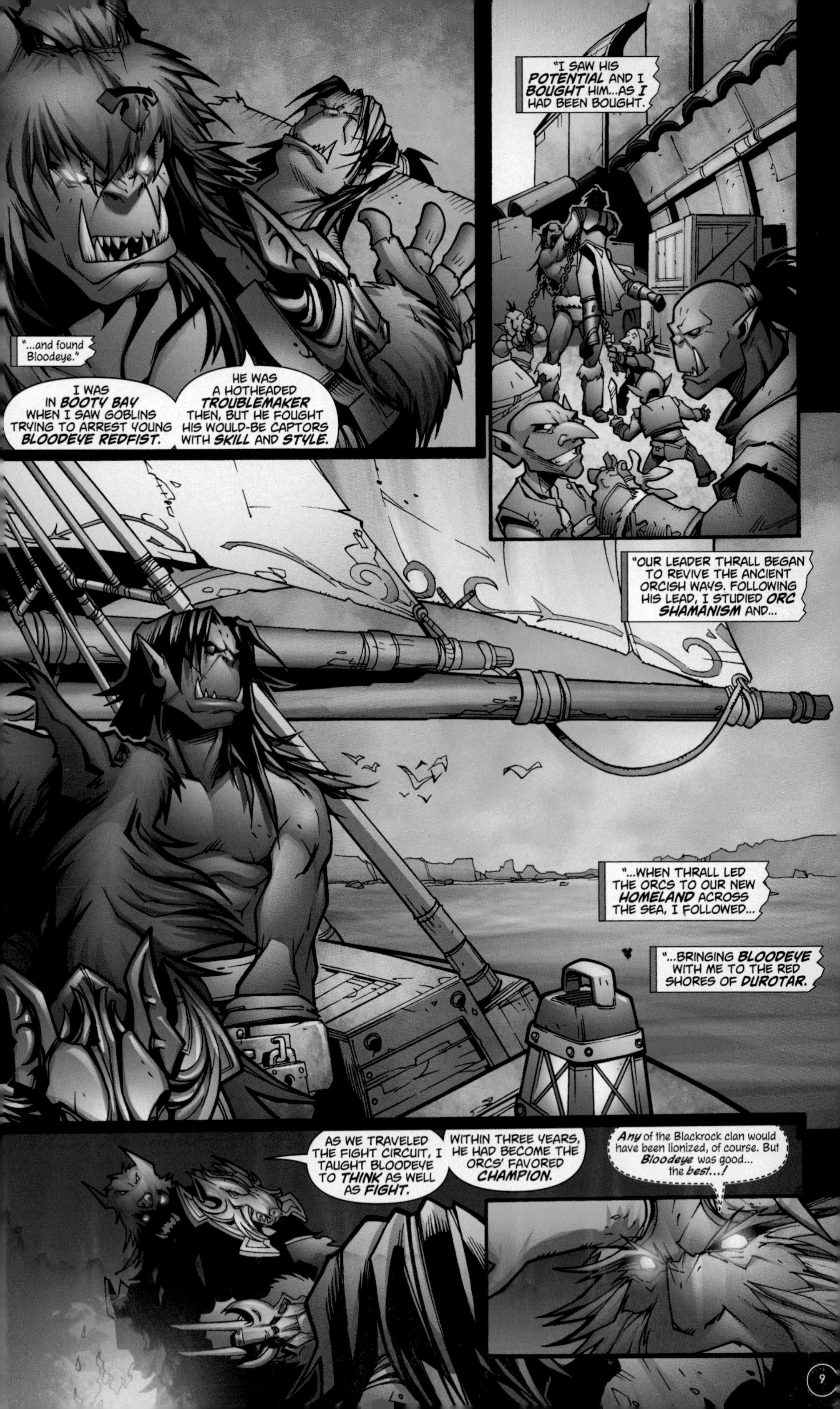
"...and found Bloodeye."
I WAS IN BOOTY BAY WHEN I SAW GOBLINS TRYING TO ARREST YOUNG BLOODEYE REDFIST.
HE WAS A HOTHEADED TROUBLEMAKER THEN, BUT HE FOUGHT HIS WOULD-BE CAPTORS WITH SKILL AND STYLE.
"I SAW HIS POTENTIAL AND I BOUGHT HIM...AS I HAD BEEN BOUGHT.
"OUR LEADER THRALL BEGAN TO REVIVE THE ANCIENT ORCISH WAYS. FOLLOWING HIS LEAD, I STUDIED ORC SHAMANISM AND...
"...WHEN THRALL LED THE ORCS TO OUR NEW HOMELAND ACROSS THE SEA, I FOLLOWED...
"...BRINGING BLOODEYE WITH ME TO THE RED SHORES OF DUROTAR.
AS WE TRAVELED THE FIGHT CIRCUIT, I TAUGHT BLOODEYE TO THINK AS WELL AS FIGHT.
WITHIN THREE YEARS, HE HAD BECOME THE ORCS' FAVORED CHAMPION.
Any of the Blackrock clan would have been lionized, of course. But Bloodeye was good... the best...!

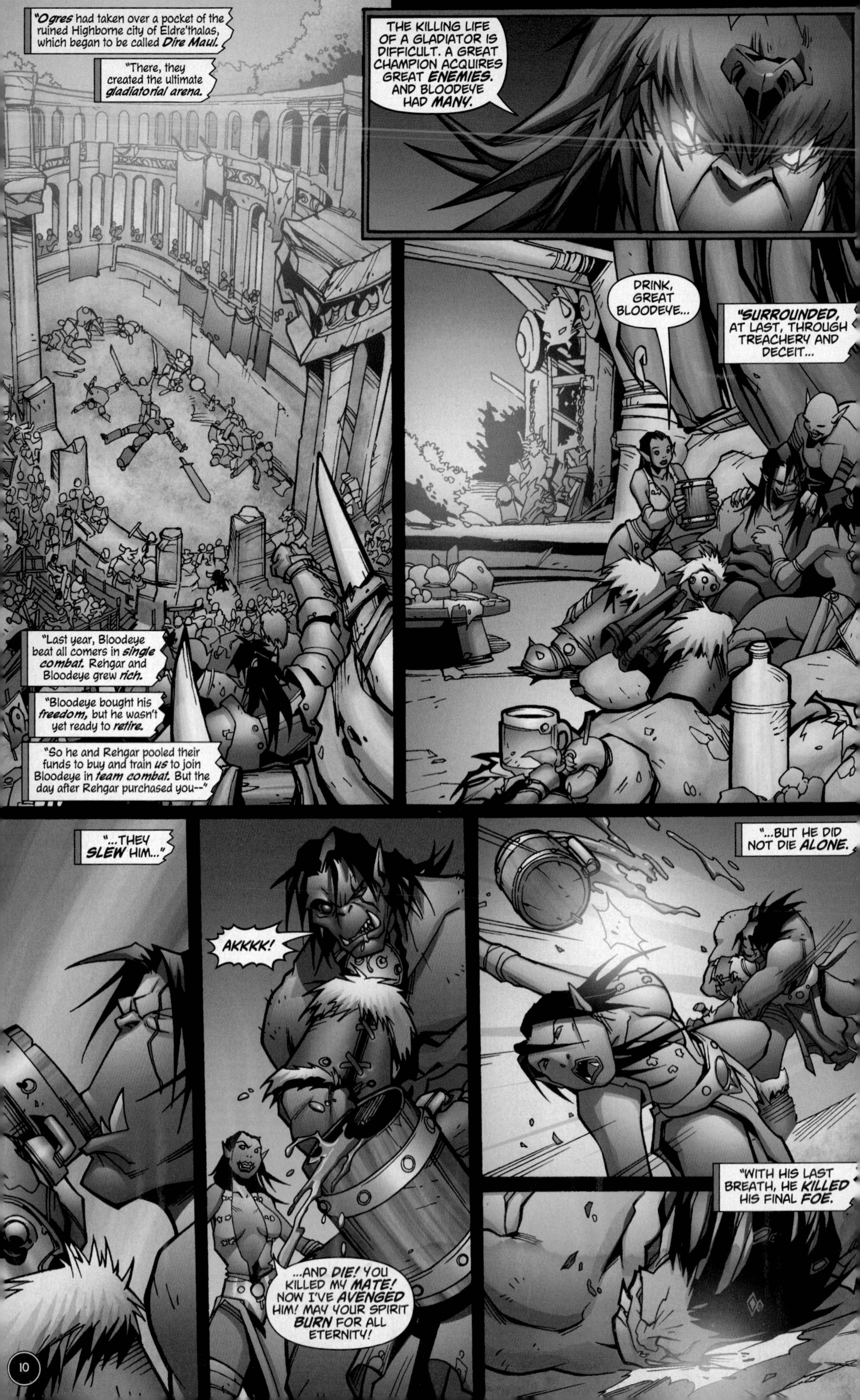
"*Ogres* had taken over a pocket of the ruined Highborne city of Eldre'thalas, which began to be called *Dire Maul.*
"There, they created the ultimate *gladiatorial arena.*
"Last year, Bloodeye beat all comers in *single combat.* Rehgar and Bloodeye grew *rich.*
"Bloodeye bought his *freedom,* but he wasn't yet ready to *retire.*
"So he and Rehgar pooled their funds to buy and train *us* to join Bloodeye in *team combat.* But the day after Rehgar purchased you--"
THE KILLING LIFE OF A GLADIATOR IS DIFFICULT. A GREAT CHAMPION ACQUIRES GREAT *ENEMIES.* AND BLOODEYE HAD *MANY.*
DRINK, GREAT BLOODEYE...
"*SURROUNDED,* AT LAST, THROUGH TREACHERY AND DECEIT...
"...THEY *SLEW* HIM..."
AKKKK!
...AND *DIE!* YOU KILLED MY *MATE!* NOW I'VE *AVENGED* HIM! MAY YOUR SPIRIT *BURN* FOR ALL ETERNITY!
"...BUT HE DID NOT DIE *ALONE.*
"WITH HIS LAST BREATH, HE *KILLED* HIS FINAL *FOE.*

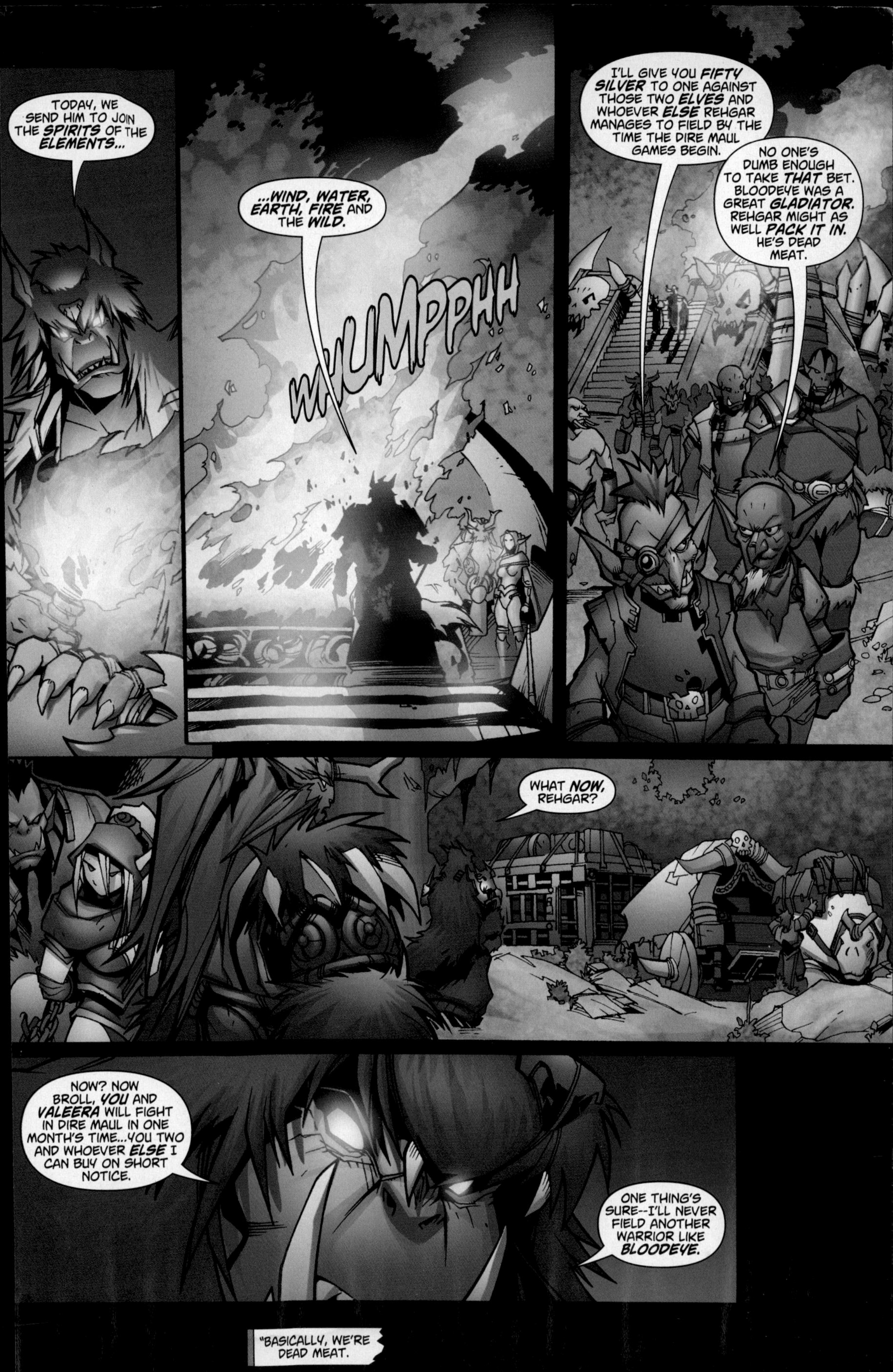
TODAY, WE SEND HIM TO JOIN THE SPIRITS OF THE ELEMENTS...
...WIND, WATER, EARTH, FIRE AND THE WILD.
WHUMPPHH
I'LL GIVE YOU FIFTY SILVER TO ONE AGAINST THOSE TWO ELVES AND WHOEVER ELSE REHGAR MANAGES TO FIELD BY THE TIME THE DIRE MAUL GAMES BEGIN.
NO ONE'S DUMB ENOUGH TO TAKE THAT BET. BLOODEYE WAS A GREAT GLADIATOR. REHGAR MIGHT AS WELL PACK IT IN. HE'S DEAD MEAT.
WHAT NOW, REHGAR?
NOW? NOW BROLL, YOU AND VALEERA WILL FIGHT IN DIRE MAUL IN ONE MONTH'S TIME...YOU TWO AND WHOEVER ELSE I CAN BUY ON SHORT NOTICE.
ONE THING'S SURE--I'LL NEVER FIELD ANOTHER WARRIOR LIKE BLOODEYE.
"BASICALLY, WE'RE DEAD MEAT.

CHAPTER I

Issue #1 Cover
by Samwise Didier

Issue #1 Cover
by Jim Lee and David Baron

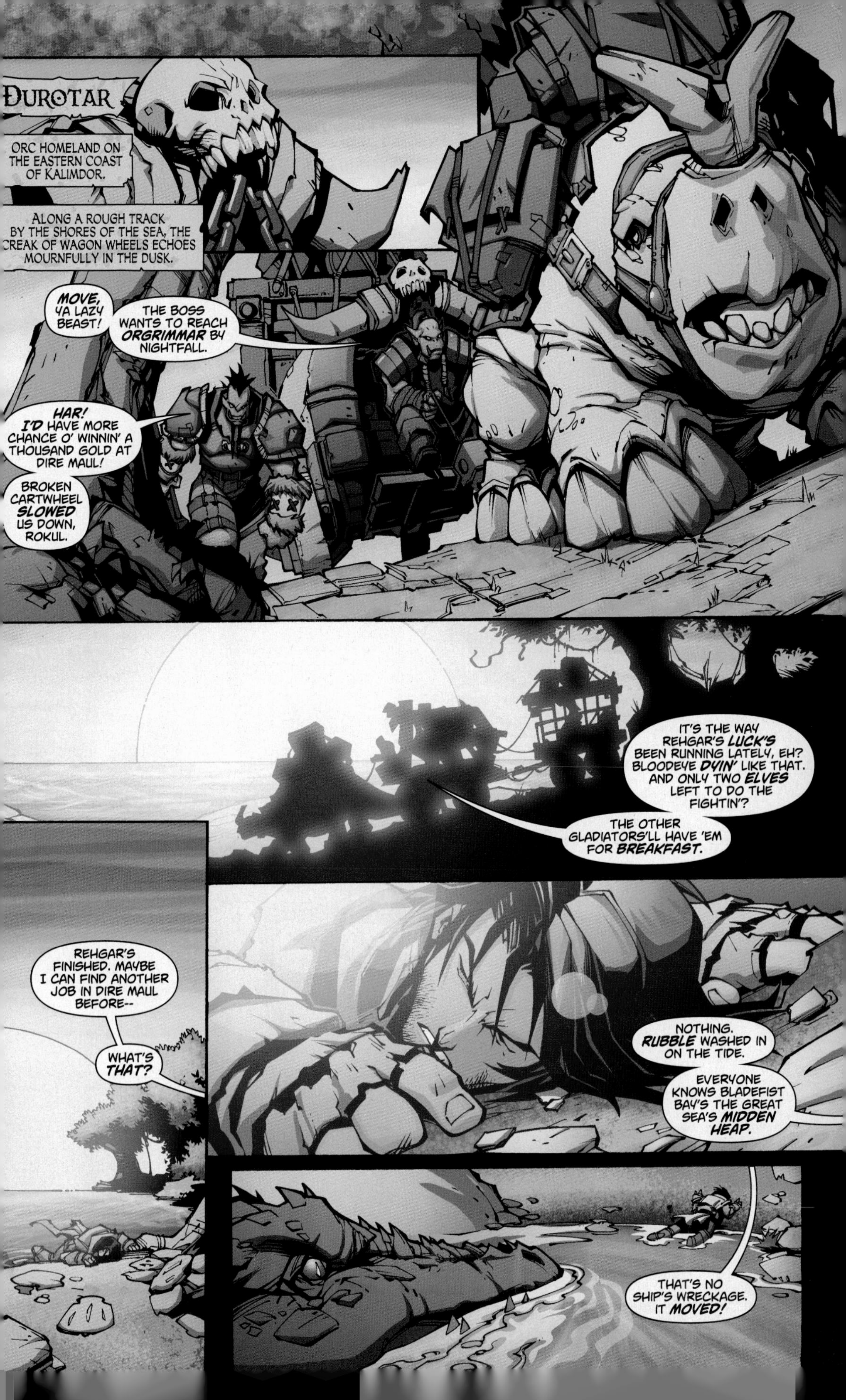
DUROTAR
ORC HOMELAND ON THE EASTERN COAST OF KALIMDOR.
ALONG A ROUGH TRACK BY THE SHORES OF THE SEA, THE CREAK OF WAGON WHEELS ECHOES MOURNFULLY IN THE DUSK.
MOVE, YA LAZY BEAST!
THE BOSS WANTS TO REACH ORGRIMMAR BY NIGHTFALL.
HAR! I'D HAVE MORE CHANCE O' WINNIN' A THOUSAND GOLD AT DIRE MAUL!
BROKEN CARTWHEEL SLOWED US DOWN, ROKUL.
IT'S THE WAY REHGAR'S LUCK'S BEEN RUNNING LATELY, EH? BLOODEYE DYIN' LIKE THAT. AND ONLY TWO ELVES LEFT TO DO THE FIGHTIN'?
THE OTHER GLADIATORS'LL HAVE 'EM FOR BREAKFAST.
REHGAR'S FINISHED. MAYBE I CAN FIND ANOTHER JOB IN DIRE MAUL BEFORE--
WHAT'S THAT?
NOTHING. RUBBLE WASHED IN ON THE TIDE.
EVERYONE KNOWS BLADEFIST BAY'S THE GREAT SEA'S MIDDEN HEAP.
THAT'S NO SHIP'S WRECKAGE. IT MOVED!

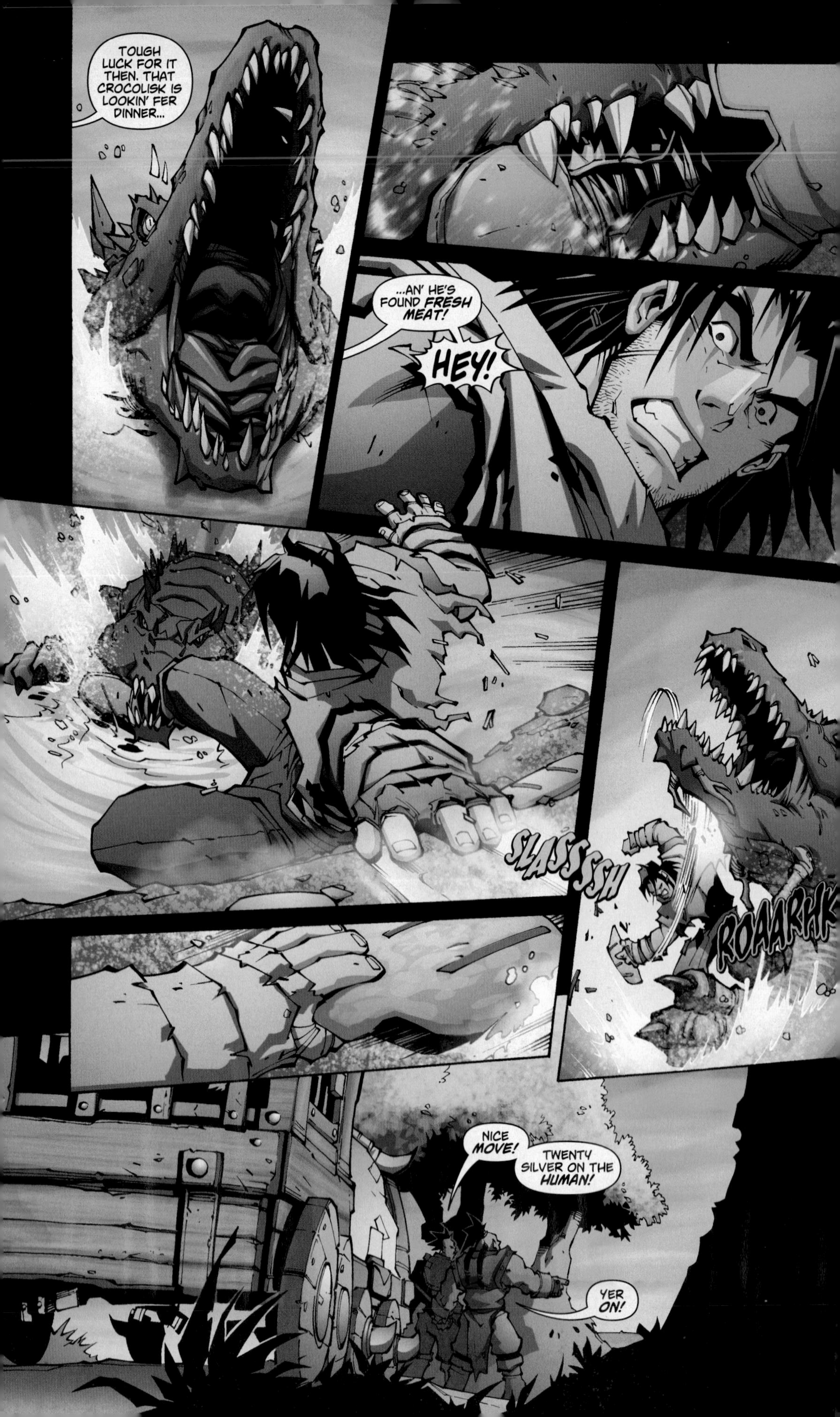
TOUGH LUCK FOR IT THEN. THAT CROCOLISK IS LOOKIN' FER DINNER...
...AN' HE'S FOUND FRESH MEAT!
HEY!
SLASSSSH
ROAARHK
NICE MOVE!
TWENTY SILVER ON THE HUMAN!
YER ON!

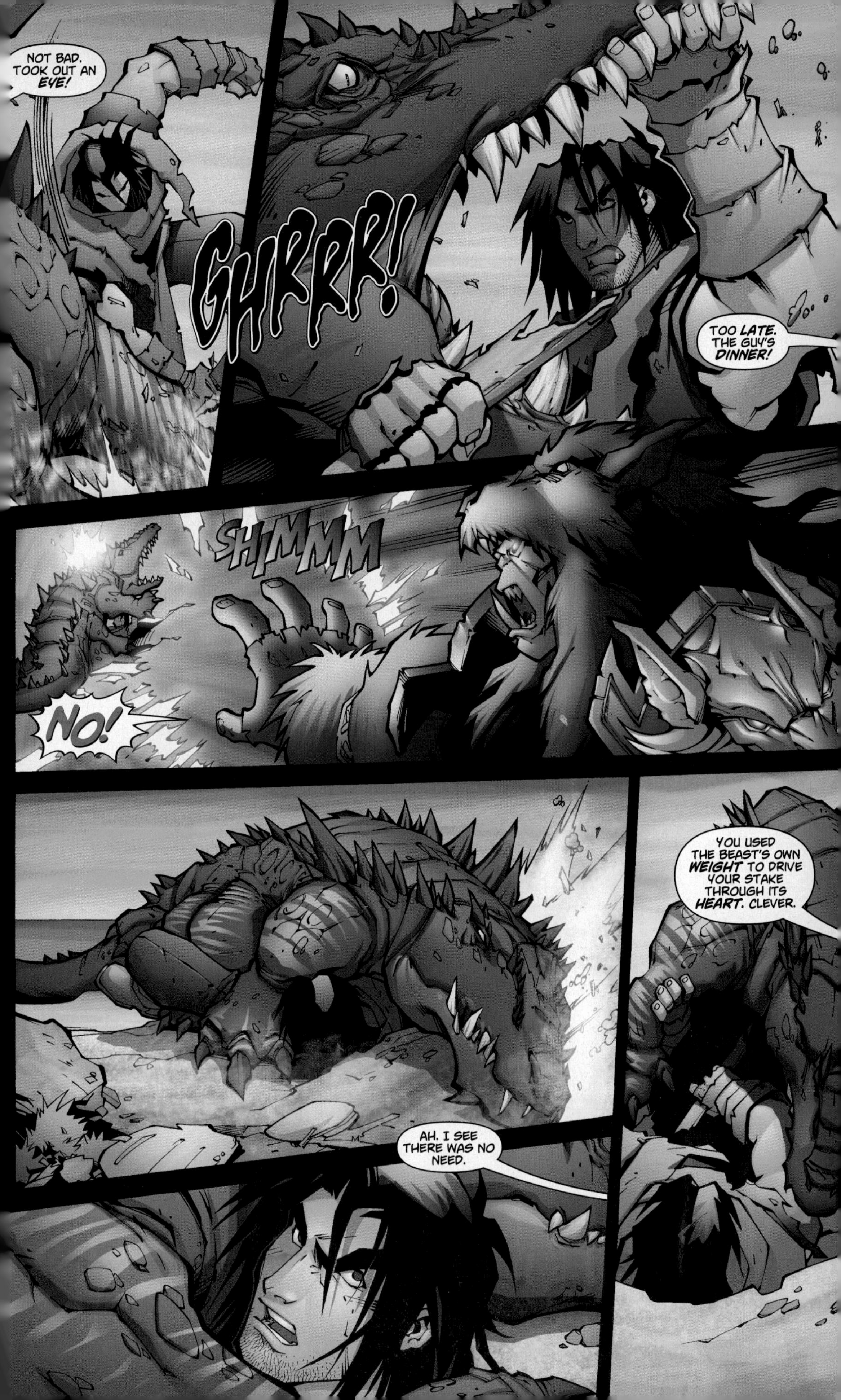
NOT BAD. TOOK OUT AN EYE!
GHRRR!
TOO LATE. THE GUY'S DINNER!
SHIMMM
NO!
YOU USED THE BEAST'S OWN WEIGHT TO DRIVE YOUR STAKE THROUGH ITS HEART. CLEVER.
AH. I SEE THERE WAS NO NEED.

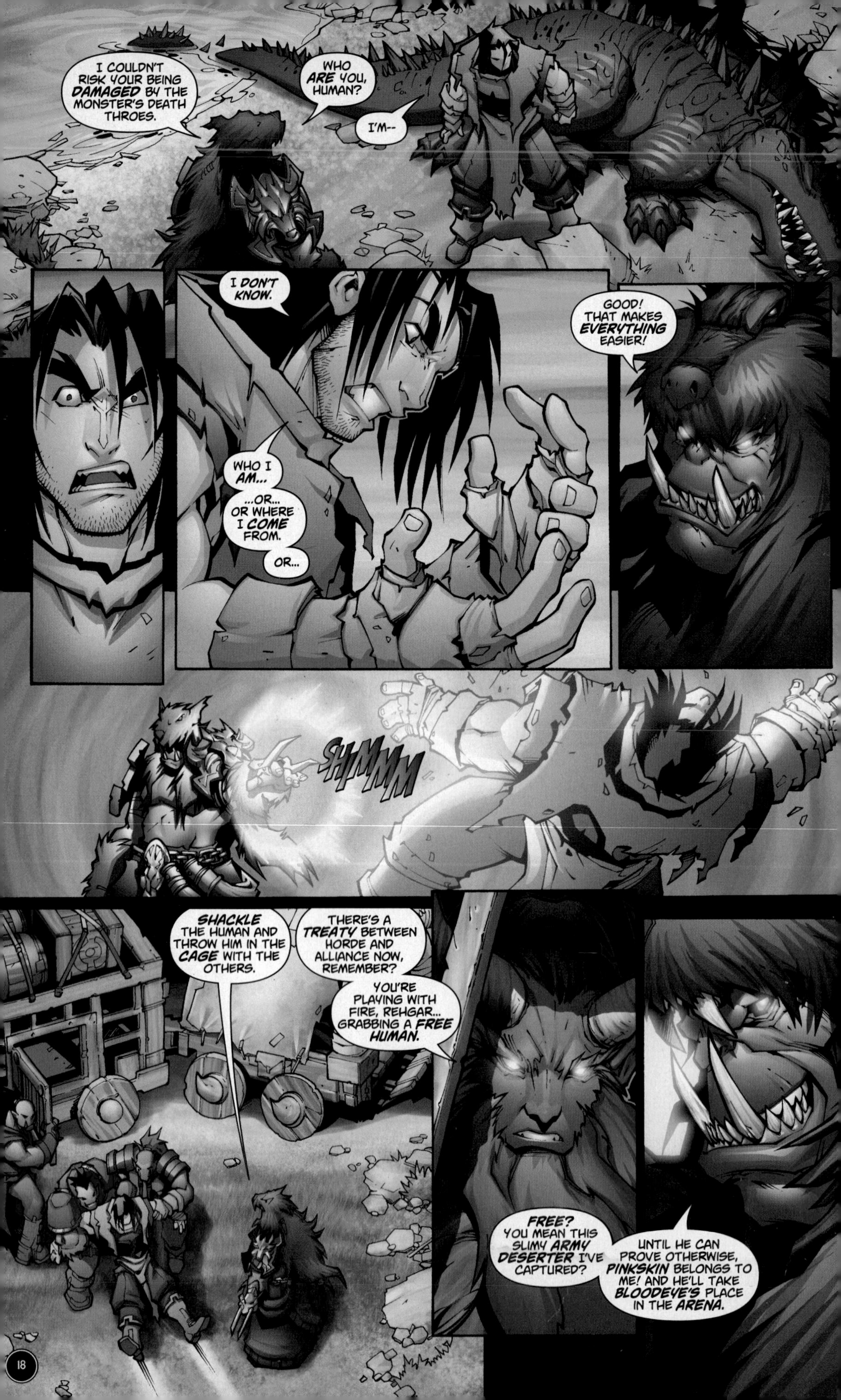
I COULDN'T RISK YOUR BEING DAMAGED BY THE MONSTER'S DEATH THROES.
WHO ARE YOU, HUMAN?
I'M--
I DON'T KNOW.
WHO I AM...
...OR... OR WHERE I COME FROM.
OR...
GOOD! THAT MAKES EVERYTHING EASIER!
SHIMMM
SHACKLE THE HUMAN AND THROW HIM IN THE CAGE WITH THE OTHERS.
THERE'S A TREATY BETWEEN HORDE AND ALLIANCE NOW, REMEMBER?
YOU'RE PLAYING WITH FIRE, REHGAR... GRABBING A FREE HUMAN.
FREE? YOU MEAN THIS SLIMY ARMY DESERTER I'VE CAPTURED?
UNTIL HE CAN PROVE OTHERWISE, PINKSKIN BELONGS TO ME! AND HE'LL TAKE BLOODEYE'S PLACE IN THE ARENA.

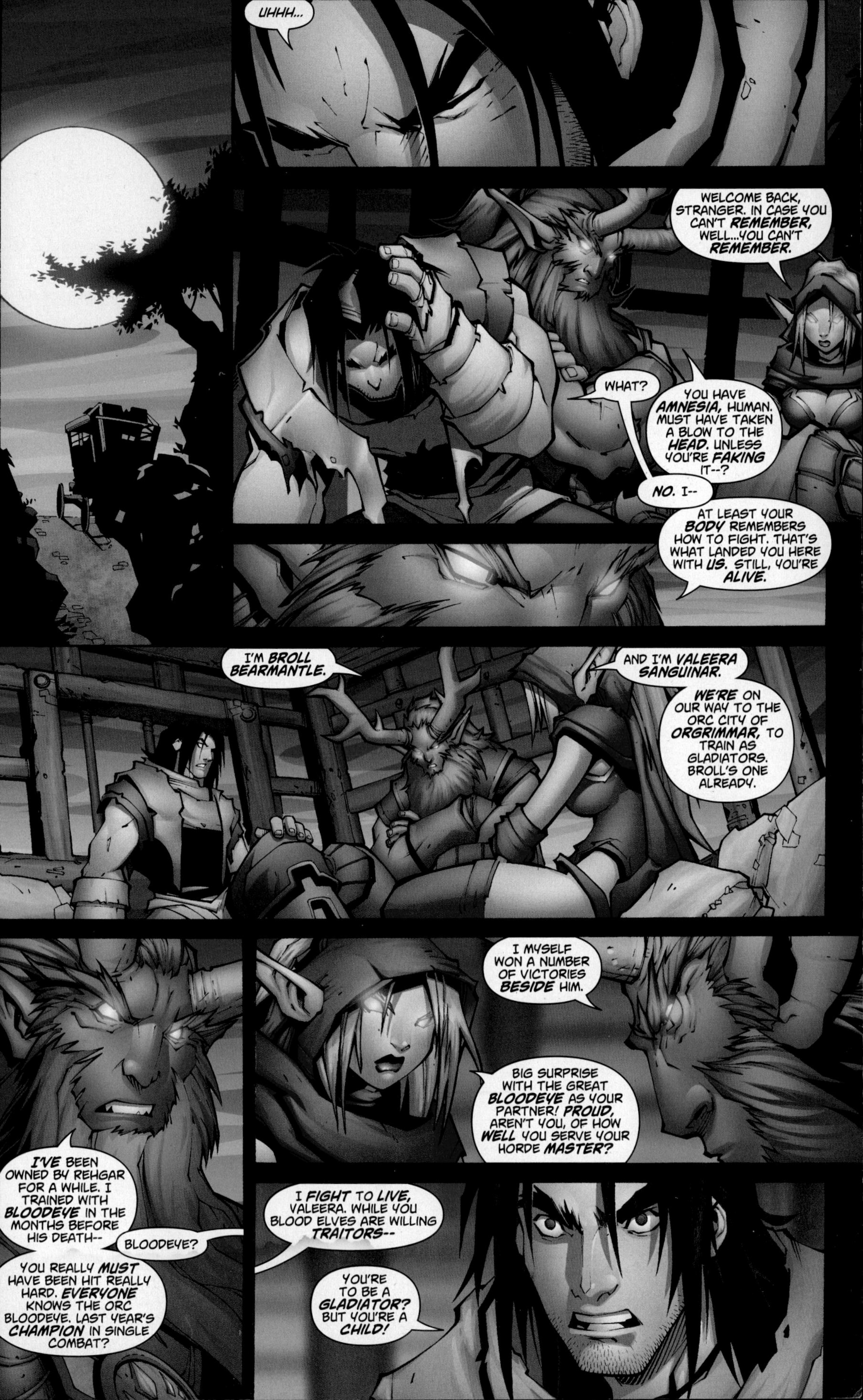
UHHH...
WELCOME BACK, STRANGER. IN CASE YOU CAN'T REMEMBER, WELL...YOU CAN'T REMEMBER.
WHAT?
YOU HAVE AMNESIA, HUMAN. MUST HAVE TAKEN A BLOW TO THE HEAD. UNLESS YOU'RE FAKING IT--?
NO. I--
AT LEAST YOUR BODY REMEMBERS HOW TO FIGHT. THAT'S WHAT LANDED YOU HERE WITH US. STILL, YOU'RE ALIVE.
I'M BROLL BEARMANTLE.
AND I'M VALEERA SANGUINAR.
WE'RE ON OUR WAY TO THE ORC CITY OF ORGRIMMAR, TO TRAIN AS GLADIATORS. BROLL'S ONE ALREADY.
I'VE BEEN OWNED BY REHGAR FOR A WHILE. I TRAINED WITH BLOODEYE IN THE MONTHS BEFORE HIS DEATH--
BLOODEYE?
YOU REALLY MUST HAVE BEEN HIT REALLY HARD. EVERYONE KNOWS THE ORC BLOODEYE. LAST YEAR'S CHAMPION IN SINGLE COMBAT?
I MYSELF WON A NUMBER OF VICTORIES BESIDE HIM.
BIG SURPRISE WITH THE GREAT BLOODEYE AS YOUR PARTNER! PROUD, AREN'T YOU, OF HOW WELL YOU SERVE YOUR HORDE MASTER?
I FIGHT TO LIVE, VALEERA. WHILE YOU BLOOD ELVES ARE WILLING TRAITORS--
YOU'RE TO BE A GLADIATOR? BUT YOU'RE A CHILD!

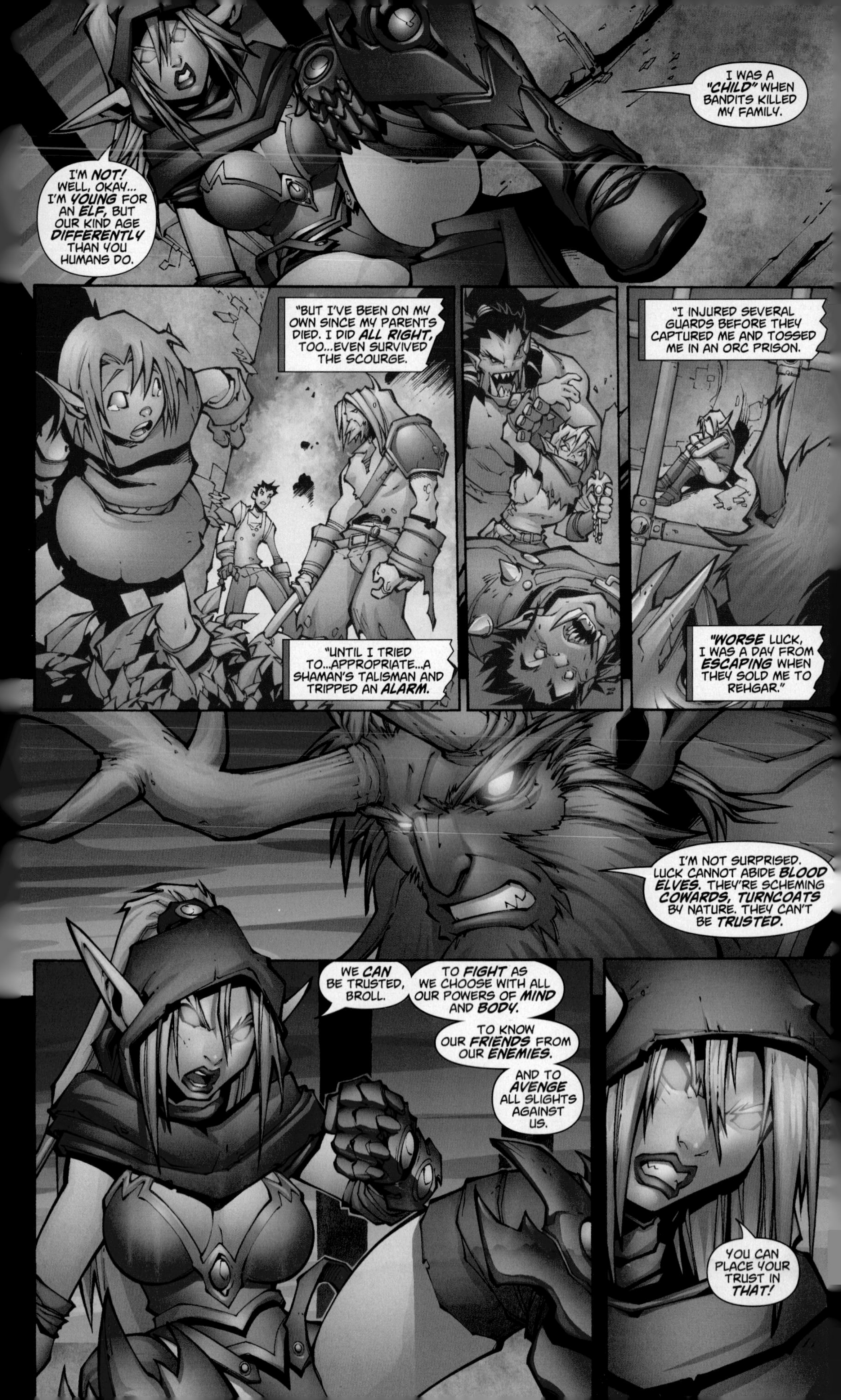

I'M NOT! WELL, OKAY... I'M YOUNG FOR AN ELF, BUT OUR KIND AGE DIFFERENTLY THAN YOU HUMANS DO.
I WAS A "CHILD" WHEN BANDITS KILLED MY FAMILY.
"BUT I'VE BEEN ON MY OWN SINCE MY PARENTS DIED. I DID ALL RIGHT, TOO...EVEN SURVIVED THE SCOURGE.
"UNTIL I TRIED TO...APPROPRIATE...A SHAMAN'S TALISMAN AND TRIPPED AN ALARM.
"I INJURED SEVERAL GUARDS BEFORE THEY CAPTURED ME AND TOSSED ME IN AN ORC PRISON.
"WORSE LUCK, I WAS A DAY FROM ESCAPING WHEN THEY SOLD ME TO REHGAR."
I'M NOT SURPRISED. LUCK CANNOT ABIDE BLOOD ELVES. THEY'RE SCHEMING COWARDS, TURNCOATS BY NATURE. THEY CAN'T BE TRUSTED.
WE CAN BE TRUSTED, BROLL.
TO FIGHT AS WE CHOOSE WITH ALL OUR POWERS OF MIND AND BODY.
TO KNOW OUR FRIENDS FROM OUR ENEMIES.
AND TO AVENGE ALL SLIGHTS AGAINST US.
YOU CAN PLACE YOUR TRUST IN THAT!

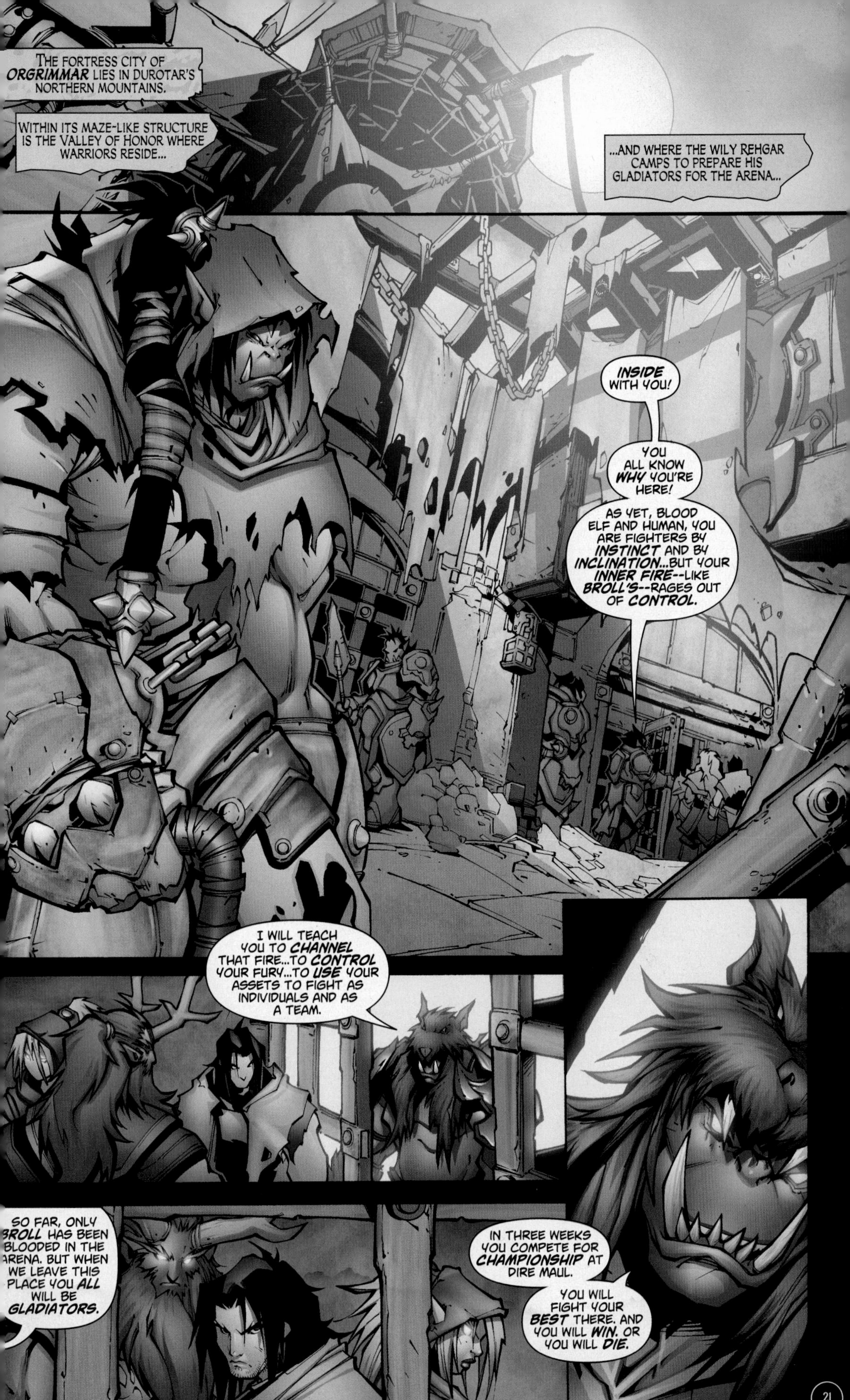

THE FORTRESS CITY OF ORGRIMMAR LIES IN DUROTAR'S NORTHERN MOUNTAINS.
WITHIN ITS MAZE-LIKE STRUCTURE IS THE VALLEY OF HONOR WHERE WARRIORS RESIDE...
...AND WHERE THE WILY REHGAR CAMPS TO PREPARE HIS GLADIATORS FOR THE ARENA...
INSIDE WITH YOU!
YOU ALL KNOW WHY YOU'RE HERE!
AS YET, BLOOD ELF AND HUMAN, YOU ARE FIGHTERS BY INSTINCT AND BY INCLINATION...BUT YOUR INNER FIRE--LIKE BROLL'S--RAGES OUT OF CONTROL.
I WILL TEACH YOU TO CHANNEL THAT FIRE...TO CONTROL YOUR FURY...TO USE YOUR ASSETS TO FIGHT AS INDIVIDUALS AND AS A TEAM.
SO FAR, ONLY BROLL HAS BEEN BLOODED IN THE ARENA. BUT WHEN WE LEAVE THIS PLACE YOU ALL WILL BE GLADIATORS.
IN THREE WEEKS YOU COMPETE FOR CHAMPIONSHIP AT DIRE MAUL.
YOU WILL FIGHT YOUR BEST THERE. AND YOU WILL WIN. OR YOU WILL DIE.

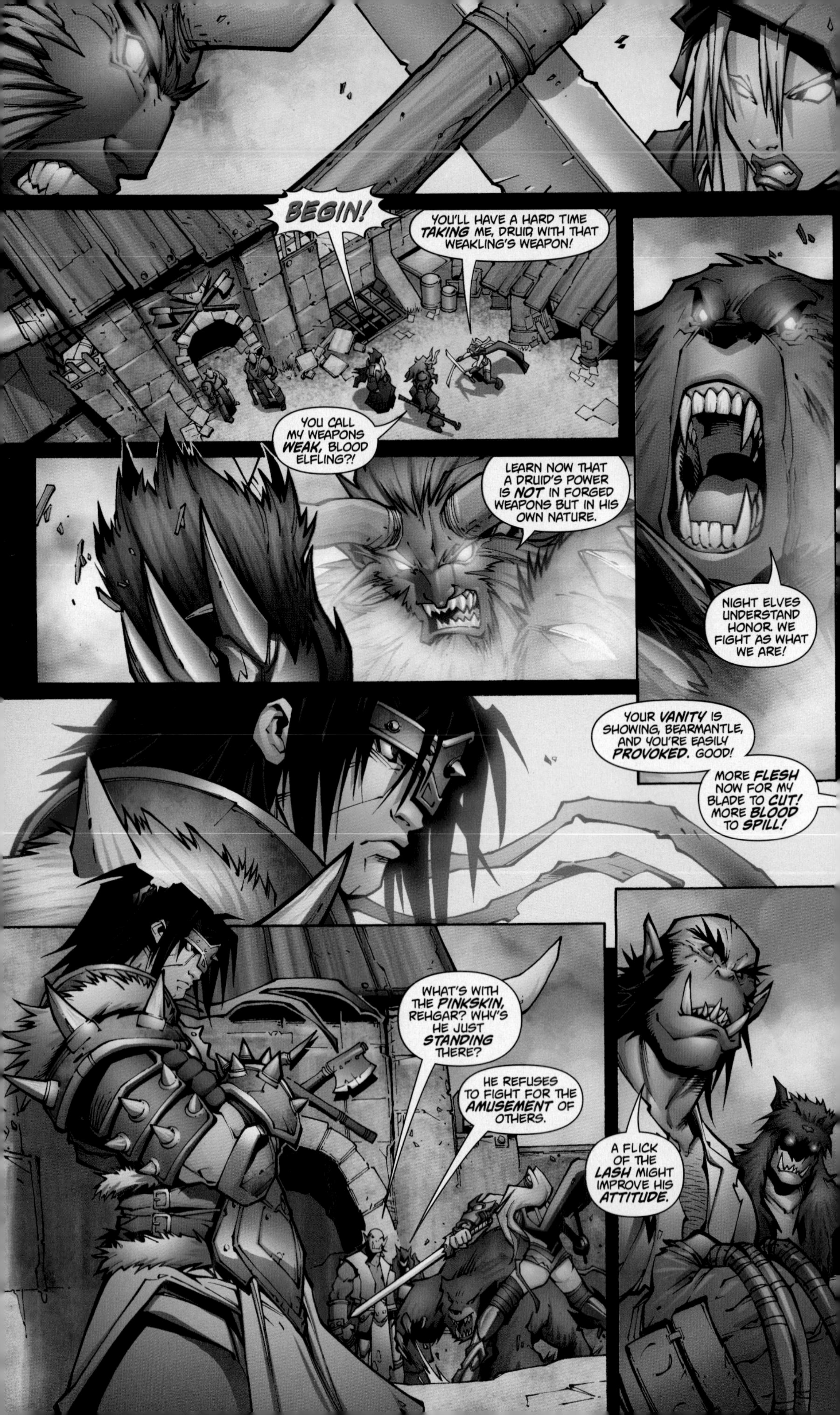
BEGIN!
YOU'LL HAVE A HARD TIME TAKING ME, DRUID WITH THAT WEAKLING'S WEAPON!
YOU CALL MY WEAPONS WEAK, BLOOD ELFLING?!
LEARN NOW THAT A DRUID'S POWER IS NOT IN FORGED WEAPONS BUT IN HIS OWN NATURE.
NIGHT ELVES UNDERSTAND HONOR. WE FIGHT AS WHAT WE ARE!
YOUR VANITY IS SHOWING, BEARMANTLE, AND YOU'RE EASILY PROVOKED. GOOD!
MORE FLESH NOW FOR MY BLADE TO CUT! MORE BLOOD TO SPILL!
WHAT'S WITH THE PINKSKIN, REHGAR? WHY'S HE JUST STANDING THERE?
HE REFUSES TO FIGHT FOR THE AMUSEMENT OF OTHERS.
A FLICK OF THE LASH MIGHT IMPROVE HIS ATTITUDE.

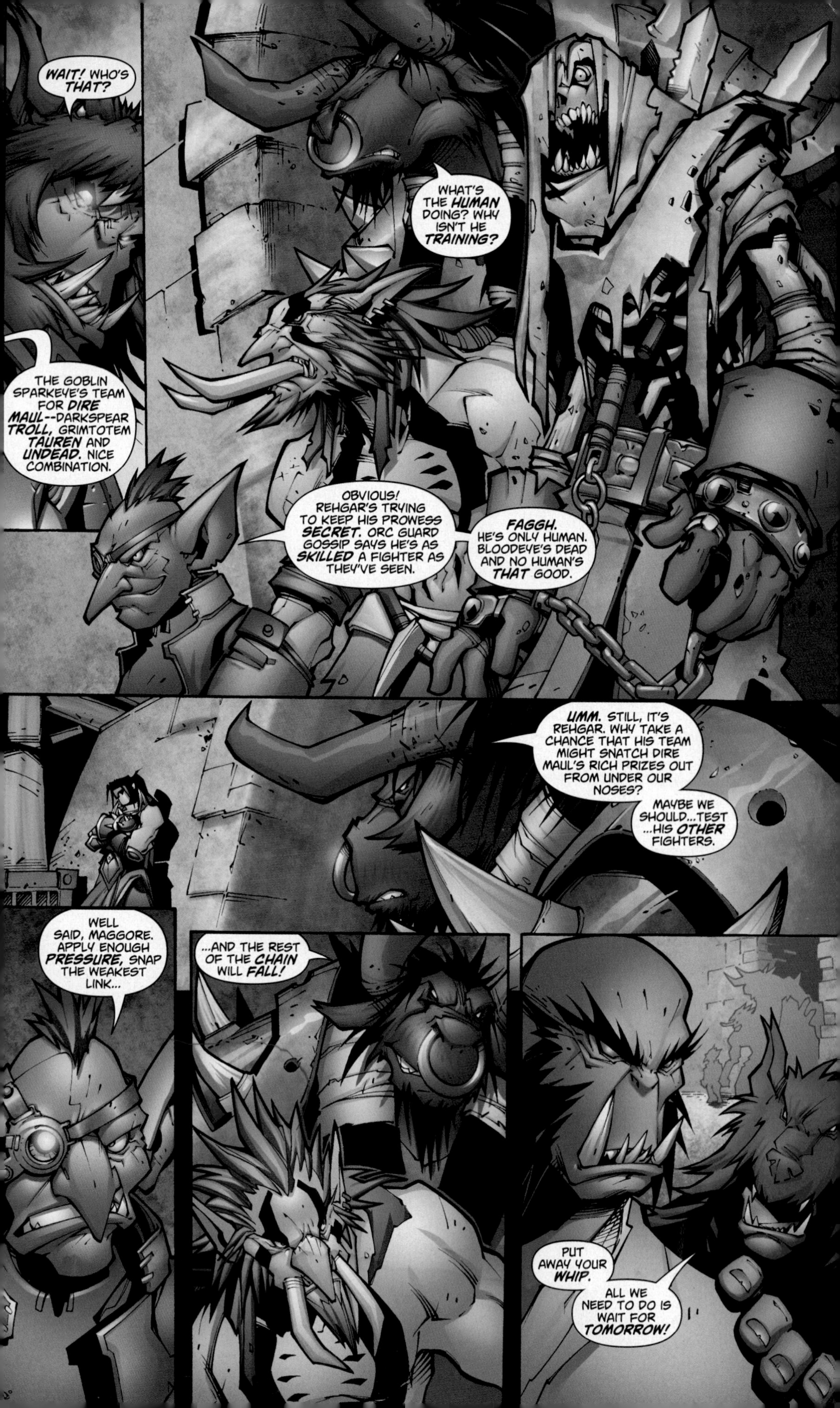

WAIT! WHO'S THAT?
WHAT'S THE HUMAN DOING? WHY ISN'T HE TRAINING?
THE GOBLIN SPARKEYE'S TEAM FOR DIRE MAUL--DARKSPEAR TROLL, GRIMTOTEM TAUREN AND UNDEAD. NICE COMBINATION.
OBVIOUS! REHGAR'S TRYING TO KEEP HIS PROWESS SECRET. ORC GUARD GOSSIP SAYS HE'S AS SKILLED A FIGHTER AS THEY'VE SEEN.
FAGGH. HE'S ONLY HUMAN. BLOODEYE'S DEAD AND NO HUMAN'S THAT GOOD.
UMM. STILL, IT'S REHGAR. WHY TAKE A CHANCE THAT HIS TEAM MIGHT SNATCH DIRE MAUL'S RICH PRIZES OUT FROM UNDER OUR NOSES?
MAYBE WE SHOULD...TEST ...HIS OTHER FIGHTERS.
WELL SAID, MAGGORE. APPLY ENOUGH PRESSURE, SNAP THE WEAKEST LINK...
...AND THE REST OF THE CHAIN WILL FALL!
PUT AWAY YOUR WHIP.
ALL WE NEED TO DO IS WAIT FOR TOMORROW!

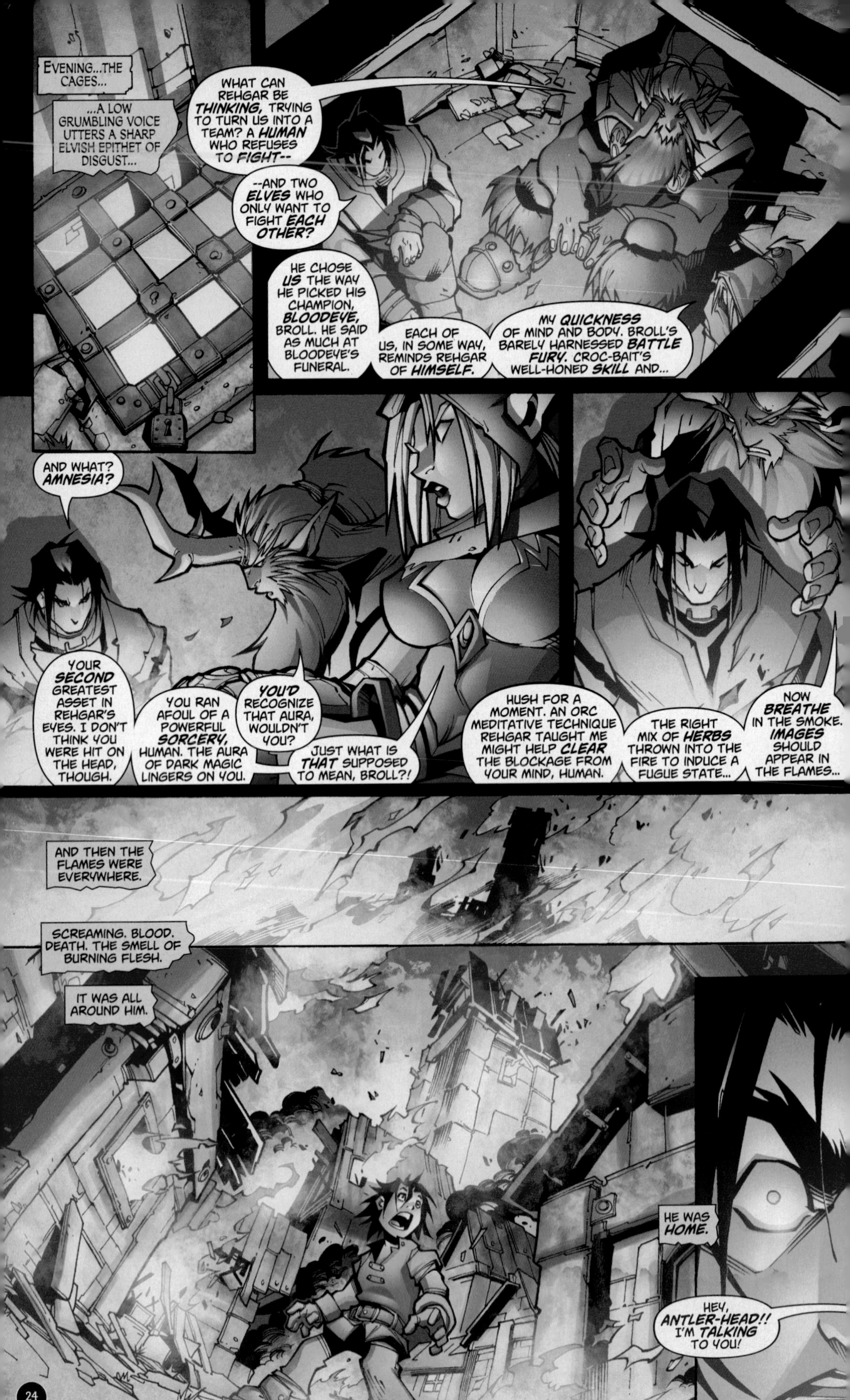

EVENING...THE CAGES...
...A LOW GRUMBLING VOICE UTTERS A SHARP ELVISH EPITHET OF DISGUST...
WHAT CAN REHGAR BE THINKING, TRYING TO TURN US INTO A TEAM? A HUMAN WHO REFUSES TO FIGHT--
--AND TWO ELVES WHO ONLY WANT TO FIGHT EACH OTHER?
HE CHOSE US THE WAY HE PICKED HIS CHAMPION, BLOODEYE, BROLL. HE SAID AS MUCH AT BLOODEYE'S FUNERAL.
EACH OF US, IN SOME WAY, REMINDS REHGAR OF HIMSELF.
MY QUICKNESS OF MIND AND BODY. BROLL'S BARELY HARNESSED BATTLE FURY. CROC-BAIT'S WELL-HONED SKILL AND...
AND WHAT? AMNESIA?
YOUR SECOND GREATEST ASSET IN REHGAR'S EYES. I DON'T THINK YOU WERE HIT ON THE HEAD, THOUGH.
YOU RAN AFOUL OF A POWERFUL SORCERY, HUMAN. THE AURA OF DARK MAGIC LINGERS ON YOU.
YOU'D RECOGNIZE THAT AURA, WOULDN'T YOU?
JUST WHAT IS THAT SUPPOSED TO MEAN, BROLL?!
HUSH FOR A MOMENT. AN ORC MEDITATIVE TECHNIQUE REHGAR TAUGHT ME MIGHT HELP CLEAR THE BLOCKAGE FROM YOUR MIND, HUMAN.
THE RIGHT MIX OF HERBS THROWN INTO THE FIRE TO INDUCE A FUGUE STATE...
NOW BREATHE IN THE SMOKE. IMAGES SHOULD APPEAR IN THE FLAMES...
AND THEN THE FLAMES WERE EVERYWHERE.
SCREAMING. BLOOD. DEATH. THE SMELL OF BURNING FLESH.
IT WAS ALL AROUND HIM.
HE WAS HOME.
HEY, ANTLER-HEAD!! I'M TALKING TO YOU!

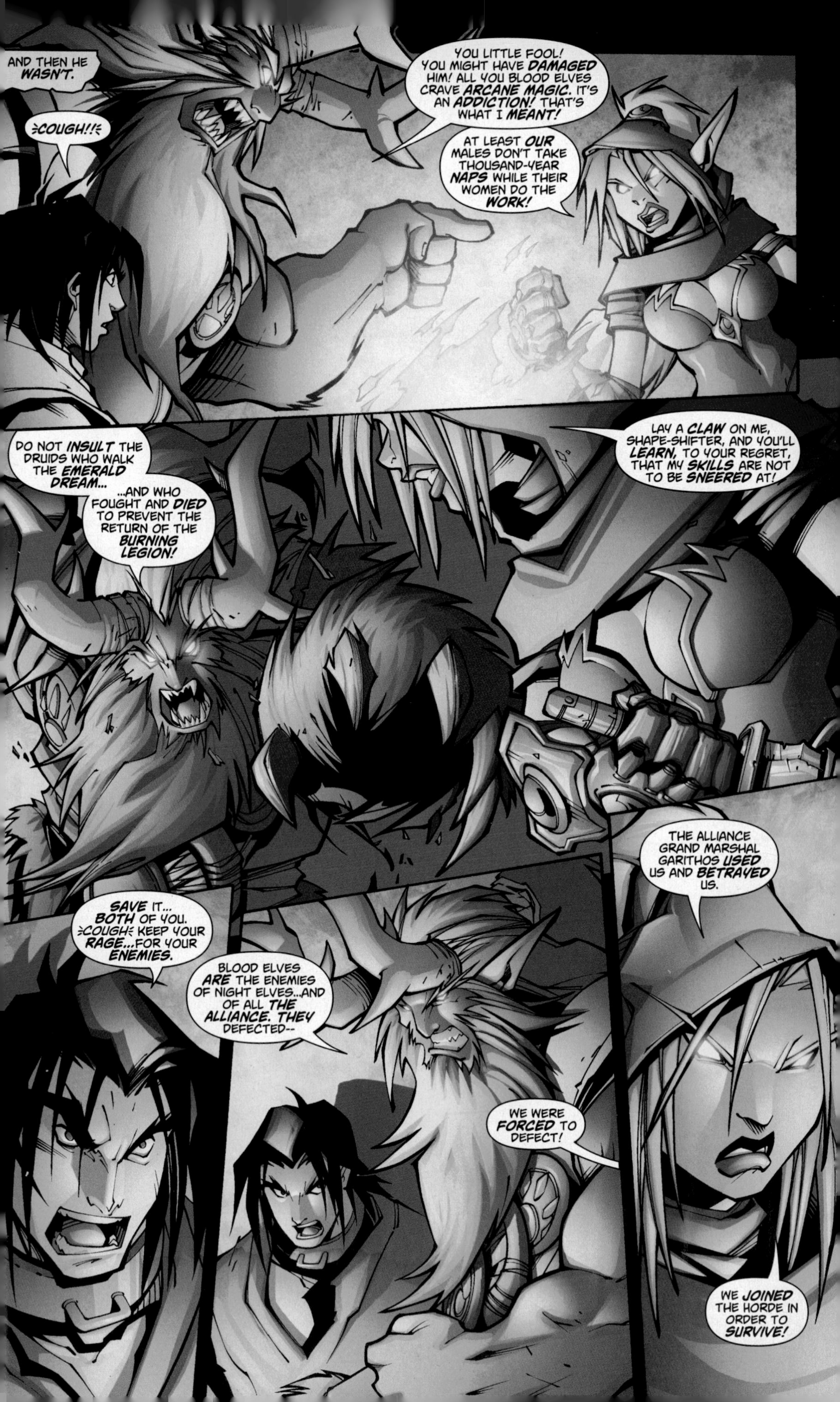
AND THEN HE WASN'T.
COUGH!!
YOU LITTLE FOOL! YOU MIGHT HAVE DAMAGED HIM! ALL YOU BLOOD ELVES CRAVE ARCANE MAGIC. IT'S AN ADDICTION! THAT'S WHAT I MEANT!
AT LEAST OUR MALES DON'T TAKE THOUSAND-YEAR NAPS WHILE THEIR WOMEN DO THE WORK!
DO NOT INSULT THE DRUIDS WHO WALK THE EMERALD DREAM...
...AND WHO FOUGHT AND DIED TO PREVENT THE RETURN OF THE BURNING LEGION!
LAY A CLAW ON ME, SHAPE-SHIFTER, AND YOU'LL LEARN, TO YOUR REGRET, THAT MY SKILLS ARE NOT TO BE SNEERED AT!
SAVE IT... BOTH OF YOU. COUGH KEEP YOUR RAGE...FOR YOUR ENEMIES.
BLOOD ELVES ARE THE ENEMIES OF NIGHT ELVES...AND OF ALL THE ALLIANCE. THEY DEFECTED--
WE WERE FORCED TO DEFECT!
THE ALLIANCE GRAND MARSHAL GARITHOS USED US AND BETRAYED US.
WE JOINED THE HORDE IN ORDER TO SURVIVE!

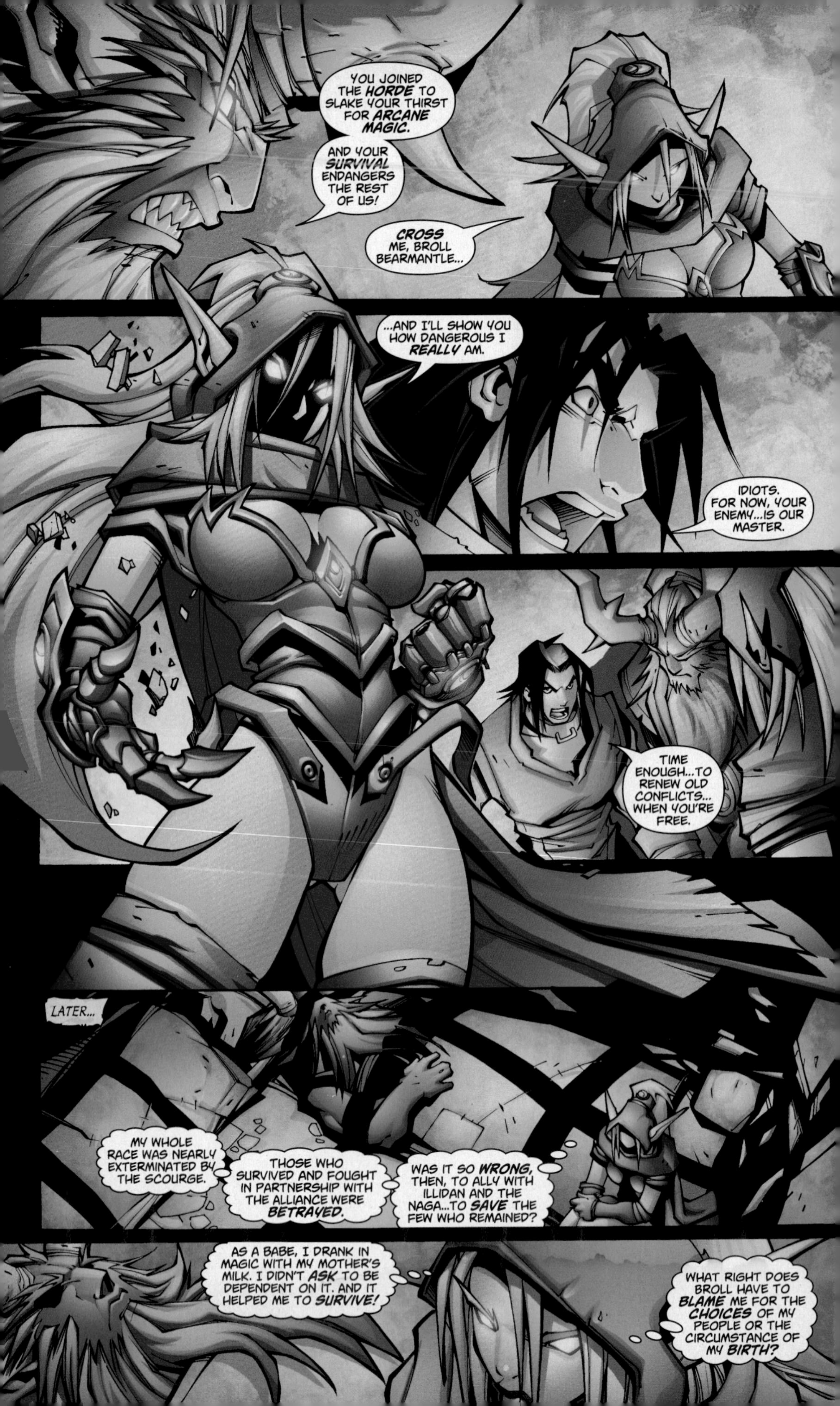
YOU JOINED THE HORDE TO SLAKE YOUR THIRST FOR ARCANE MAGIC.
AND YOUR SURVIVAL ENDANGERS THE REST OF US!
CROSS ME, BROLL BEARMANTLE...
...AND I'LL SHOW YOU HOW DANGEROUS I REALLY AM.
IDIOTS. FOR NOW, YOUR ENEMY...IS OUR MASTER.
TIME ENOUGH...TO RENEW OLD CONFLICTS... WHEN YOU'RE FREE.
LATER...
MY WHOLE RACE WAS NEARLY EXTERMINATED BY THE SCOURGE.
THOSE WHO SURVIVED AND FOUGHT IN PARTNERSHIP WITH THE ALLIANCE WERE BETRAYED.
WAS IT SO WRONG, THEN, TO ALLY WITH ILLIDAN AND THE NAGA...TO SAVE THE FEW WHO REMAINED?
AS A BABE, I DRANK IN MAGIC WITH MY MOTHER'S MILK. I DIDN'T ASK TO BE DEPENDENT ON IT. AND IT HELPED ME TO SURVIVE!
WHAT RIGHT DOES BROLL HAVE TO BLAME ME FOR THE CHOICES OF MY PEOPLE OR THE CIRCUMSTANCE OF MY BIRTH?

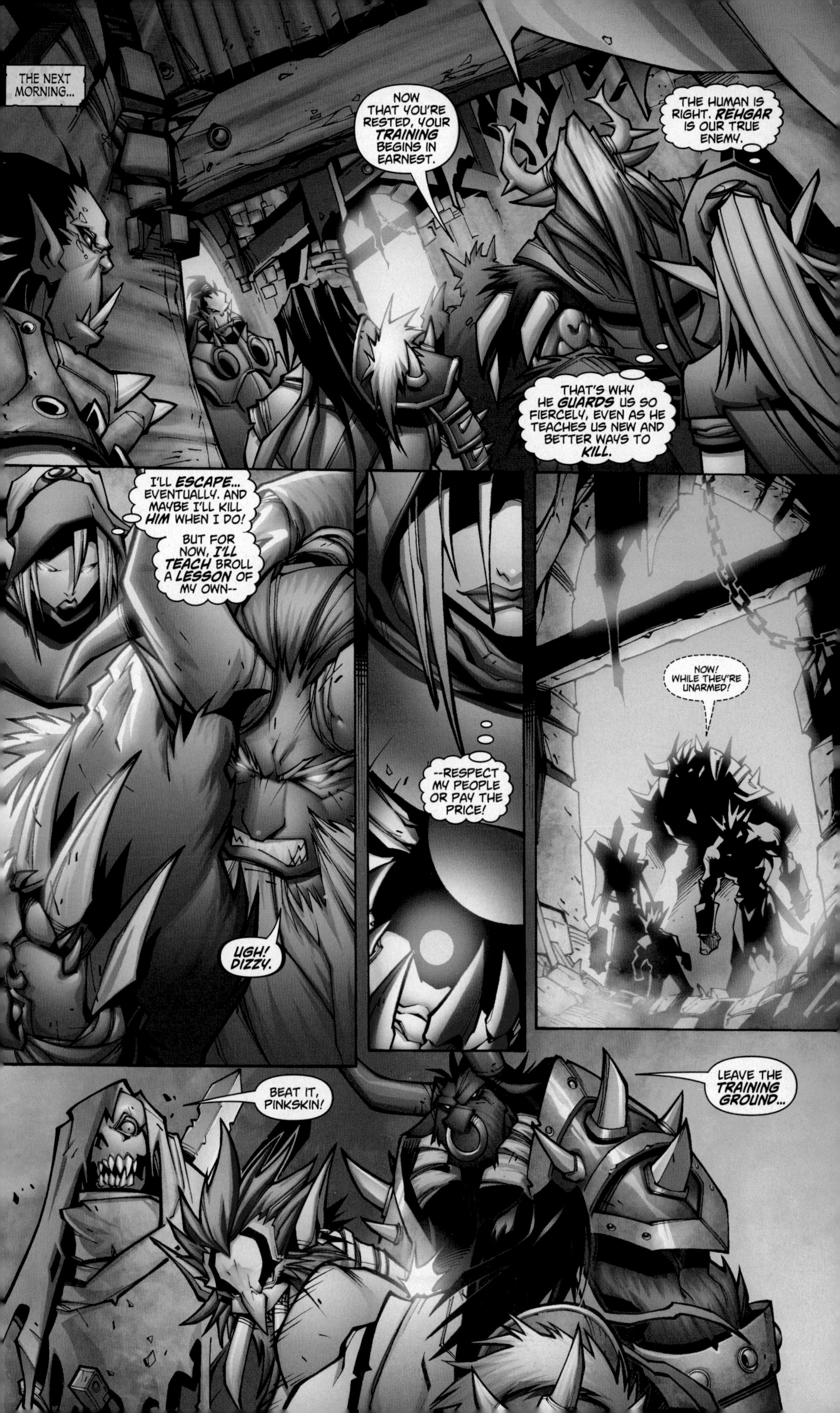
THE NEXT MORNING...
NOW THAT YOU'RE RESTED, YOUR TRAINING BEGINS IN EARNEST.
THE HUMAN IS RIGHT. REHGAR IS OUR TRUE ENEMY.
THAT'S WHY HE GUARDS US SO FIERCELY, EVEN AS HE TEACHES US NEW AND BETTER WAYS TO KILL.
I'LL ESCAPE... EVENTUALLY. AND MAYBE I'LL KILL HIM WHEN I DO!
BUT FOR NOW, I'LL TEACH BROLL A LESSON OF MY OWN--
UGH! DIZZY.
--RESPECT MY PEOPLE OR PAY THE PRICE!
NOW! WHILE THEY'RE UNARMED!
BEAT IT, PINKSKIN!
LEAVE THE TRAINING GROUND...

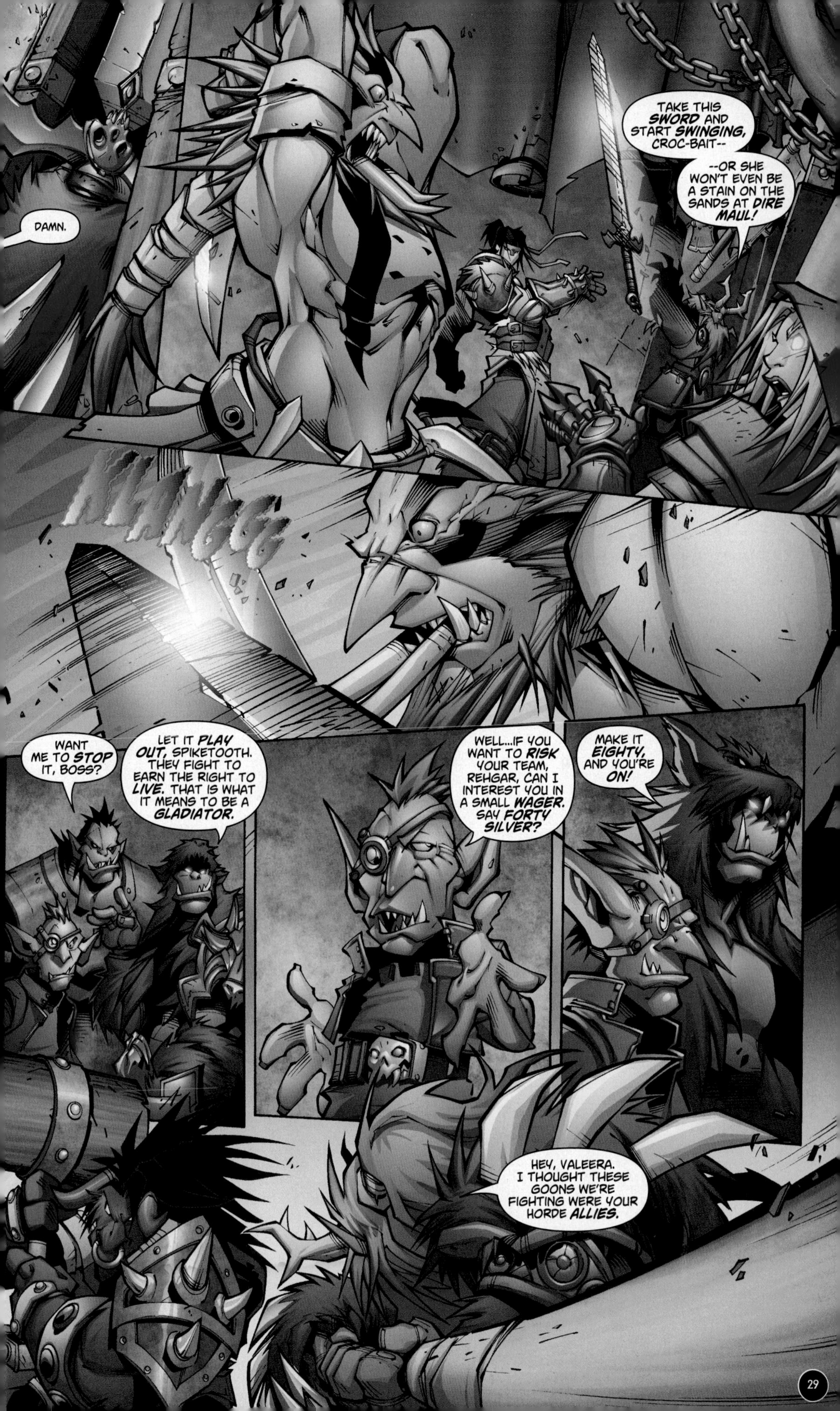

DAMN.
TAKE THIS SWORD AND START SWINGING, CROC-BAIT--
--OR SHE WON'T EVEN BE A STAIN ON THE SANDS AT DIRE MAUL!
WANT ME TO STOP IT, BOSS?
LET IT PLAY OUT, SPIKETOOTH. THEY FIGHT TO EARN THE RIGHT TO LIVE. THAT IS WHAT IT MEANS TO BE A GLADIATOR.
WELL...IF YOU WANT TO RISK YOUR TEAM, REHGAR, CAN I INTEREST YOU IN A SMALL WAGER. SAY FORTY SILVER?
MAKE IT EIGHTY, AND YOU'RE ON!
HEY, VALEERA. I THOUGHT THESE GOONS WE'RE FIGHTING WERE YOUR HORDE ALLIES.

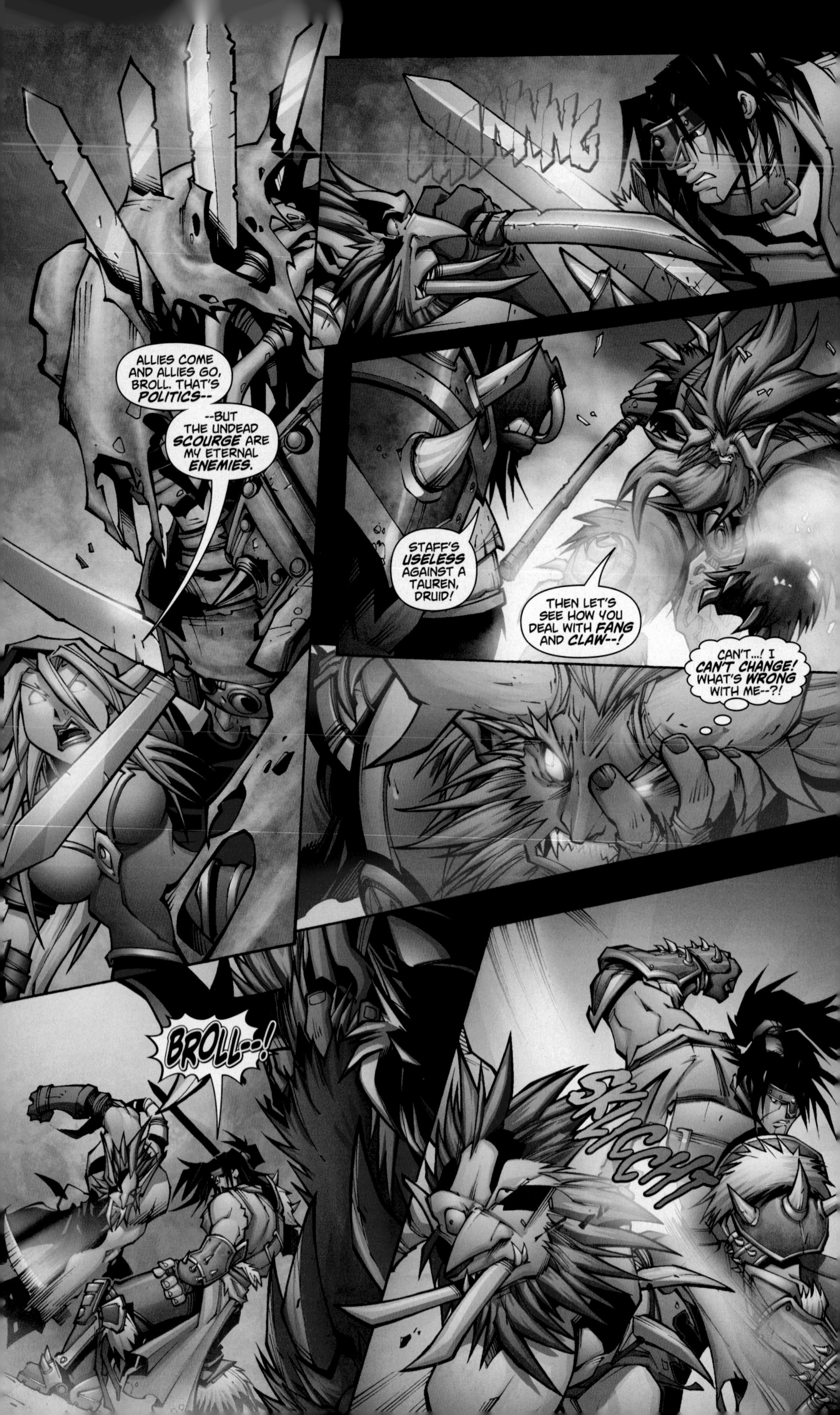

CHANNNG
ALLIES COME AND ALLIES GO, BROLL. THAT'S POLITICS--
--BUT THE UNDEAD SCOURGE ARE MY ETERNAL ENEMIES.
STAFF'S USELESS AGAINST A TAUREN, DRUID!
THEN LET'S SEE HOW YOU DEAL WITH FANG AND CLAW--!
CAN'T...! I CAN'T CHANGE! WHAT'S WRONG WITH ME--?!
BROLL--!
SHCHT

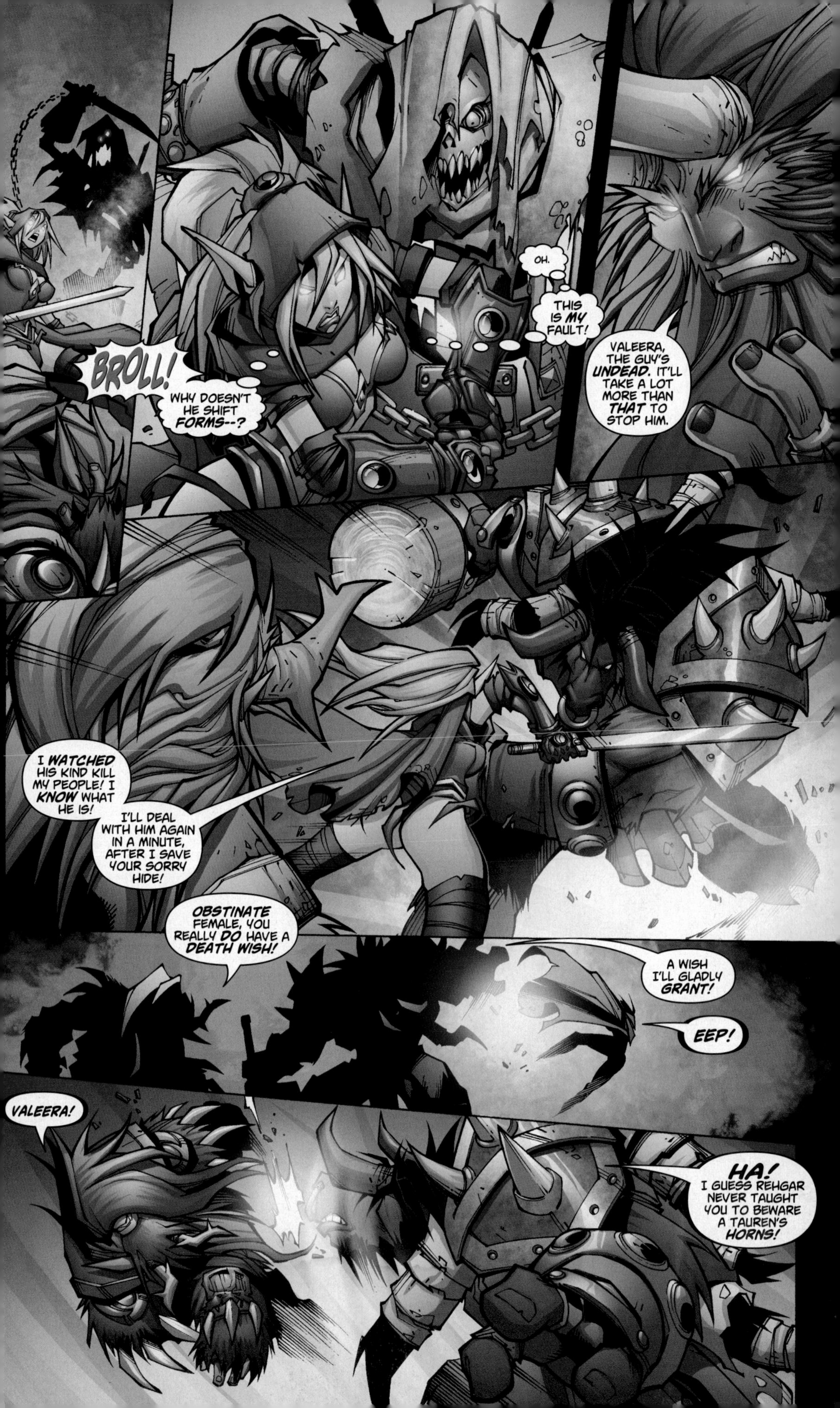
OH.
THIS IS MY FAULT!
VALEERA, THE GUY'S UNDEAD. IT'LL TAKE A LOT MORE THAN THAT TO STOP HIM.
BROLL!
WHY DOESN'T HE SHIFT FORMS--?
I WATCHED HIS KIND KILL MY PEOPLE! I KNOW WHAT HE IS!
I'LL DEAL WITH HIM AGAIN IN A MINUTE, AFTER I SAVE YOUR SORRY HIDE!
OBSTINATE FEMALE, YOU REALLY DO HAVE A DEATH WISH!
A WISH I'LL GLADLY GRANT!
EEP!
VALEERA!
HA! I GUESS REHGAR NEVER TAUGHT YOU TO BEWARE A TAUREN'S HORNS!

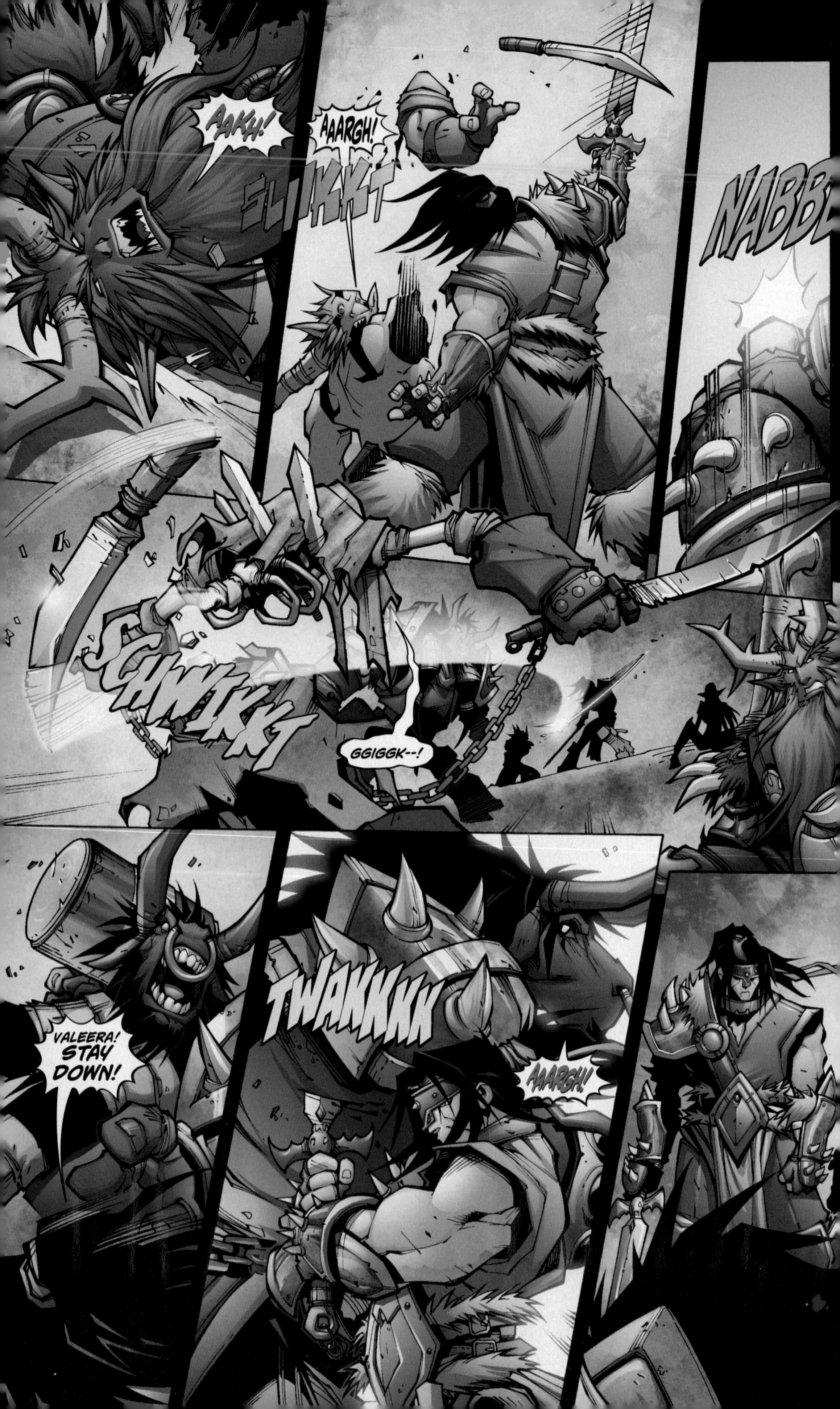
AAKH!
AAARGH!
SLIKKT
NABBE
SCHWIKKT
GGIGGK--!
VALEERA! STAY DOWN!
TWAKKKK
AAARGH!

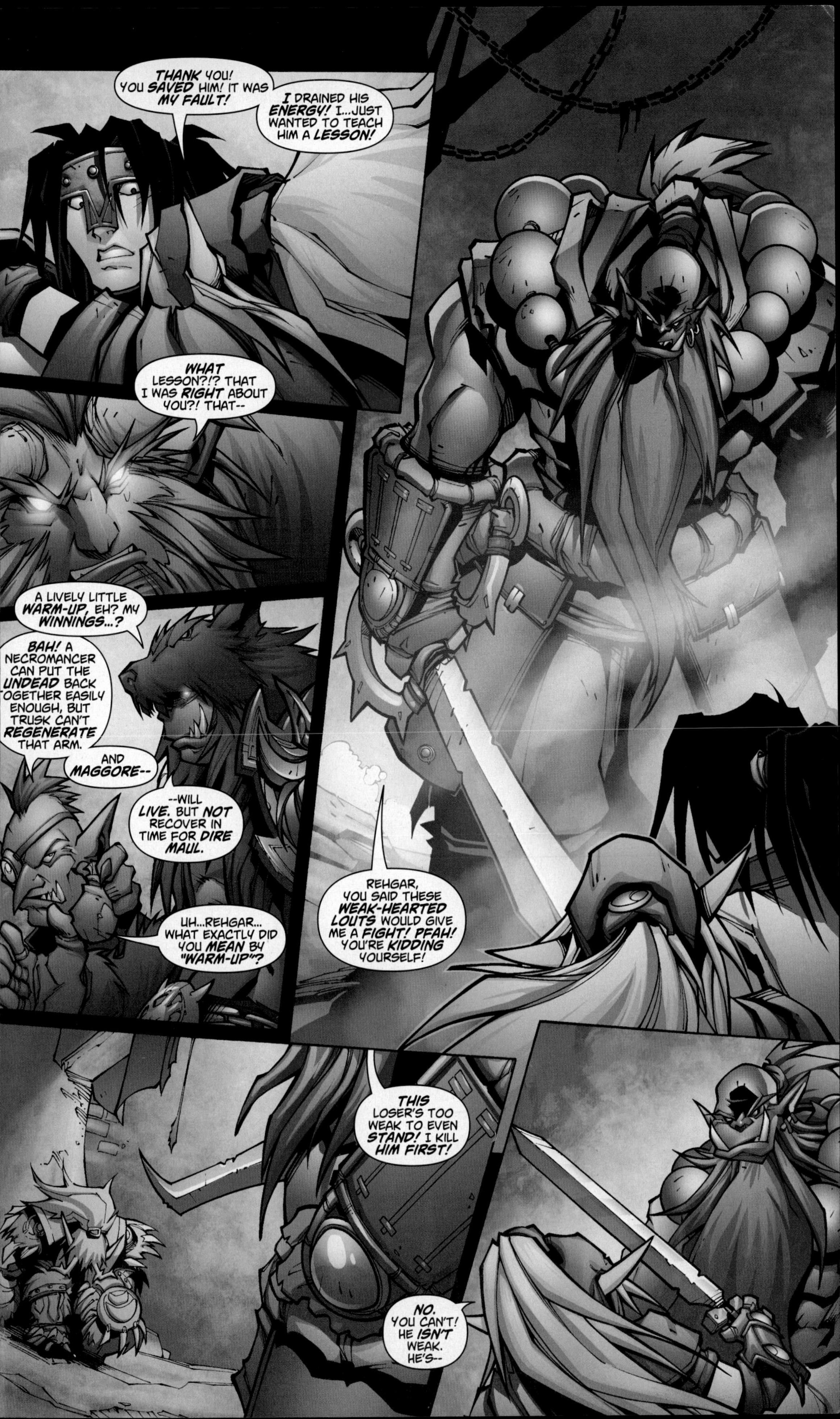
THANK YOU! YOU SAVED HIM! IT WAS MY FAULT!
I DRAINED HIS ENERGY! I...JUST WANTED TO TEACH HIM A LESSON!
WHAT LESSON?!? THAT I WAS RIGHT ABOUT YOU?! THAT--
A LIVELY LITTLE WARM-UP, EH? MY WINNINGS...?
BAH! A NECROMANCER CAN PUT THE UNDEAD BACK TOGETHER EASILY ENOUGH, BUT TRUSK CAN'T REGENERATE THAT ARM.
AND MAGGORE--
--WILL LIVE. BUT NOT RECOVER IN TIME FOR DIRE MAUL.
UH...REHGAR... WHAT EXACTLY DID YOU MEAN BY "WARM-UP"?
REHGAR, YOU SAID THESE WEAK-HEARTED LOUTS WOULD GIVE ME A FIGHT! PFAH! YOU'RE KIDDING YOURSELF!
THIS LOSER'S TOO WEAK TO EVEN STAND! I KILL HIM FIRST!
NO. YOU CAN'T! HE ISN'T WEAK. HE'S--

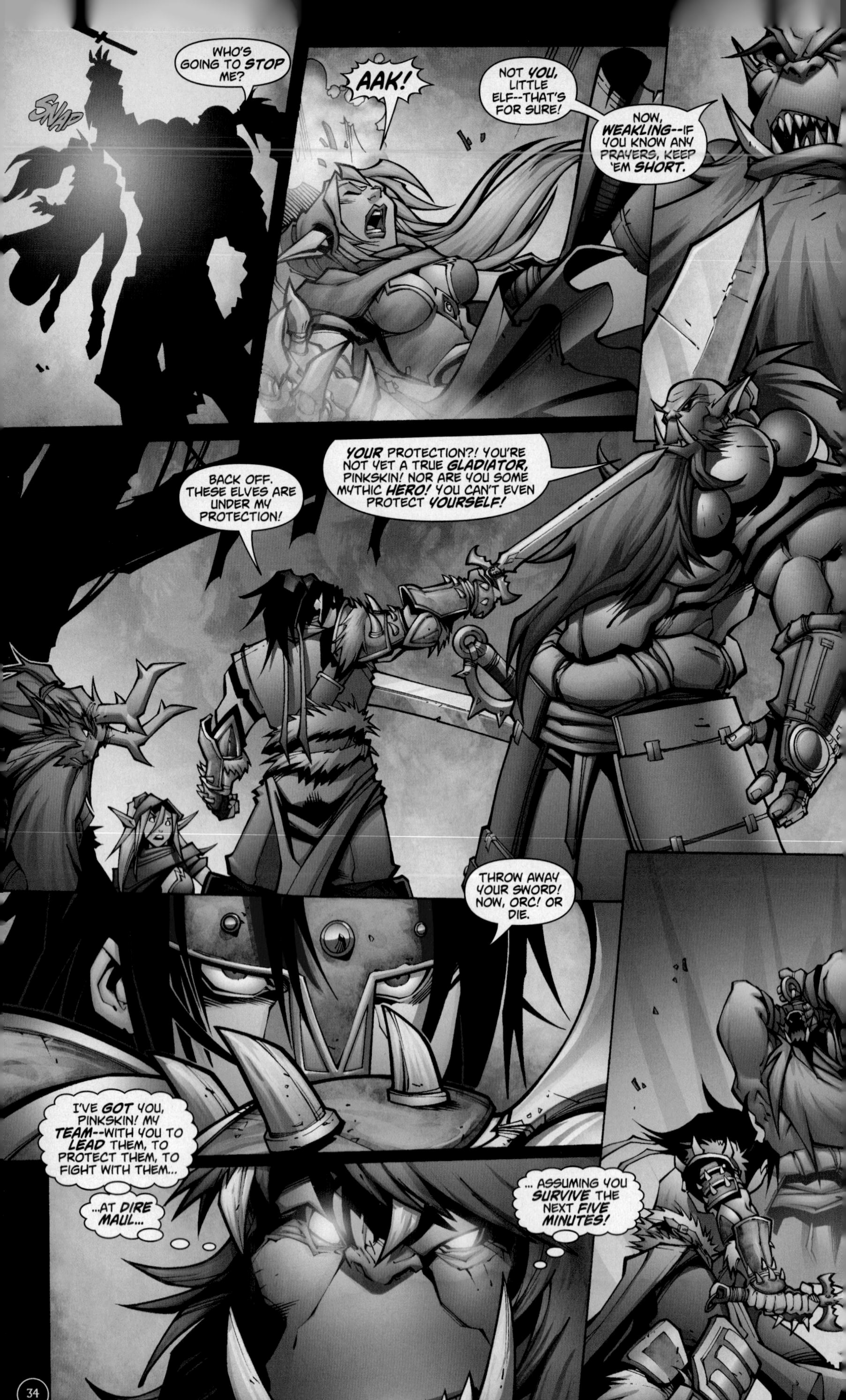
WHO'S GOING TO STOP ME?
SNAP
AAK!
NOT YOU, LITTLE ELF--THAT'S FOR SURE!
NOW, WEAKLING--IF YOU KNOW ANY PRAYERS, KEEP 'EM SHORT.
BACK OFF. THESE ELVES ARE UNDER MY PROTECTION!
YOUR PROTECTION?! YOU'RE NOT YET A TRUE GLADIATOR, PINKSKIN! NOR ARE YOU SOME MYTHIC HERO! YOU CAN'T EVEN PROTECT YOURSELF!
THROW AWAY YOUR SWORD! NOW, ORC! OR DIE.
I'VE GOT YOU, PINKSKIN! MY TEAM--WITH YOU TO LEAD THEM, TO PROTECT THEM, TO FIGHT WITH THEM...
...AT DIRE MAUL...
... ASSUMING YOU SURVIVE THE NEXT FIVE MINUTES!

CHAPTER 2

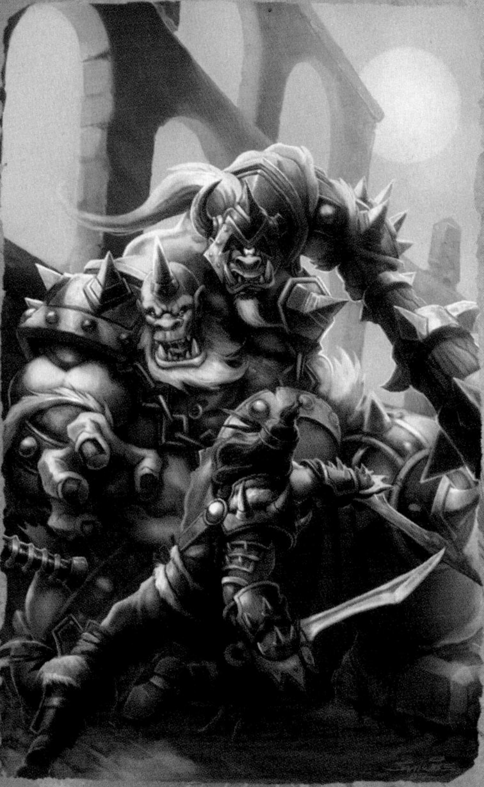

Issue #2 Cover
by Samwise Didier

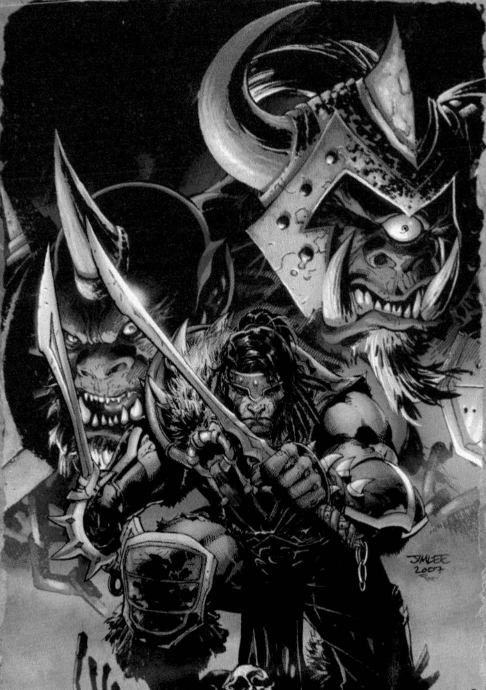

Issue #2 Cover
by Jim Lee and Alex Sinclair

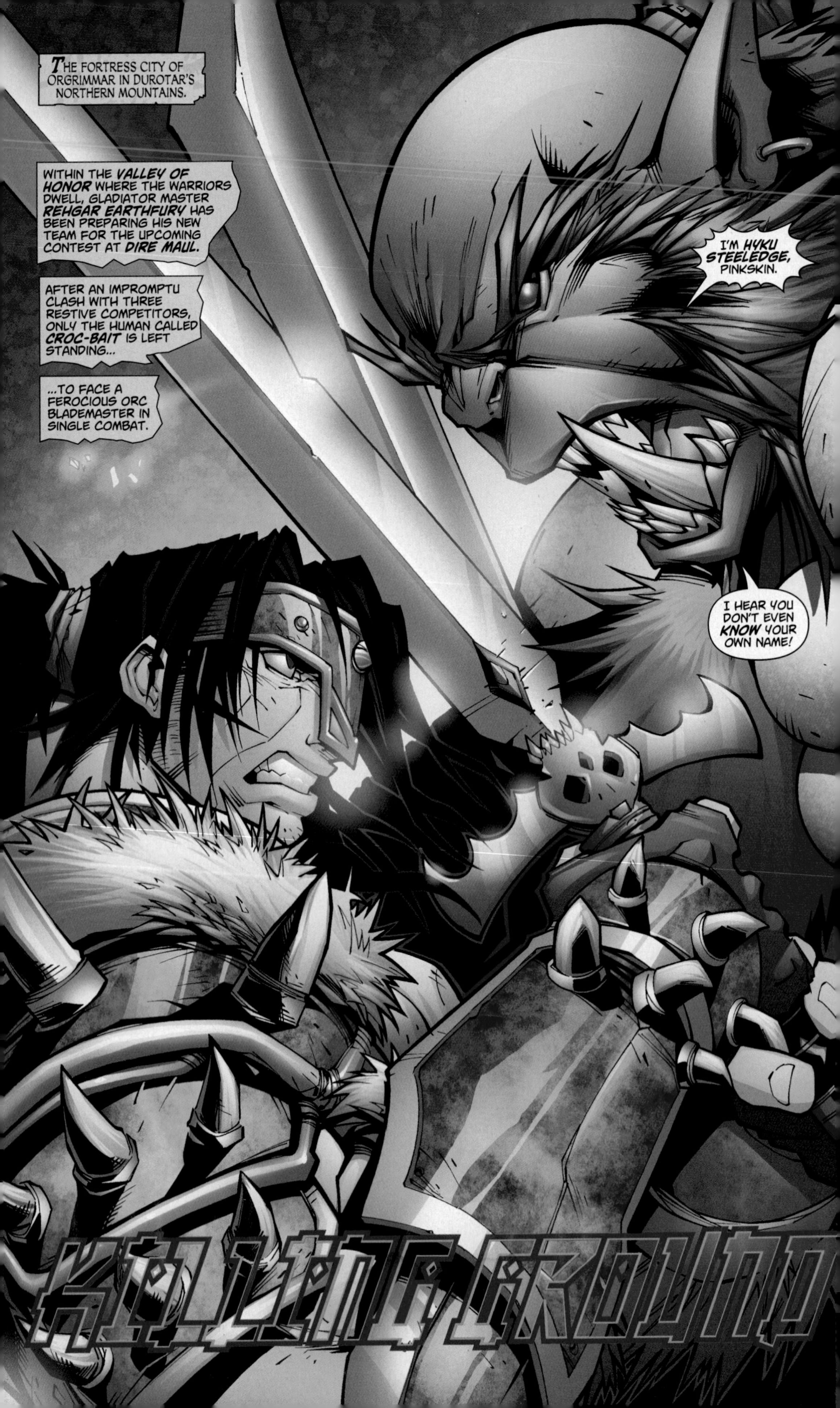
THE FORTRESS CITY OF ORGRIMMAR IN DUROTAR'S NORTHERN MOUNTAINS.
WITHIN THE VALLEY OF HONOR WHERE THE WARRIORS DWELL, GLADIATOR MASTER REHGAR EARTHFURY HAS BEEN PREPARING HIS NEW TEAM FOR THE UPCOMING CONTEST AT DIRE MAUL.
AFTER AN IMPROMPTU CLASH WITH THREE RESTIVE COMPETITORS, ONLY THE HUMAN CALLED CROC-BAIT IS LEFT STANDING...
...TO FACE A FEROCIOUS ORC BLADEMASTER IN SINGLE COMBAT.
I'M HYKU STEELEDGE, PINKSKIN.
I HEAR YOU DON'T EVEN KNOW YOUR OWN NAME!
KILLING GROUND

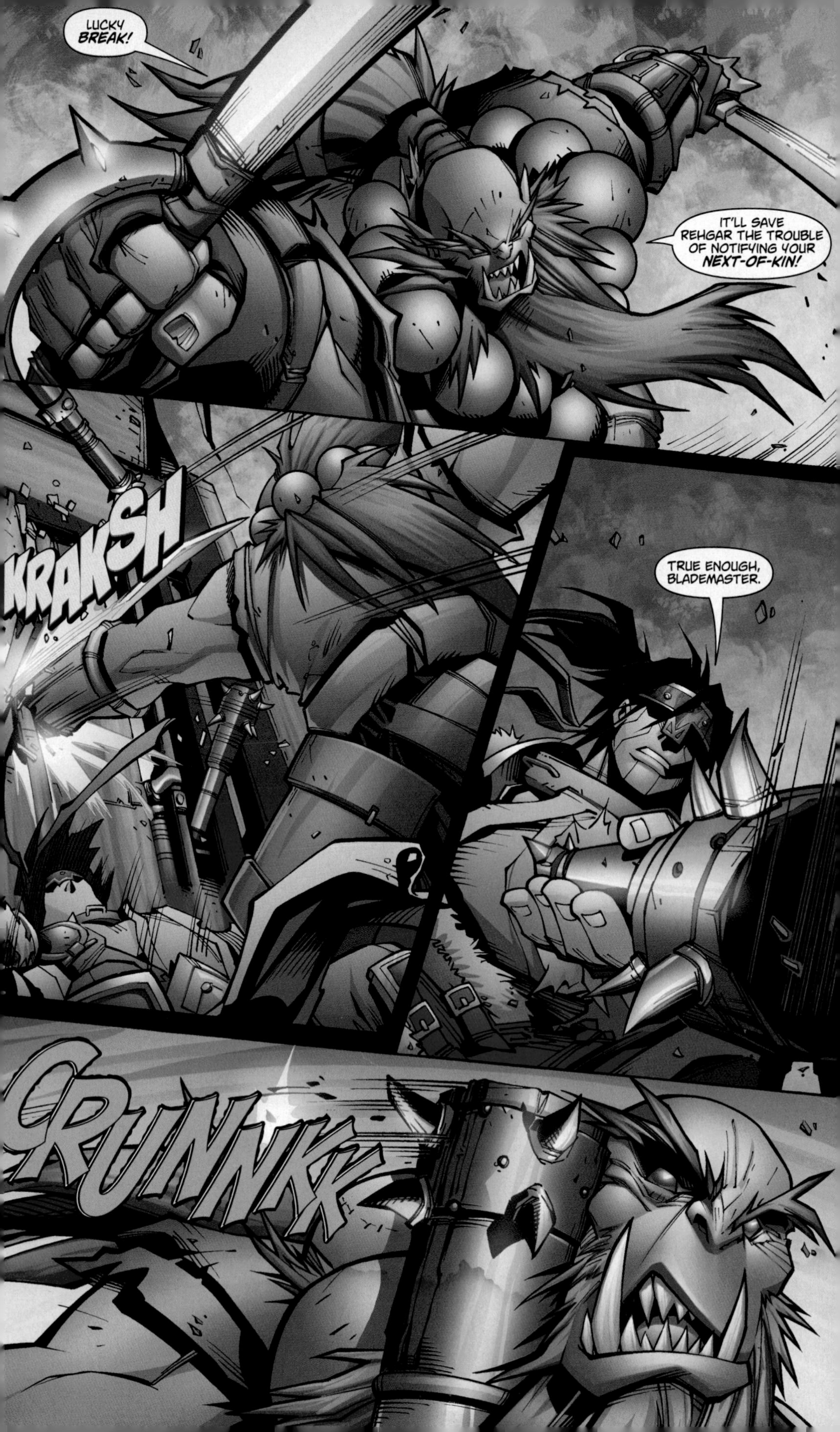
LUCKY BREAK!
IT'LL SAVE REHGAR THE TROUBLE OF NOTIFYING YOUR NEXT-OF-KIN!
KRAKSH
TRUE ENOUGH, BLADEMASTER.
CRUNNKK

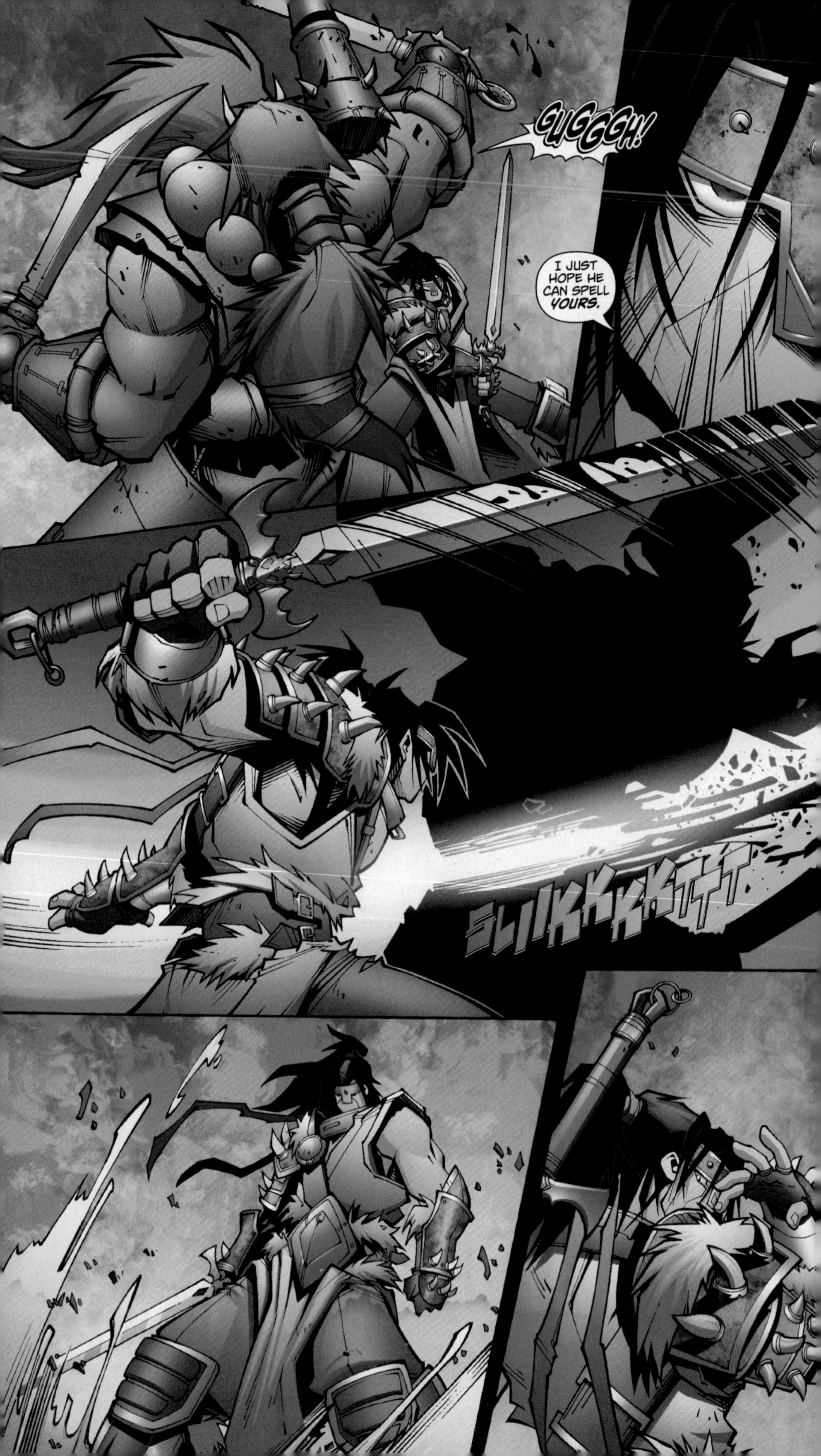
GUGGGH!
I JUST HOPE HE CAN SPELL YOURS.
SLIIKKKKTTT

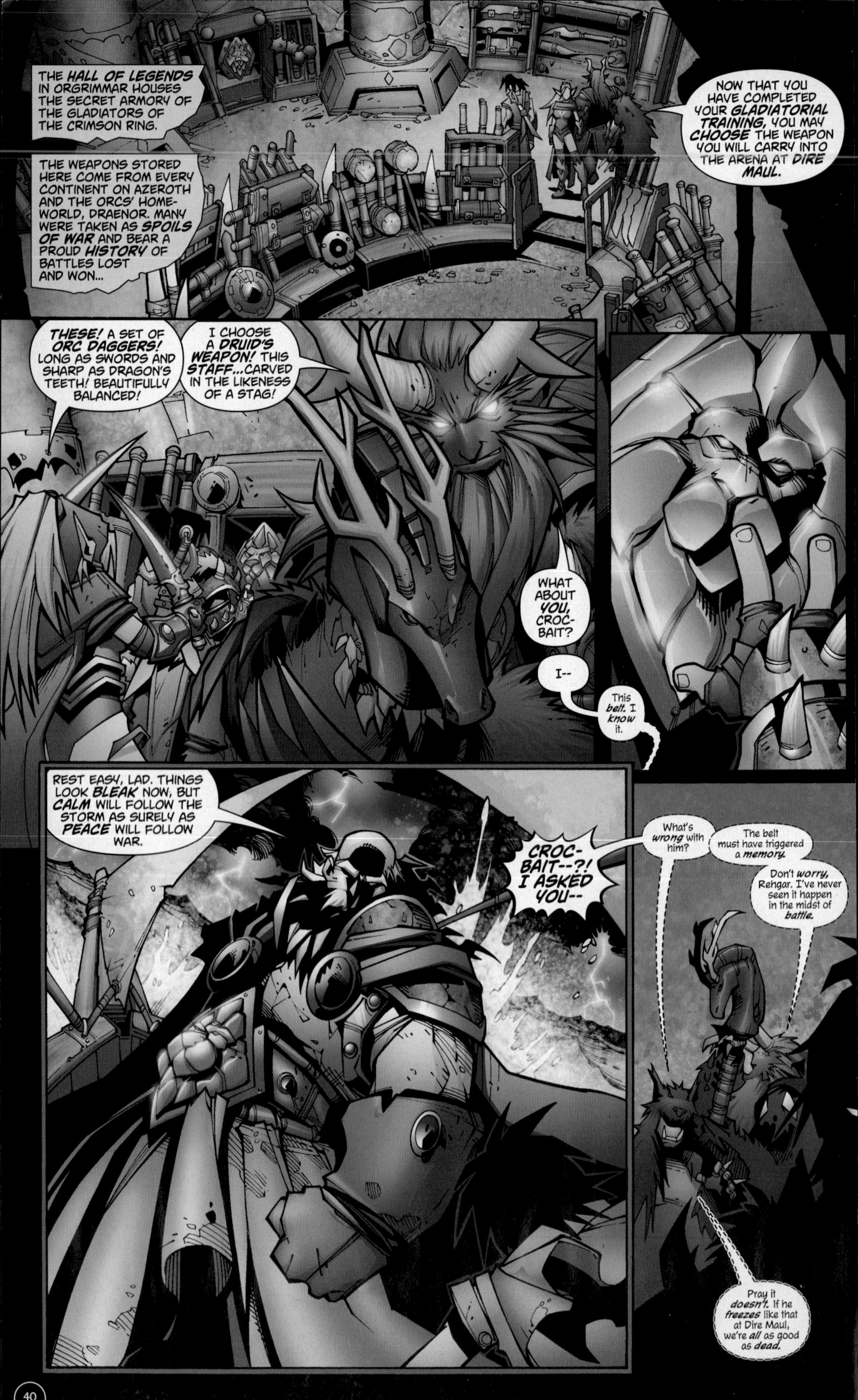
THE HALL OF LEGENDS IN ORGRIMMAR HOUSES THE SECRET ARMORY OF THE GLADIATORS OF THE CRIMSON RING.
THE WEAPONS STORED HERE COME FROM EVERY CONTINENT ON AZEROTH AND THE ORCS' HOME-WORLD, DRAENOR. MANY WERE TAKEN AS SPOILS OF WAR AND BEAR A PROUD HISTORY OF BATTLES LOST AND WON...
NOW THAT YOU HAVE COMPLETED YOUR GLADIATORIAL TRAINING, YOU MAY CHOOSE THE WEAPON YOU WILL CARRY INTO THE ARENA AT DIRE MAUL.
THESE! A SET OF ORC DAGGERS! LONG AS SWORDS AND SHARP AS DRAGON'S TEETH! BEAUTIFULLY BALANCED!
I CHOOSE A DRUID'S WEAPON! THIS STAFF...CARVED IN THE LIKENESS OF A STAG!
WHAT ABOUT YOU, CROC-BAIT?
I--
This belt. I know it.
REST EASY, LAD. THINGS LOOK BLEAK NOW, BUT CALM WILL FOLLOW THE STORM AS SURELY AS PEACE WILL FOLLOW WAR.
CROC-BAIT--?! I ASKED YOU--
What's wrong with him?
The belt must have triggered a memory.
Don't worry, Rehgar. I've never seen it happen in the midst of battle.
Pray it doesn't. If he freezes like that at Dire Maul, we're all as good as dead.

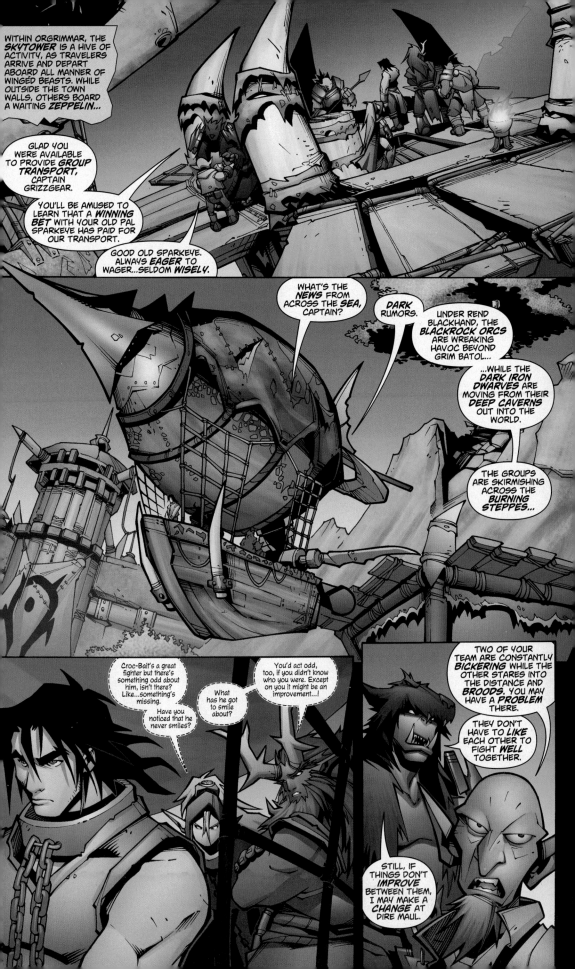

WITHIN ORGRIMMAR, THE *SKYTOWER* IS A HIVE OF ACTIVITY, AS TRAVELERS ARRIVE AND DEPART ABOARD ALL MANNER OF WINGED BEASTS. WHILE OUTSIDE THE TOWN WALLS, OTHERS BOARD A WAITING *ZEPPELIN*...

GLAD YOU WERE AVAILABLE TO PROVIDE *GROUP TRANSPORT*, CAPTAIN GRIZZGEAR.

YOU'LL BE AMUSED TO LEARN THAT A *WINNING BET* WITH YOUR OLD PAL SPARKEYE HAS PAID FOR OUR TRANSPORT.

GOOD OLD SPARKEYE. ALWAYS *EAGER* TO WAGER...SELDOM *WISELY*.

WHAT'S THE *NEWS* FROM ACROSS THE *SEA*, CAPTAIN?

DARK RUMORS.

UNDER REND BLACKHAND, THE *BLACKROCK ORCS* ARE WREAKING HAVOC BEYOND GRIM BATOL...

...WHILE THE *DARK IRON DWARVES* ARE MOVING FROM THEIR *DEEP CAVERNS* OUT INTO THE WORLD.

THE GROUPS ARE SKIRMISHING ACROSS THE *BURNING STEPPES*...

Croc-Bait's a great fighter but there's something odd about him, isn't there? Like...something's missing.

Have you noticed that he never smiles?

What has he got to smile about?

You'd act odd, too, if you didn't know who you were. Except on you it might be an improvement...!

TWO OF YOUR TEAM ARE CONSTANTLY *BICKERING* WHILE THE OTHER STARES INTO THE DISTANCE AND BROODS. YOU MAY HAVE A *PROBLEM* THERE.

THEY DON'T HAVE TO *LIKE* EACH OTHER TO FIGHT *WELL* TOGETHER.

STILL, IF THINGS DON'T *IMPROVE* BETWEEN THEM, I MAY MAKE A *CHANGE* AT DIRE MAUL.

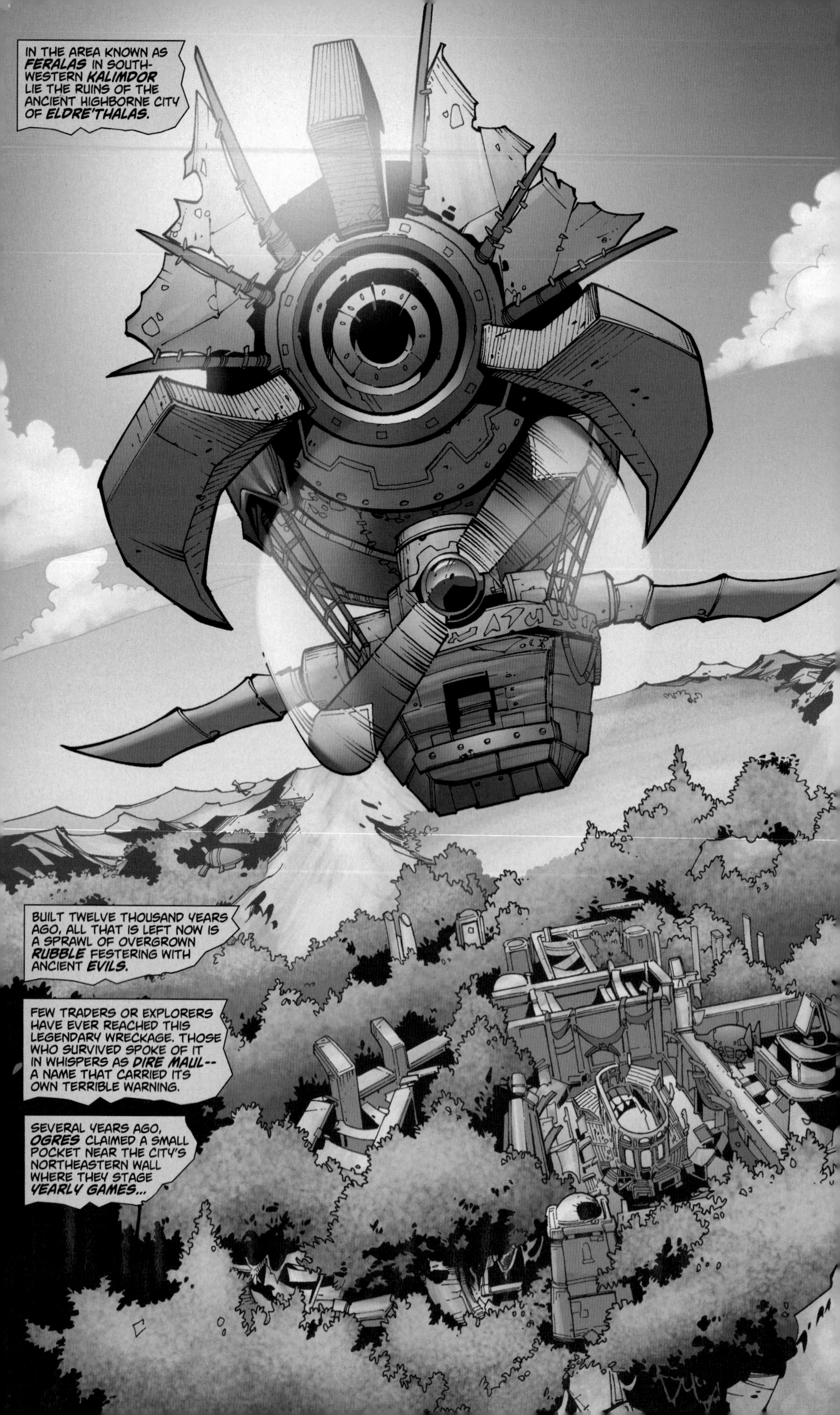
IN THE AREA KNOWN AS FERALAS IN SOUTH-WESTERN KALIMDOR LIE THE RUINS OF THE ANCIENT HIGHBORNE CITY OF ELDRE'THALAS.
BUILT TWELVE THOUSAND YEARS AGO, ALL THAT IS LEFT NOW IS A SPRAWL OF OVERGROWN RUBBLE FESTERING WITH ANCIENT EVILS.
FEW TRADERS OR EXPLORERS HAVE EVER REACHED THIS LEGENDARY WRECKAGE. THOSE WHO SURVIVED SPOKE OF IT IN WHISPERS AS DIRE MAUL-- A NAME THAT CARRIED ITS OWN TERRIBLE WARNING.
SEVERAL YEARS AGO, OGRES CLAIMED A SMALL POCKET NEAR THE CITY'S NORTHEASTERN WALL WHERE THEY STAGE YEARLY GAMES...

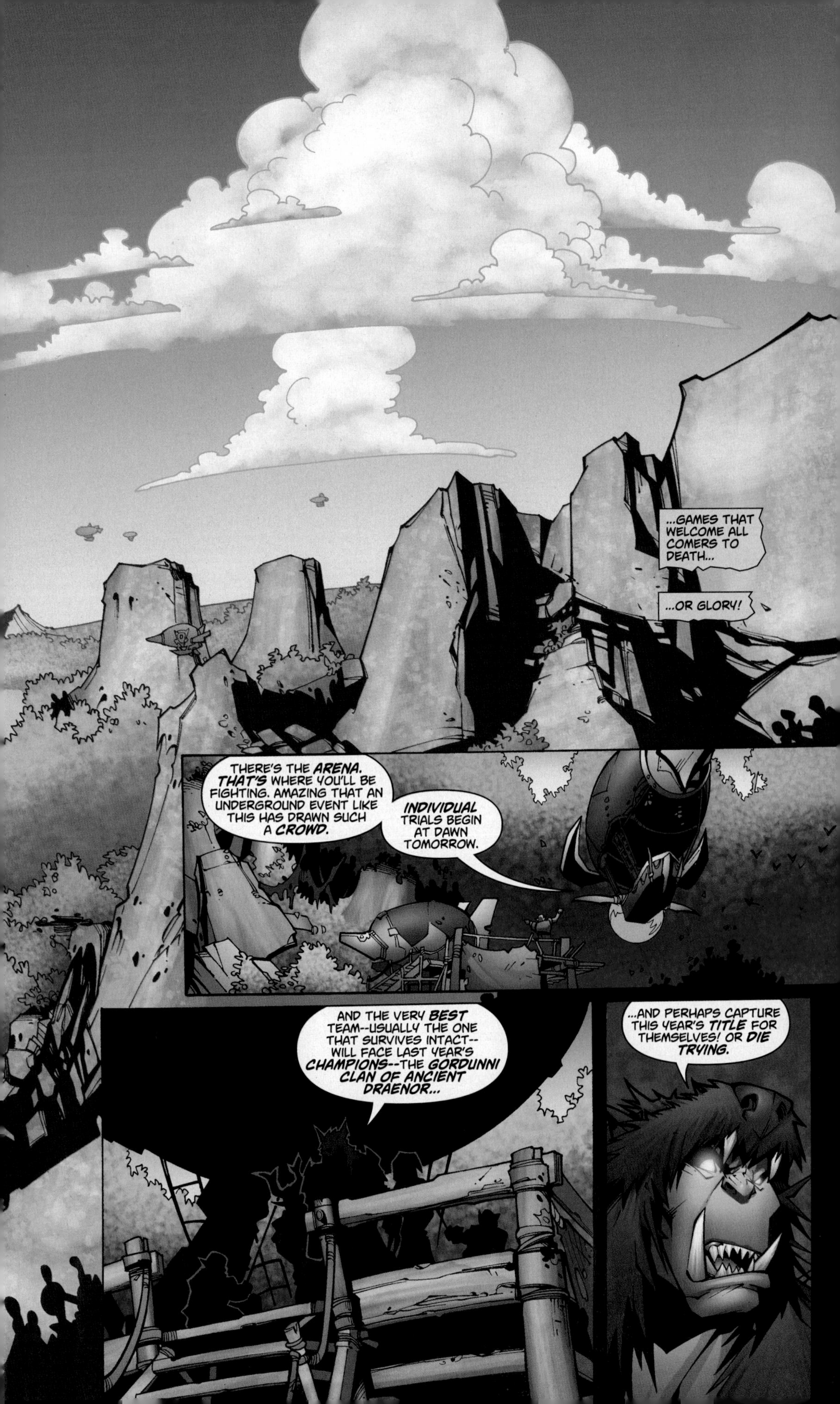
...GAMES THAT WELCOME ALL COMERS TO DEATH...
...OR GLORY!
THERE'S THE ARENA. THAT'S WHERE YOU'LL BE FIGHTING. AMAZING THAT AN UNDERGROUND EVENT LIKE THIS HAS DRAWN SUCH A CROWD.
INDIVIDUAL TRIALS BEGIN AT DAWN TOMORROW.
AND THE VERY BEST TEAM--USUALLY THE ONE THAT SURVIVES INTACT--WILL FACE LAST YEAR'S CHAMPIONS--THE GORDUNNI CLAN OF ANCIENT DRAENOR...
...AND PERHAPS CAPTURE THIS YEAR'S TITLE FOR THEMSELVES! OR DIE TRYING.

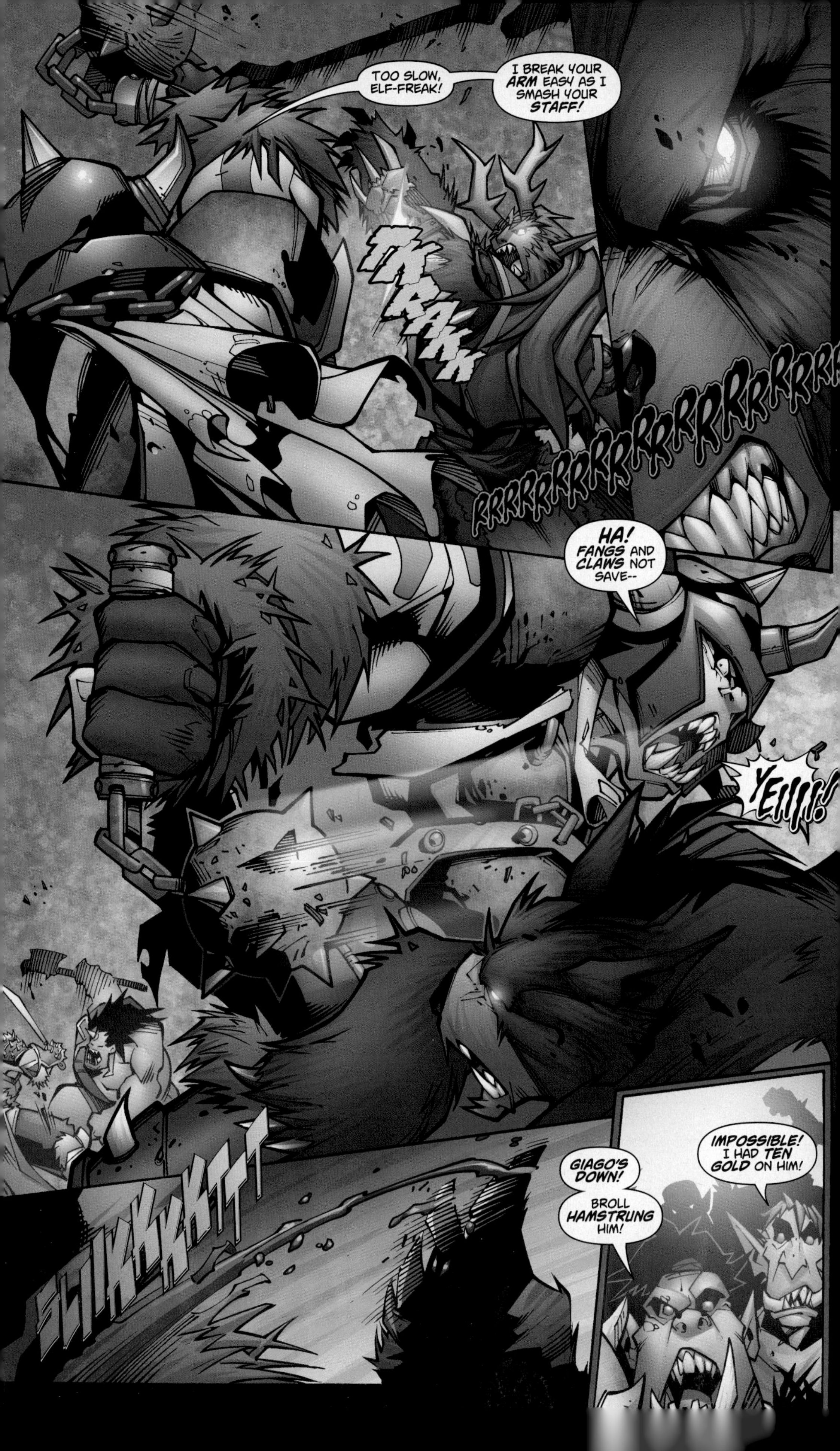
TOO SLOW, ELF-FREAK!
I BREAK YOUR ARM EASY AS I SMASH YOUR STAFF!
TKRAKK
RRRRRRRRRRRRRRRRRRRRRRR
HA! FANGS AND CLAWS NOT SAVE--
YEIIII!
SCHKKKTTT
GIAGO'S DOWN!
BROLL HAMSTRUNG HIM!
IMPOSSIBLE! I HAD TEN GOLD ON HIM!

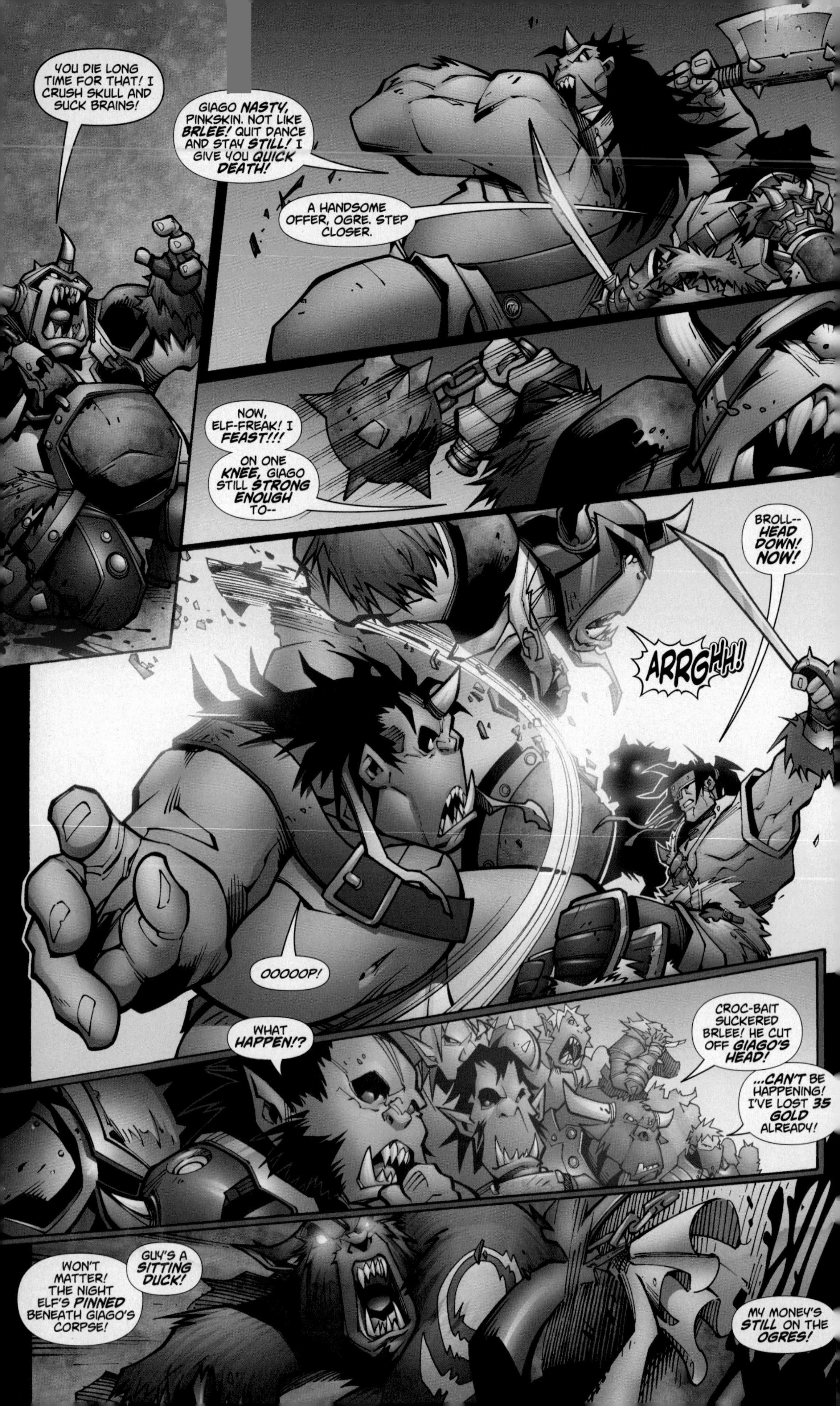
YOU DIE LONG TIME FOR THAT! I CRUSH SKULL AND SUCK BRAINS!
GIAGO NASTY, PINKSKIN. NOT LIKE BRLEE! QUIT DANCE AND STAY STILL! I GIVE YOU QUICK DEATH!
A HANDSOME OFFER, OGRE. STEP CLOSER.
NOW, ELF-FREAK! I FEAST!!!
ON ONE KNEE, GIAGO STILL STRONG ENOUGH TO--
BROLL-- HEAD DOWN! NOW!
ARRGHH!
OOOOOP!
WHAT HAPPEN!?
CROC-BAIT SUCKERED BRLEE! HE CUT OFF GIAGO'S HEAD!
...CAN'T BE HAPPENING! I'VE LOST 35 GOLD ALREADY!
WON'T MATTER! THE NIGHT ELF'S PINNED BENEATH GIAGO'S CORPSE!
GUY'S A SITTING DUCK!
MY MONEY'S STILL ON THE OGRES!

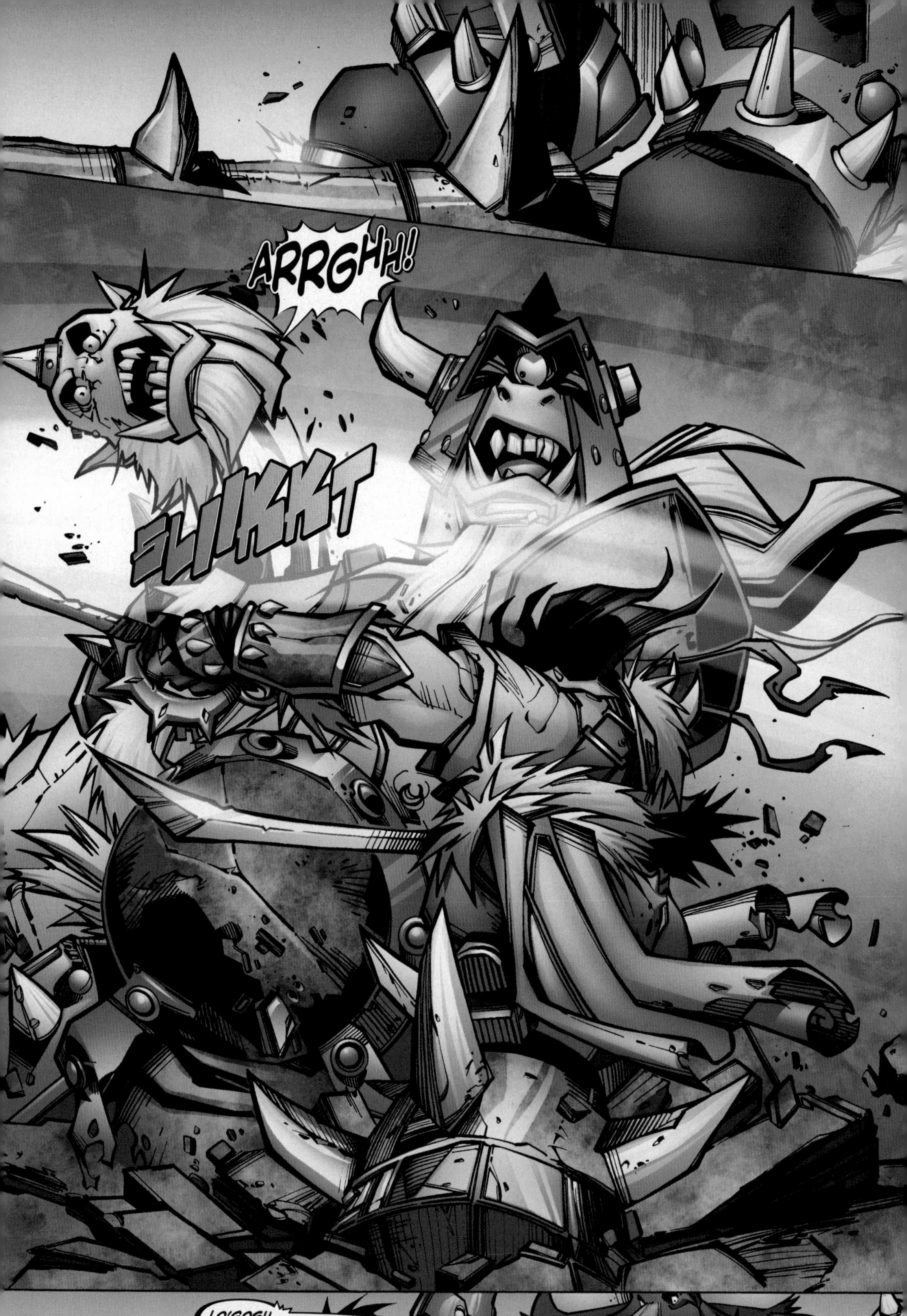
ARRGHH!
SLIIKKT
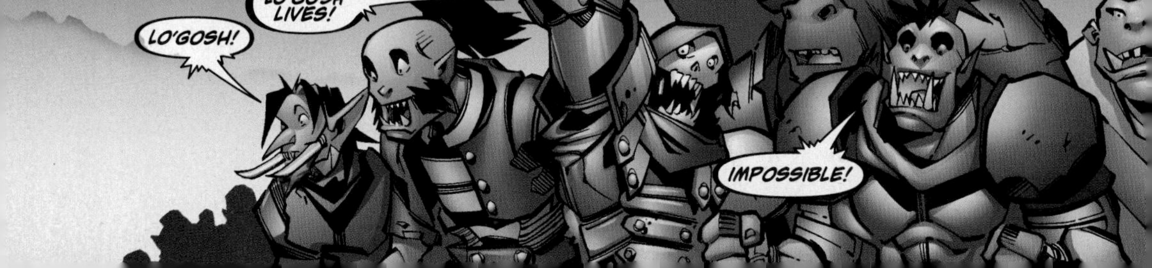
LO'GOSH LIVES!
LO'GOSH!
IMPOSSIBLE!

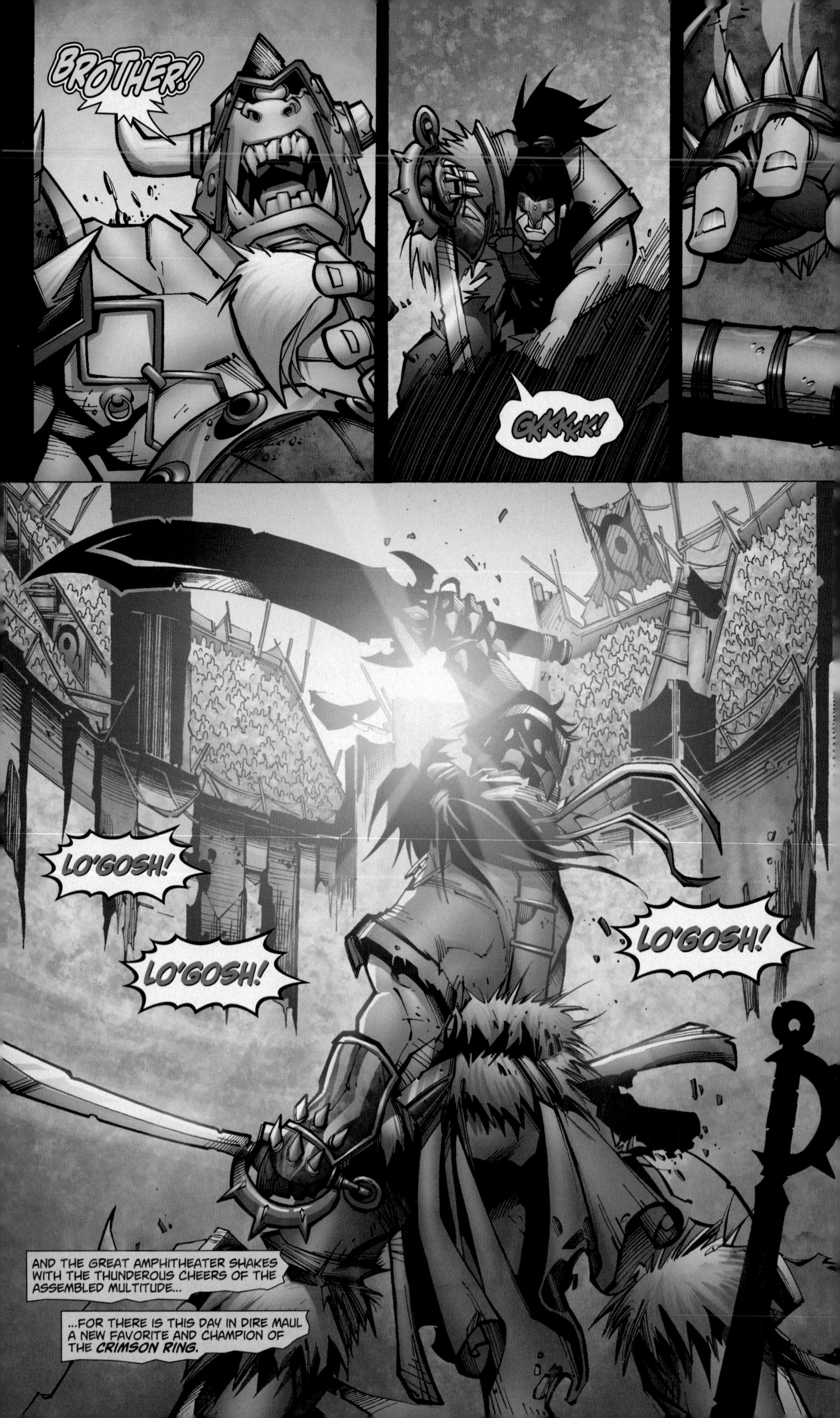
BROTHER!
GKKKK!
LO'GOSH!
LO'GOSH!
LO'GOSH!
AND THE GREAT AMPHITHEATER SHAKES WITH THE THUNDEROUS CHEERS OF THE ASSEMBLED MULTITUDE...
...FOR THERE IS THIS DAY IN DIRE MAUL A NEW FAVORITE AND CHAMPION OF THE *CRIMSON RING*.

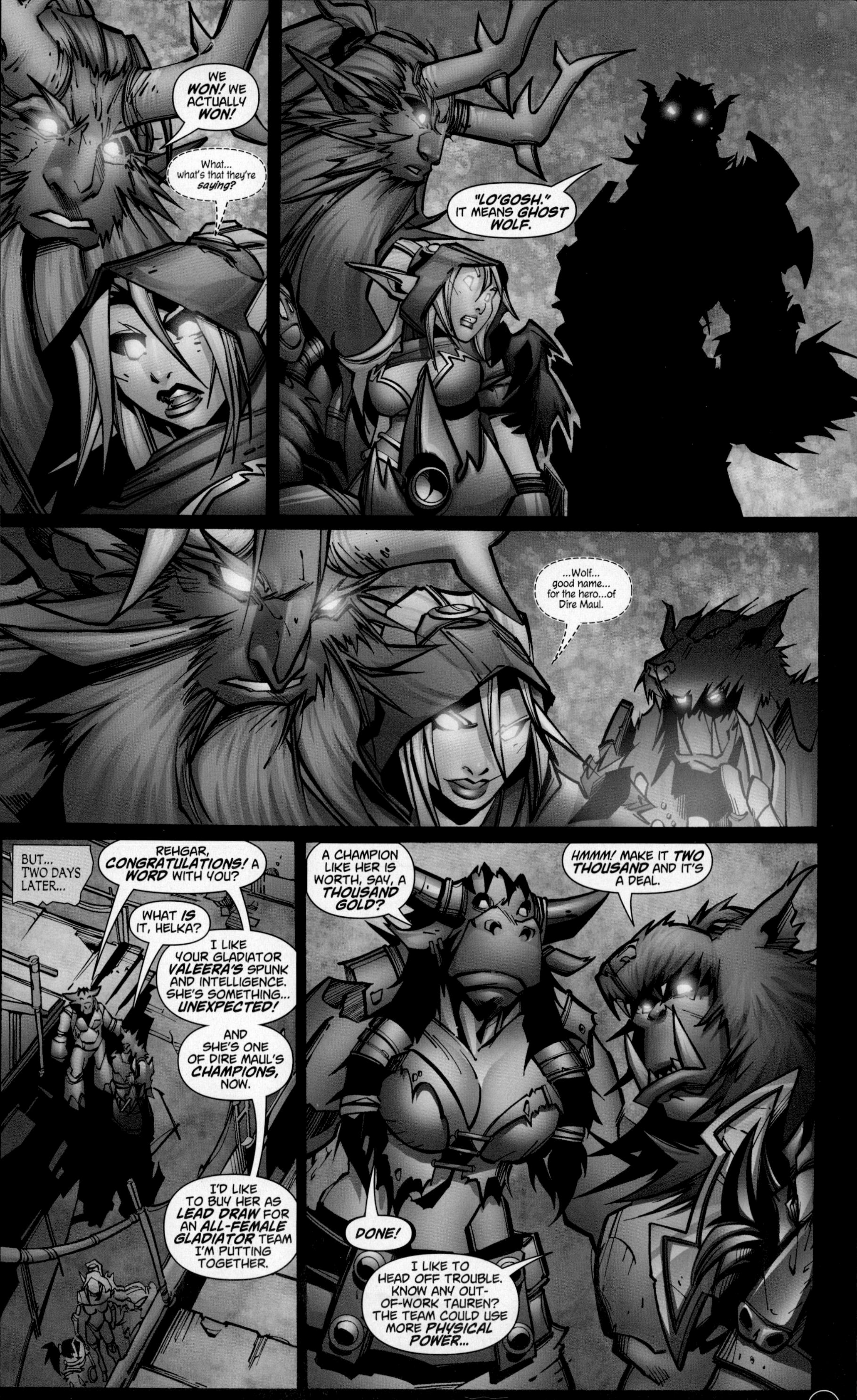
WE WON! WE ACTUALLY WON!
What... what's that they're saying?
"LO'GOSH." IT MEANS GHOST WOLF.
...Wolf... good name... for the hero...of Dire Maul.
BUT... TWO DAYS LATER...
REHGAR, CONGRATULATIONS! A WORD WITH YOU?
WHAT IS IT, HELKA?
I LIKE YOUR GLADIATOR VALEERA'S SPUNK AND INTELLIGENCE. SHE'S SOMETHING... UNEXPECTED!
AND SHE'S ONE OF DIRE MAUL'S CHAMPIONS, NOW.
I'D LIKE TO BUY HER AS LEAD DRAW FOR AN ALL-FEMALE GLADIATOR TEAM I'M PUTTING TOGETHER.
A CHAMPION LIKE HER IS WORTH, SAY, A THOUSAND GOLD?
HMMM! MAKE IT TWO THOUSAND AND IT'S A DEAL.
DONE!
I LIKE TO HEAD OFF TROUBLE. KNOW ANY OUT-OF-WORK TAUREN? THE TEAM COULD USE MORE PHYSICAL POWER...

Sketches By Ludo Lullabi

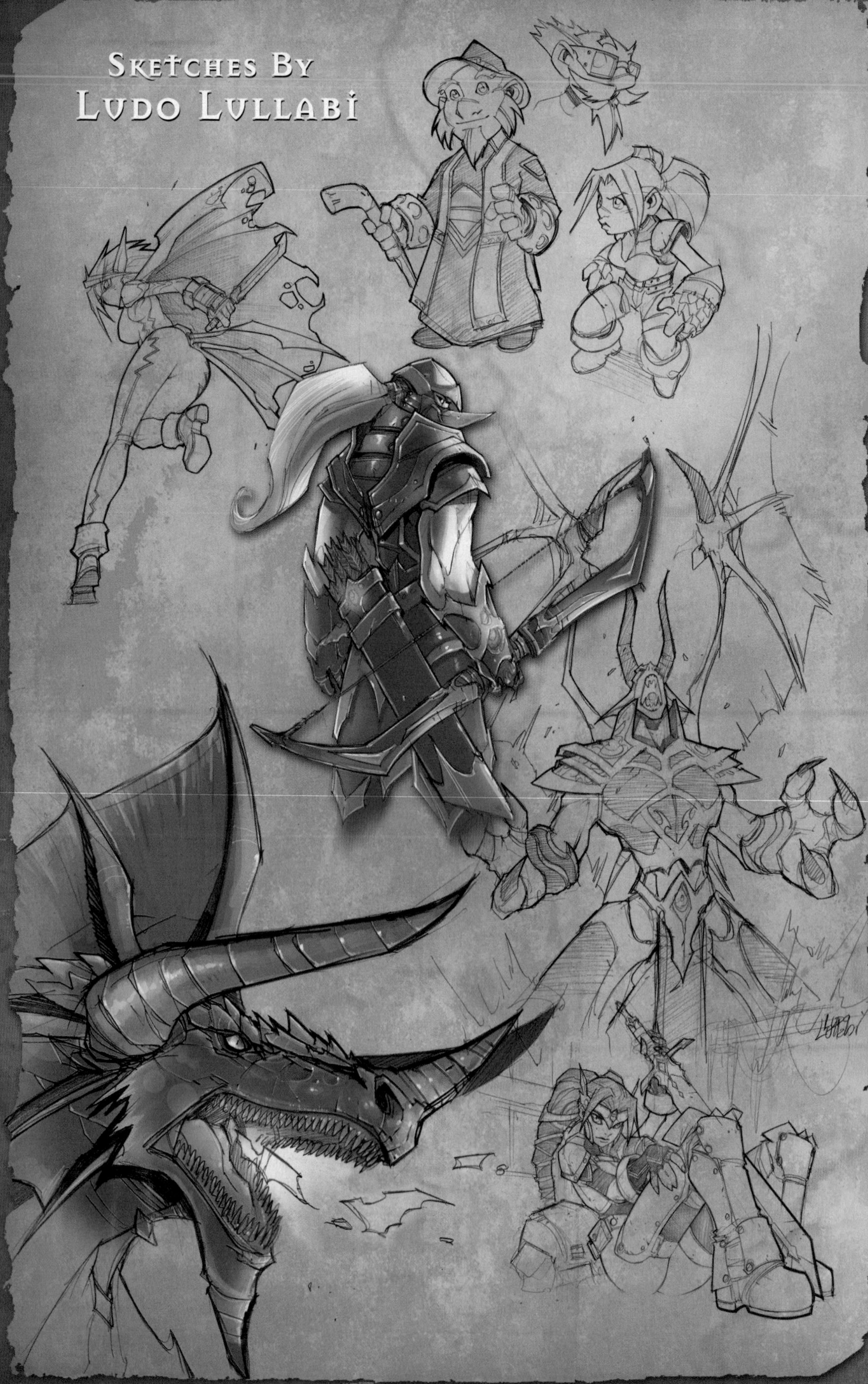

CHAPTER 3

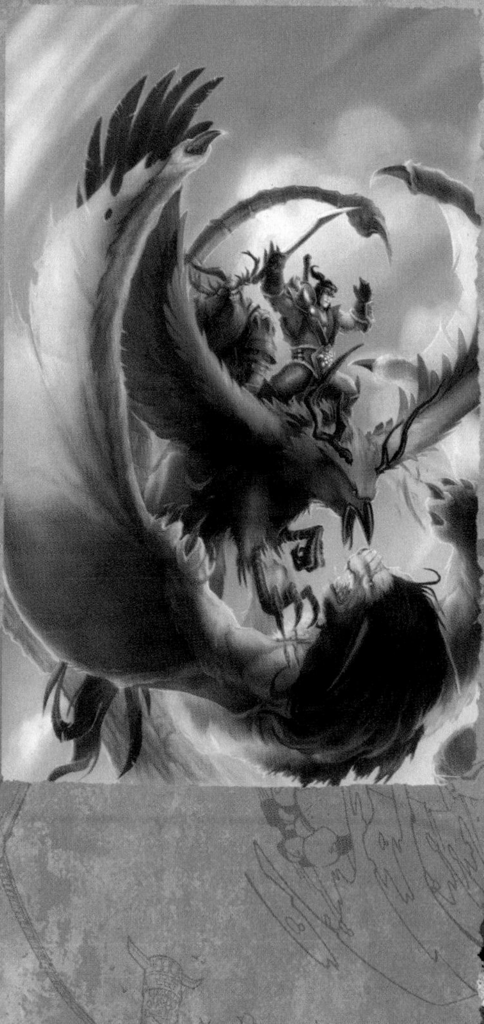

Issue #3 Cover
by Samwise Didier

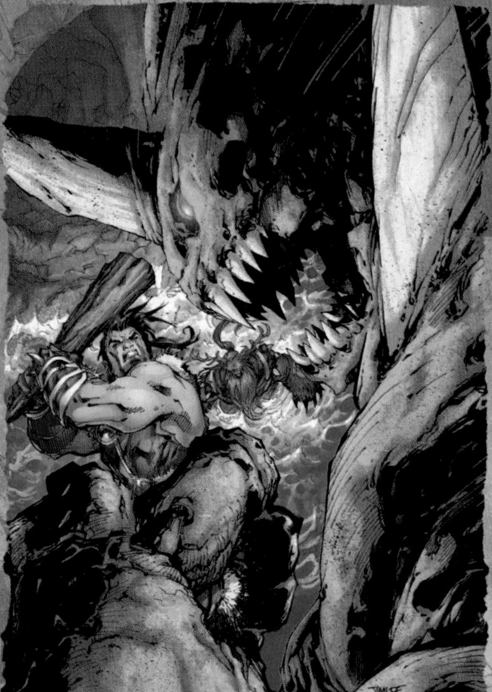

Issue #3 Cover
by Jim Lee and Alex Sinclair

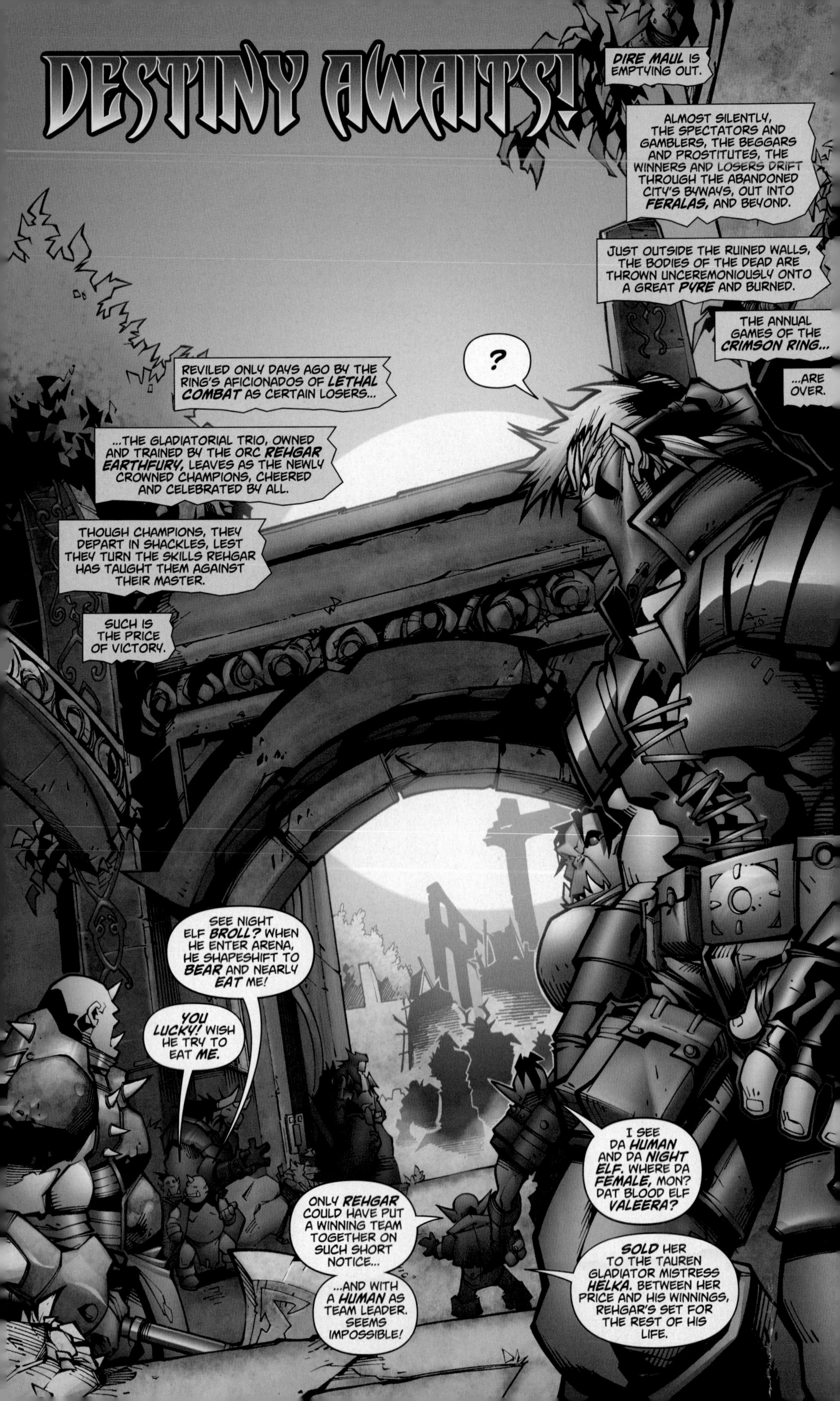

DESTINY AWAITS!
DIRE MAUL IS EMPTYING OUT.
ALMOST SILENTLY, THE SPECTATORS AND GAMBLERS, THE BEGGARS AND PROSTITUTES, THE WINNERS AND LOSERS DRIFT THROUGH THE ABANDONED CITY'S BYWAYS, OUT INTO FERALAS, AND BEYOND.
JUST OUTSIDE THE RUINED WALLS, THE BODIES OF THE DEAD ARE THROWN UNCEREMONIOUSLY ONTO A GREAT PYRE AND BURNED.
THE ANNUAL GAMES OF THE CRIMSON RING...
...ARE OVER.
?
REVILED ONLY DAYS AGO BY THE RING'S AFICIONADOS OF LETHAL COMBAT AS CERTAIN LOSERS...
...THE GLADIATORIAL TRIO, OWNED AND TRAINED BY THE ORC REHGAR EARTHFURY, LEAVES AS THE NEWLY CROWNED CHAMPIONS, CHEERED AND CELEBRATED BY ALL.
THOUGH CHAMPIONS, THEY DEPART IN SHACKLES, LEST THEY TURN THE SKILLS REHGAR HAS TAUGHT THEM AGAINST THEIR MASTER.
SUCH IS THE PRICE OF VICTORY.
SEE NIGHT ELF BROLL? WHEN HE ENTER ARENA, HE SHAPESHIFT TO BEAR AND NEARLY EAT ME!
YOU LUCKY! WISH HE TRY TO EAT ME.
ONLY REHGAR COULD HAVE PUT A WINNING TEAM TOGETHER ON SUCH SHORT NOTICE...
...AND WITH A HUMAN AS TEAM LEADER. SEEMS IMPOSSIBLE!
I SEE DA HUMAN AND DA NIGHT ELF. WHERE DA FEMALE, MON? DAT BLOOD ELF VALEERA?
SOLD HER TO THE TAUREN GLADIATOR MISTRESS HELKA. BETWEEN HER PRICE AND HIS WINNINGS, REHGAR'S SET FOR THE REST OF HIS LIFE.

FLUSH WITH HIS WINNINGS, REHGAR *TRANSPORTS* HIS ENTOURAGE ABOARD THE *DIRIGIBLE* BELONGING TO HIS FRIEND, THE GOBLIN CAPTAIN GRIZZGEAR...

FORGET IT, REHGAR. THIS TRIP'S ON *ME.* I *BET* ALL THE GOLD I HAD ON YOUR TEAM... *QUIETLY,* AS YOU ADVISED. MADE A *FORTUNE.* IF I DIDN'T ENJOY MY WORK SO MUCH, I'D *RETIRE!*

RUMOR SAYS YOU'RE REPLACING THE NIGHT ELF WITH A *TAUREN.* THAT WHY WE'RE HEADED TO *THUNDER BLUFF?* YOU'LL TALK TO *MAGATHA?*

HELKA WILL HAVE SENT WORD TO HER AUNT. I EXPECT THE *OLD HAG* WILL BE WAITING WITH A LIST OF LIKELY PROSPECTS...

VALEERA WAS *GOOD COMPANY.* SHE MADE ME WANT TO *LAUGH* AS OFTEN AS I WANTED TO *THROTTLE* HER.

WHY DID REHGAR *SELL* HER?

GOLD. AS OUR MASTER, IT WAS HIS *RIGHT.*

AND I THINK HE FELT WE WERE ILL MATCHED. HE WAS *WRONG* THERE.

"TO BE A *GLADIATOR* IS TO COURT DEATH. TO BE A *SLAVE* IS TO DO YOUR MASTER'S WILL."

AN *UNPROMISING* FUTURE, DON'T YOU THINK?

YOU PLAN TO *ESCAPE?* BUT, YOU HAVE *AMNESIA.* IF YOU AREN'T LO'GOSH THE GLADIATOR CHAMPION, YOU'RE NOBODY.

I'LL ASK REHGAR IF WE MIGHT PARTAKE OF A *CLEANSING RITUAL* THERE. IT MIGHT HELP RESTORE YOUR *MEMORY.*

LOOK, THERE ARE SPRINGS AT THUNDER BLUFF CALLED THE *POOLS OF VISION.* IT'S RUMORED THAT THEY DELIVER *MESSAGES...* FROM THE DEAD.

WE...? YOU WANT TO TALK TO THE DEAD?

I...LOST A *DAUGHTER.* QUICK, FUNNY, AND BRAVE... LIKE *VALEERA.* MAYBE...

BROLL'S VOICE TRAILS OFF.

THE BROKEN COMMONS.

HELKA AND HER CREW QUEUE UP FOR THEIR FLIGHT.

TARM, YOU'LL TAKE *VALEERA* ON BRISTLEFUR.

GOT IT.

Bristlefur?

PRRR RRRRRR RRT!

NO MORE PRIVATE *DIRIGIBLES* FOR YOU, BLOOD ELF. HELKA'S OUTFIT TRAVELS STRICTLY *SECOND CLASS!*

YOU FLY ON *WYVERN* BACK. *AND* SHARE DA MOUNT!

Excellent!

KICK

EEEE EEEEEE EEK!

HEY! NOT SO *FAST*, GIRL!

OHH, TARM! SHE JUST...*BOLTED.* I'M *SCARED.* I *HATE* BEING UP HIGH.

SHE'S A *LIVELY* ONE! NOTHING TO WORRY ABOUT WITH ME ABOARD.

BUT I'M AMAZED A KID LIKE YOU SURVIVED DIRE MAUL.

LUCK MOSTLY. I *WAS* HURT PRETTY BAD. I WAS *LOUSY.* THAT'S WHY REHGAR *SOLD* ME.

WELL, YOU'RE *SAFE* ENOUGH WITH OLD *TARM.*

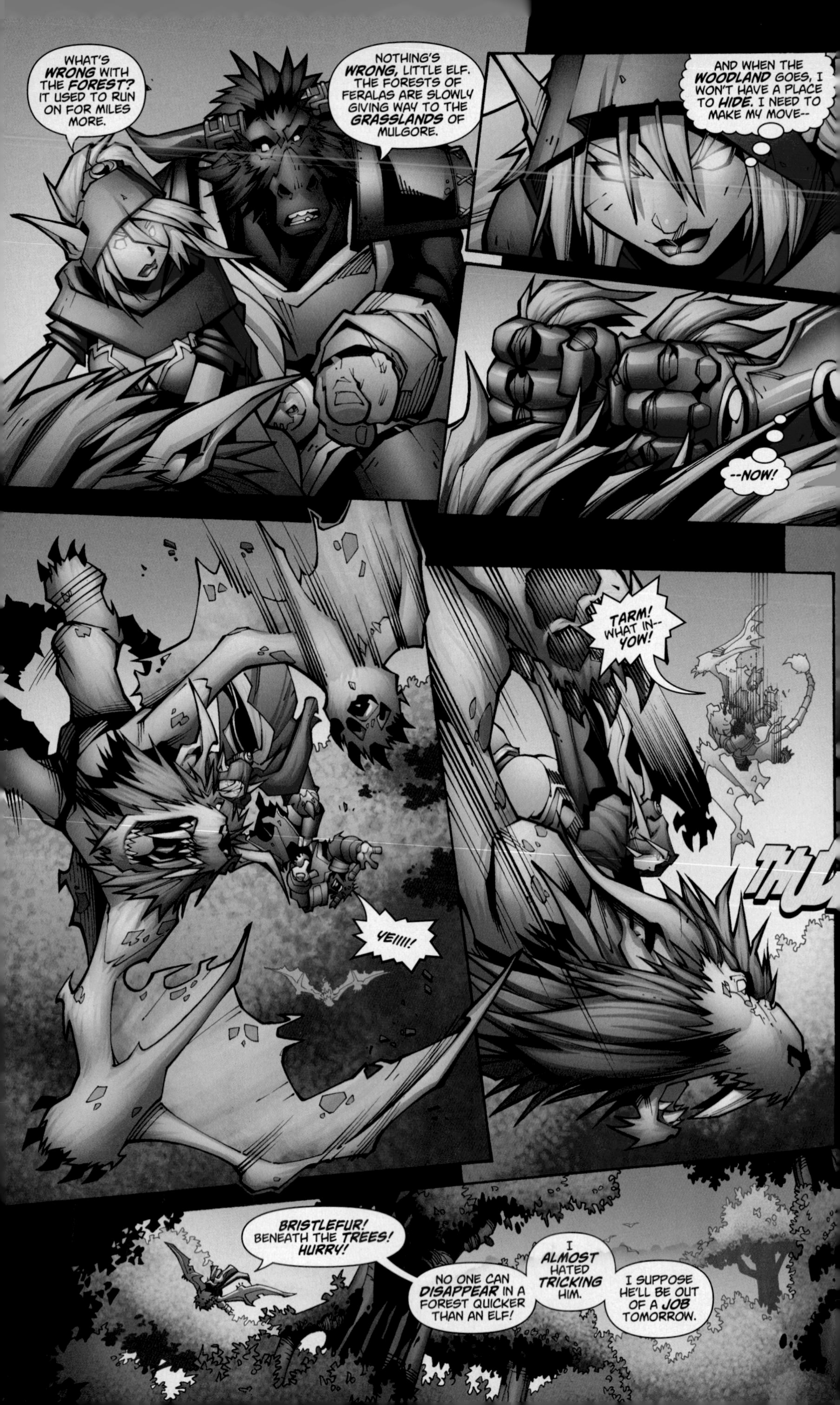
WHAT'S **WRONG** WITH THE **FOREST?** IT USED TO RUN ON FOR MILES MORE.
NOTHING'S **WRONG**, LITTLE ELF. THE FORESTS OF FERALAS ARE SLOWLY GIVING WAY TO THE **GRASSLANDS** OF MULGORE.
AND WHEN THE **WOODLAND** GOES, I WON'T HAVE A PLACE TO **HIDE**. I NEED TO MAKE MY MOVE--
--NOW!
YE!!!!!
TARM! WHAT IN-- **YOW!**
BRISTLEFUR! BENEATH THE TREES! HURRY!
NO ONE CAN **DISAPPEAR** IN A FOREST QUICKER THAN AN ELF!
I **ALMOST** HATED **TRICKING** HIM.
I SUPPOSE HE'LL BE OUT OF A **JOB** TOMORROW.

THE LATE AFTERNOON SUN RIMS THE MESAS IN GOLD AS MAGATHA AND HER GRIMTOTEM CLAN WATCH LO'GOSH AND BROLL CROSS THE SPAN TO *SPIRIT RISE* AND FOLLOW THE PATH TO THE *POOLS OF VISION*.

WE'RE IN LUCK. *REHGAR* ISN'T COMING.

WHILE WE ENGAGE IN THE PURIFI-CATION RITUAL, HE'LL DINE WITH THE ARCHDRUID *HAMUUL RUNETOTEM* ON ELDER RISE. CAIRNE'S AWAY.

THAT OLD HAG *MAGATHA* ISN'T PLEASED. SHE THOUGHT SHE'D HAVE REHGAR IN HER POCKET, BUT HE'S TOO WILY.

THESE CAVERNS ARE...*ASTONISHING*, BROLL.

BUT MAGATHA WAS RIGHT. NO ONE'S *HERE*. EVERYONE HAS *FLED*. EVEN THE FORSAKEN WHO HAUNT THESE CAVERNS. I DON'T LIKE IT.

STILL...I DON'T *SEE* ANY MONSTER. OUR GUARDS THOUGHT IT WAS A BIG JOKE.

REHGAR TOLD US TO REMOVE YOUR *CHAINS* SINCE THERE'S NO OTHER WAY OUT OF THE CAVES.

BUT YOU'LL HAVE TO LEAVE YOUR *WEAPONS* WITH US AND WE'LL *GUARD* THE ENTRANCE.

SHOUT IF YOU *CHAMPIONS* NEED HELP WITH THE BIG, SCARY *MONSTER! HA!*

IF THERE *IS* A MONSTER, *MAGATHA* PROBABLY CONJURED IT, HOPING IT'LL KILL US AND LEAVE REHGAR FREE TO TRAIN HER WHOLE *CLAN* FOR BATTLE.

I'M TEMPTED TO *FORGET* THE WHOLE THING, EXCEPT FOR THOSE FLASHES OF MEMORY THAT FREEZE YOU INTO *IMMOBILITY*.

IF IT WERE TO HAPPEN IN THE MIDST OF A *FIGHT*...

GOOD *POINT*. WHAT *NOW*?

WE SIT AND STARE INTO THE *WATER*...

...AND ASK THE POOLS FOR *REVELATION*.

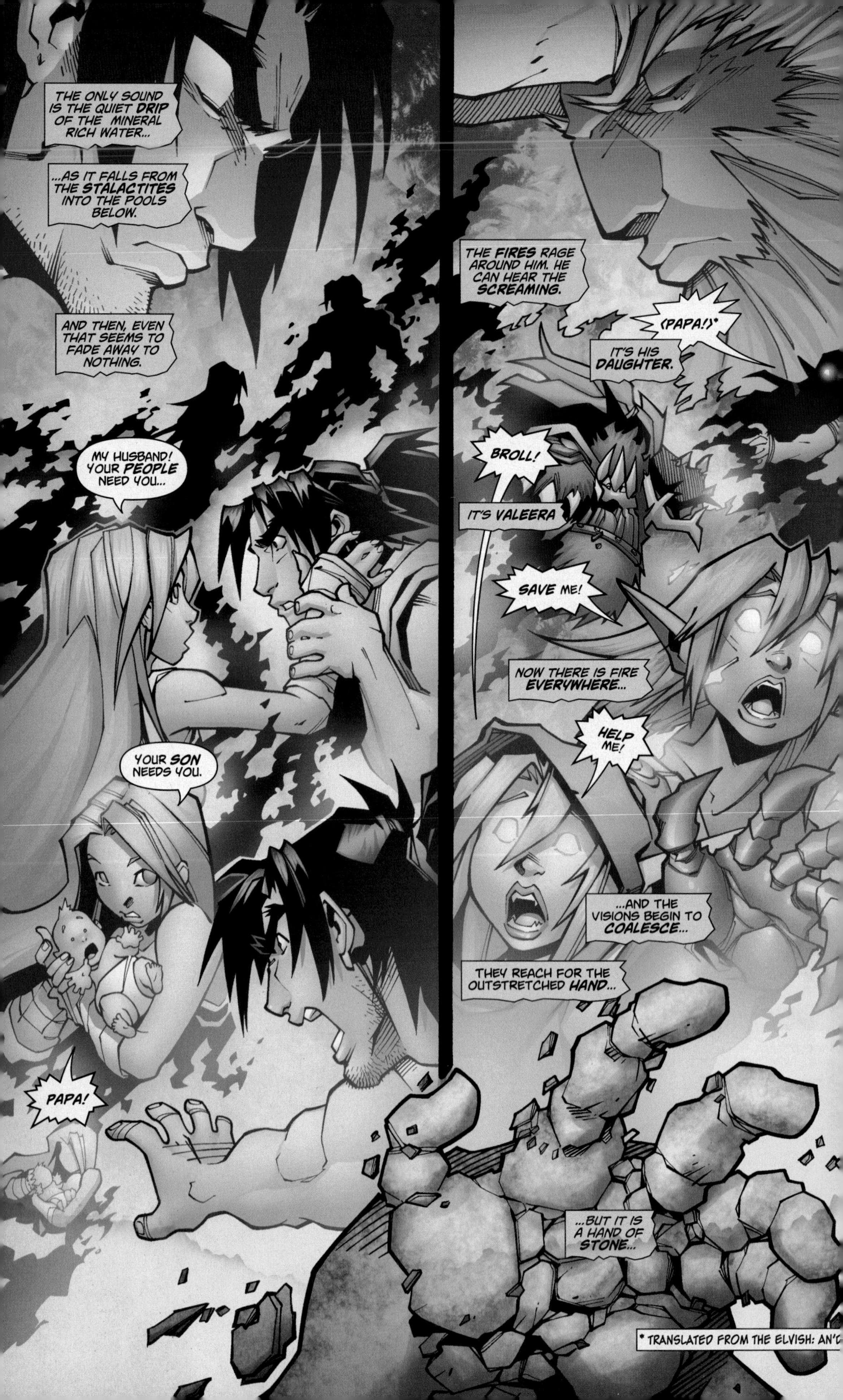
THE ONLY SOUND IS THE QUIET DRIP OF THE MINERAL RICH WATER...
...AS IT FALLS FROM THE STALACTITES INTO THE POOLS BELOW.
AND THEN, EVEN THAT SEEMS TO FADE AWAY TO NOTHING.
MY HUSBAND! YOUR PEOPLE NEED YOU...
YOUR SON NEEDS YOU.
PAPA!
THE FIRES RAGE AROUND HIM. HE CAN HEAR THE SCREAMING.
‹PAPA!›*
IT'S HIS DAUGHTER.
BROLL!
IT'S VALEERA
SAVE ME!
NOW THERE IS FIRE EVERYWHERE...
HELP ME!
...AND THE VISIONS BEGIN TO COALESCE...
THEY REACH FOR THE OUTSTRETCHED HAND...
...BUT IT IS A HAND OF STONE...

* TRANSLATED FROM THE ELVISH: AN'D

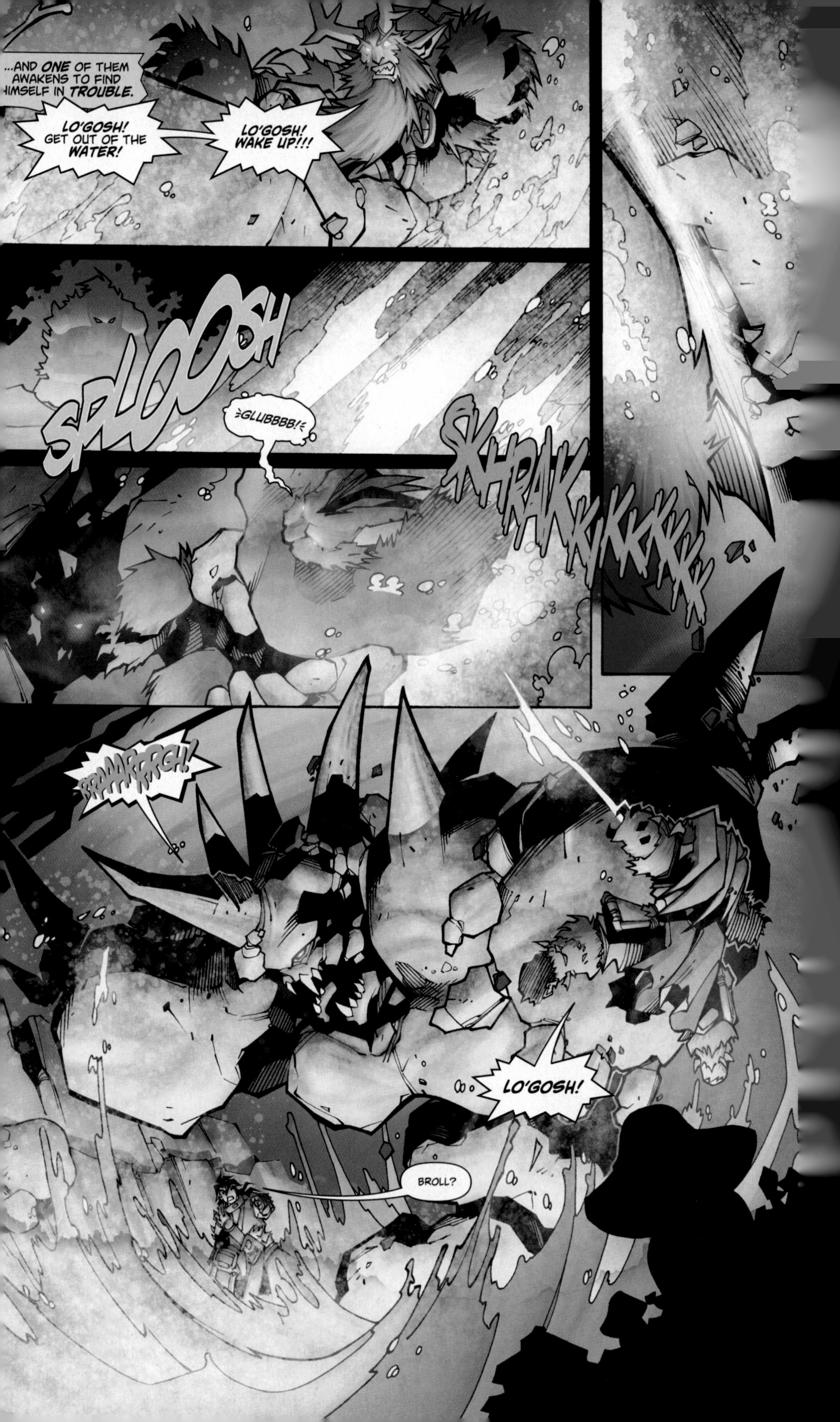
...AND ONE OF THEM AWAKENS TO FIND HIMSELF IN TROUBLE.
LO'GOSH! GET OUT OF THE WATER!
LO'GOSH! WAKE UP!!!
SPLOOOSH
GLUBBBB!
SKHRAKKKKKKKK
BRAAARRRGH!
LO'GOSH!
BROLL?

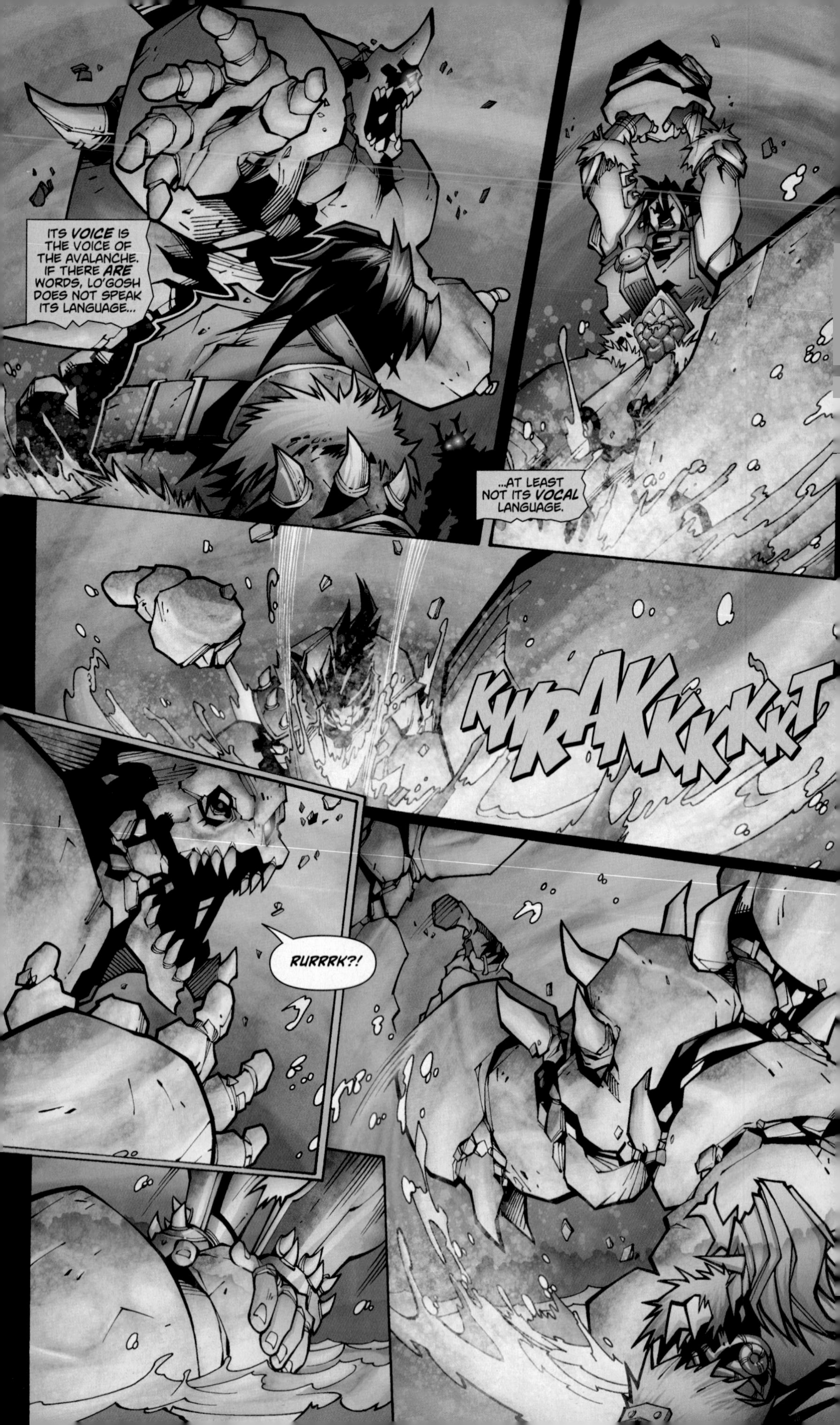
ITS VOICE IS THE VOICE OF THE AVALANCHE. IF THERE ARE WORDS, LO'GOSH DOES NOT SPEAK ITS LANGUAGE...
...AT LEAST NOT ITS VOCAL LANGUAGE.
KWRAKKKKKT
RURRRK?!

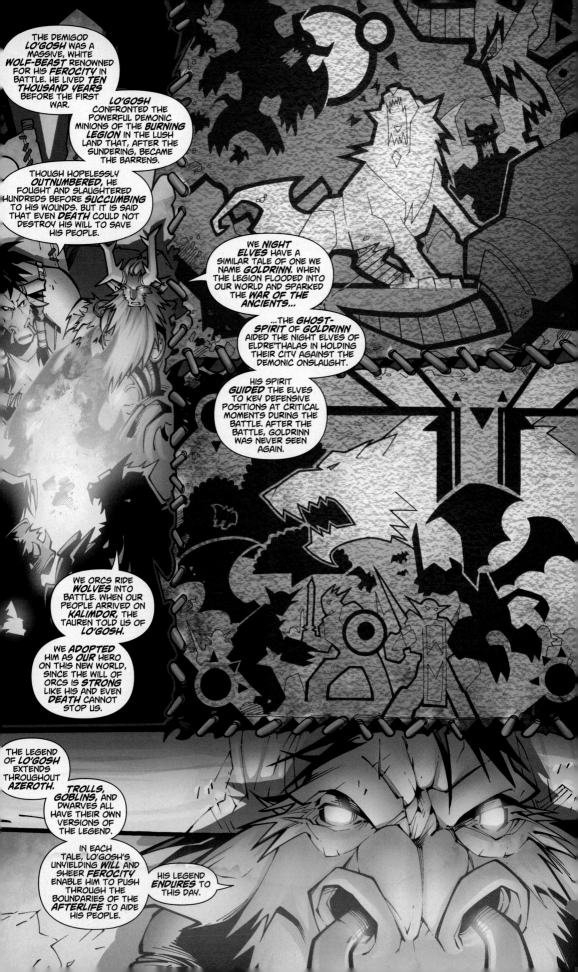

THE DEMIGOD *LO'GOSH* WAS A MASSIVE, WHITE *WOLF-BEAST* RENOWNED FOR HIS *FEROCITY* IN BATTLE. HE LIVED *TEN THOUSAND YEARS* BEFORE THE FIRST WAR.

LO'GOSH CONFRONTED THE POWERFUL DEMONIC MINIONS OF THE *BURNING LEGION* IN THE LUSH LAND THAT, AFTER THE SUNDERING, BECAME THE BARRENS.

THOUGH HOPELESSLY *OUTNUMBERED,* HE FOUGHT AND SLAUGHTERED HUNDREDS BEFORE *SUCCUMBING* TO HIS WOUNDS. BUT IT IS SAID THAT EVEN *DEATH* COULD NOT DESTROY HIS WILL TO SAVE HIS PEOPLE.

WE *NIGHT ELVES* HAVE A SIMILAR TALE OF ONE WE NAME *GOLDRINN.* WHEN THE LEGION FLOODED INTO OUR WORLD AND SPARKED THE *WAR OF THE ANCIENTS...*

...THE *GHOST-SPIRIT* OF *GOLDRINN* AIDED THE NIGHT ELVES OF ELDRE'THALAS IN HOLDING THEIR CITY AGAINST THE DEMONIC ONSLAUGHT.

HIS SPIRIT *GUIDED* THE ELVES TO KEY DEFENSIVE POSITIONS AT CRITICAL MOMENTS DURING THE BATTLE. AFTER THE BATTLE, GOLDRINN WAS NEVER SEEN AGAIN.

WE ORCS RIDE *WOLVES* INTO BATTLE. WHEN OUR PEOPLE ARRIVED ON *KALIMDOR,* THE TAUREN TOLD US OF *LO'GOSH.*

WE *ADOPTED* HIM AS *OUR* HERO ON THIS NEW WORLD, SINCE THE WILL OF ORCS IS *STRONG* LIKE HIS AND EVEN *DEATH* CANNOT STOP US.

THE LEGEND OF *LO'GOSH* EXTENDS THROUGHOUT *AZEROTH.*

TROLLS, GOBLINS, AND *DWARVES* ALL HAVE THEIR OWN VERSIONS OF THE LEGEND.

IN EACH TALE, LO'GOSH'S UNYIELDING *WILL* AND SHEER *FEROCITY* ENABLE HIM TO PUSH THROUGH THE BOUNDARIES OF THE *AFTERLIFE* TO AIDE HIS PEOPLE.

HIS LEGEND *ENDURES* TO THIS DAY.

CHAPTER 4

Issue #4 Cover
by Samwise Didier

Issue #4 Cover
by Jim Lee and Alex Sinclair

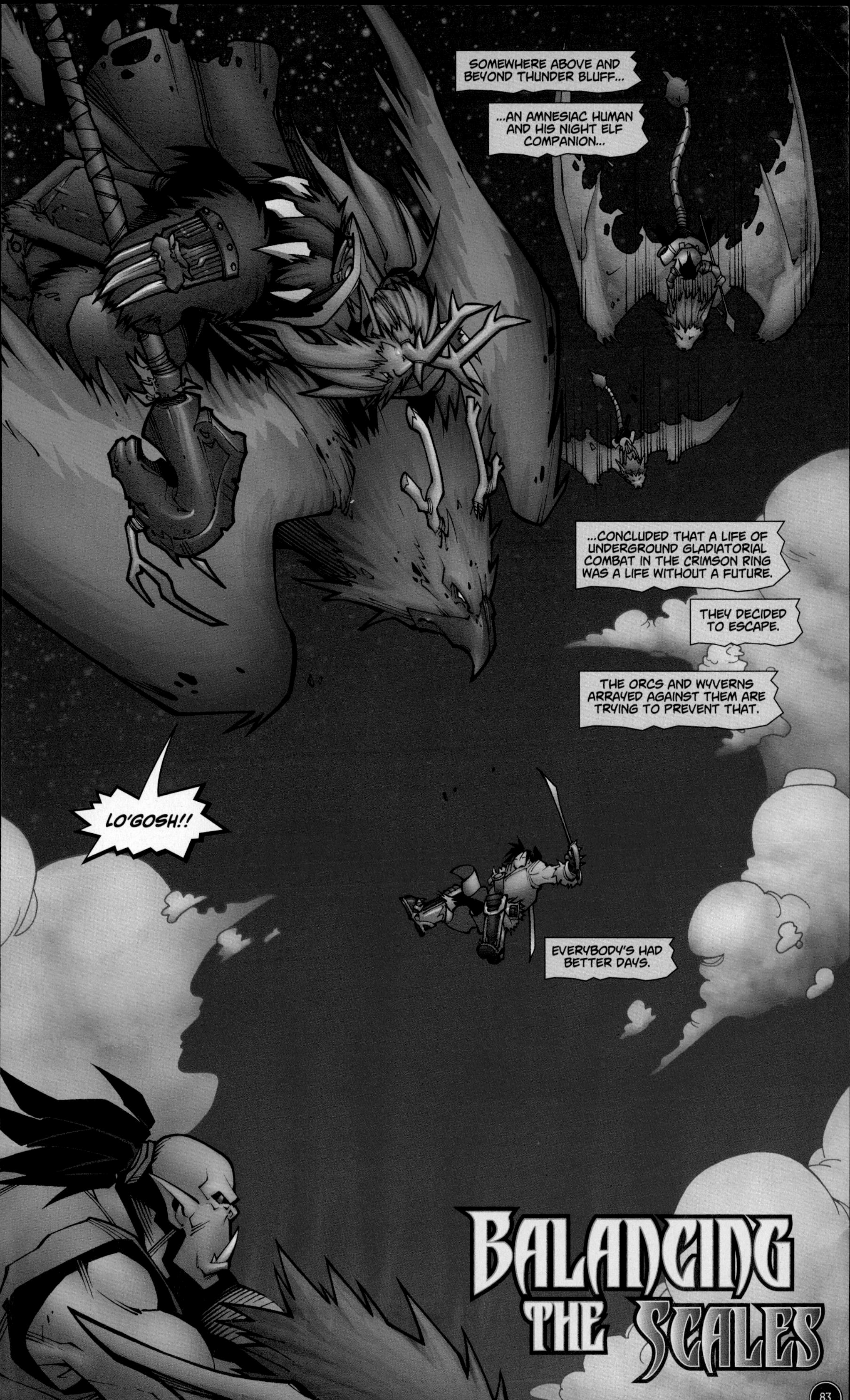
SOMEWHERE ABOVE AND BEYOND THUNDER BLUFF...
...AN AMNESIAC HUMAN AND HIS NIGHT ELF COMPANION...
...CONCLUDED THAT A LIFE OF UNDERGROUND GLADIATORIAL COMBAT IN THE CRIMSON RING WAS A LIFE WITHOUT A FUTURE.
THEY DECIDED TO ESCAPE.
THE ORCS AND WYVERNS ARRAYED AGAINST THEM ARE TRYING TO PREVENT THAT.
LO'GOSH!!
EVERYBODY'S HAD BETTER DAYS.
BALANCING THE SCALES

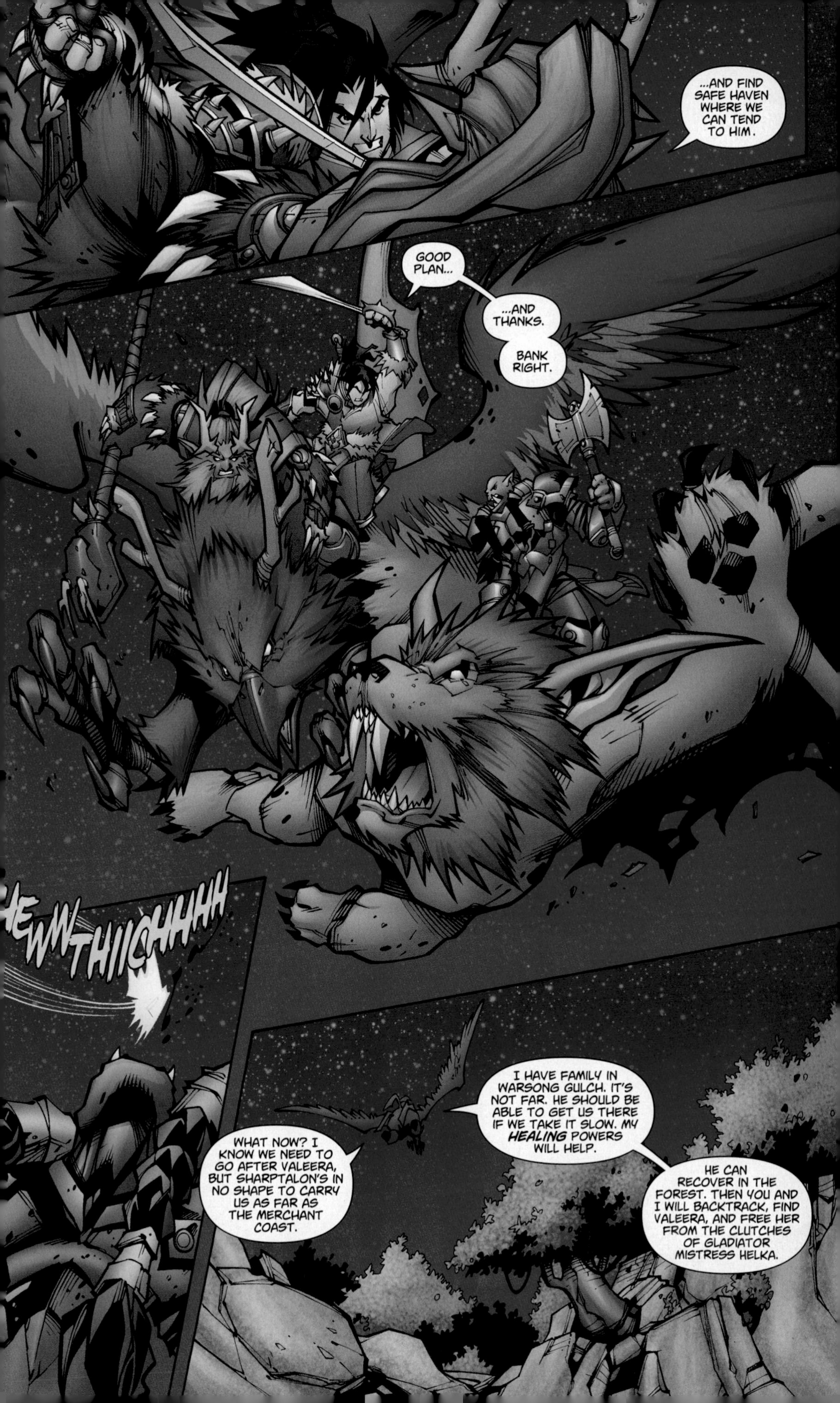

...AND FIND SAFE HAVEN WHERE WE CAN TEND TO HIM.
GOOD PLAN...
...AND THANKS.
BANK RIGHT.
FWEWWTHIICHHHH
I HAVE FAMILY IN WARSONG GULCH. IT'S NOT FAR. HE SHOULD BE ABLE TO GET US THERE IF WE TAKE IT SLOW. MY HEALING POWERS WILL HELP.
WHAT NOW? I KNOW WE NEED TO GO AFTER VALEERA, BUT SHARPTALON'S IN NO SHAPE TO CARRY US AS FAR AS THE MERCHANT COAST.
HE CAN RECOVER IN THE FOREST. THEN YOU AND I WILL BACKTRACK, FIND VALEERA, AND FREE HER FROM THE CLUTCHES OF GLADIATOR MISTRESS HELKA.

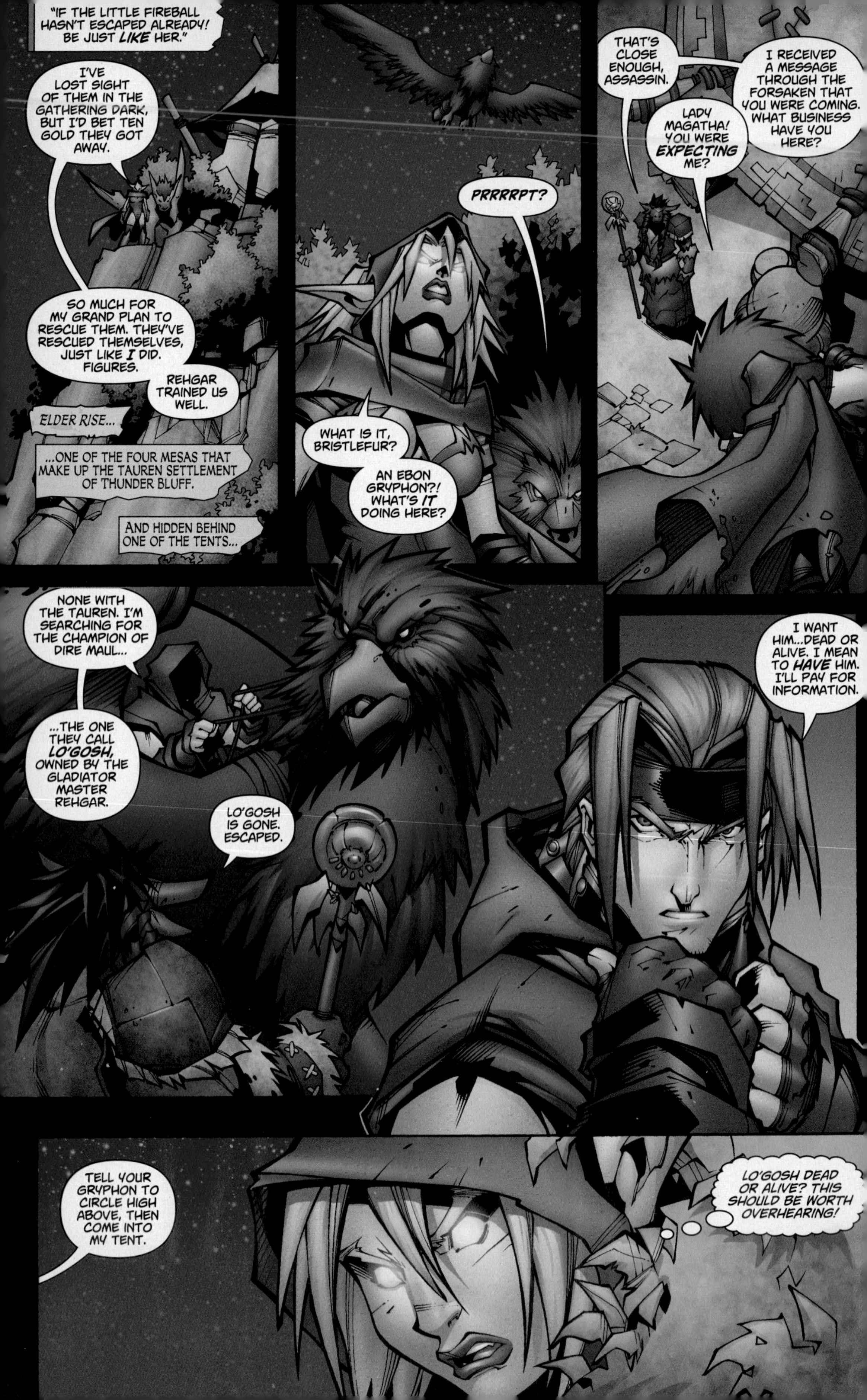

"IF THE LITTLE FIREBALL HASN'T ESCAPED ALREADY! BE JUST LIKE HER."
I'VE LOST SIGHT OF THEM IN THE GATHERING DARK, BUT I'D BET TEN GOLD THEY GOT AWAY.
SO MUCH FOR MY GRAND PLAN TO RESCUE THEM. THEY'VE RESCUED THEMSELVES, JUST LIKE I DID. FIGURES.
REHGAR TRAINED US WELL.
ELDER RISE...
...ONE OF THE FOUR MESAS THAT MAKE UP THE TAUREN SETTLEMENT OF THUNDER BLUFF.
AND HIDDEN BEHIND ONE OF THE TENTS...
PRRRRPT?
WHAT IS IT, BRISTLEFUR?
AN EBON GRYPHON?! WHAT'S IT DOING HERE?
THAT'S CLOSE ENOUGH, ASSASSIN.
LADY MAGATHA! YOU WERE EXPECTING ME?
I RECEIVED A MESSAGE THROUGH THE FORSAKEN THAT YOU WERE COMING. WHAT BUSINESS HAVE YOU HERE?
NONE WITH THE TAUREN. I'M SEARCHING FOR THE CHAMPION OF DIRE MAUL...
...THE ONE THEY CALL LO'GOSH, OWNED BY THE GLADIATOR MASTER REHGAR.
LO'GOSH IS GONE. ESCAPED.
I WANT HIM...DEAD OR ALIVE. I MEAN TO HAVE HIM. I'LL PAY FOR INFORMATION.
TELL YOUR GRYPHON TO CIRCLE HIGH ABOVE, THEN COME INTO MY TENT.
LO'GOSH DEAD OR ALIVE? THIS SHOULD BE WORTH OVERHEARING!

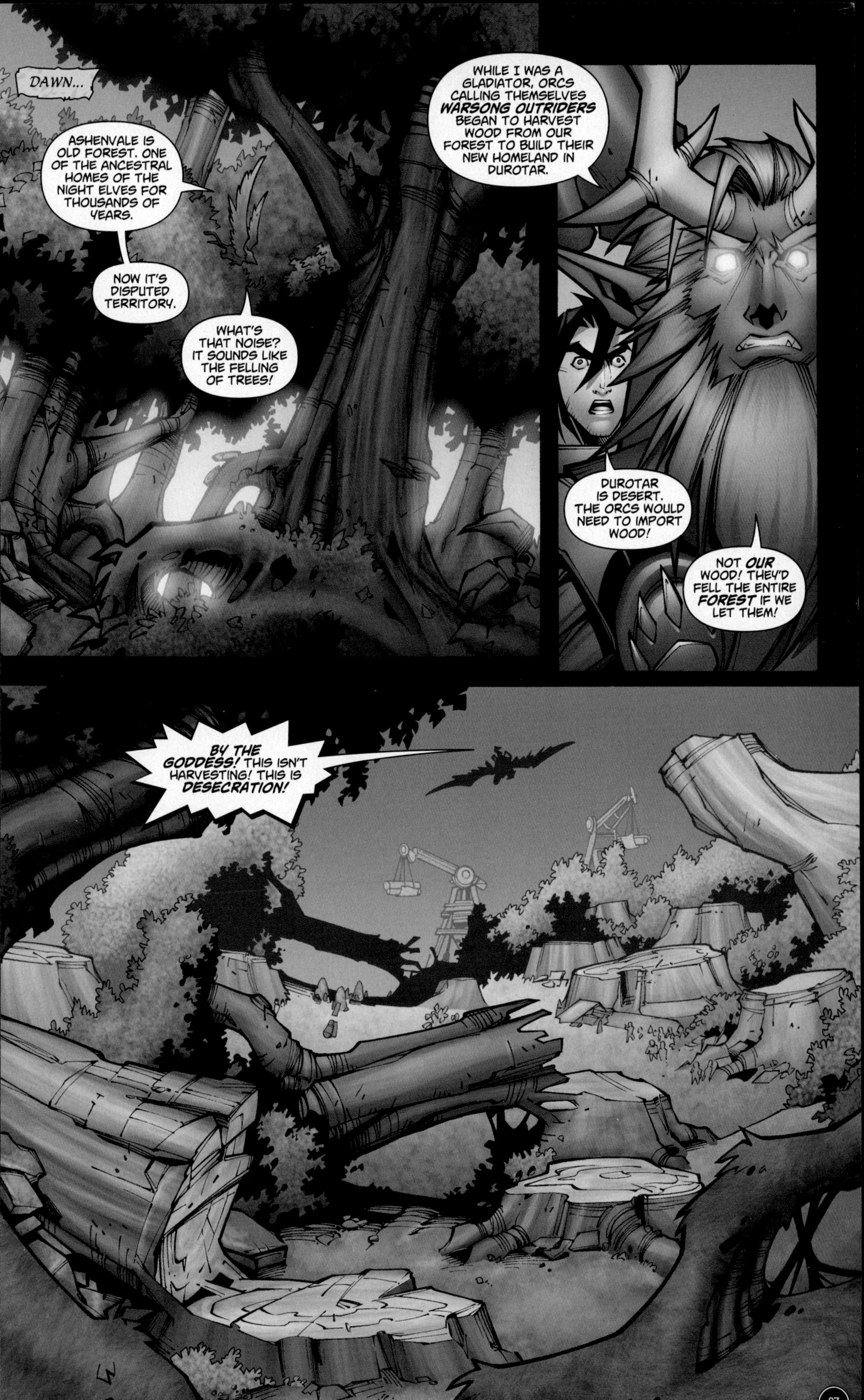
DAWN...
ASHENVALE IS OLD FOREST. ONE OF THE ANCESTRAL HOMES OF THE NIGHT ELVES FOR THOUSANDS OF YEARS.
NOW IT'S DISPUTED TERRITORY.
WHAT'S THAT NOISE? IT SOUNDS LIKE THE FELLING OF TREES!
WHILE I WAS A GLADIATOR, ORCS CALLING THEMSELVES **WARSONG OUTRIDERS** BEGAN TO HARVEST WOOD FROM OUR FOREST TO BUILD THEIR NEW HOMELAND IN DUROTAR.
DUROTAR IS DESERT. THE ORCS WOULD NEED TO IMPORT WOOD!
NOT ***OUR*** WOOD! THEY'D FELL THE ENTIRE ***FOREST*** IF WE LET THEM!
BY THE GODDESS! THIS ISN'T HARVESTING! THIS IS ***DESECRATION!***

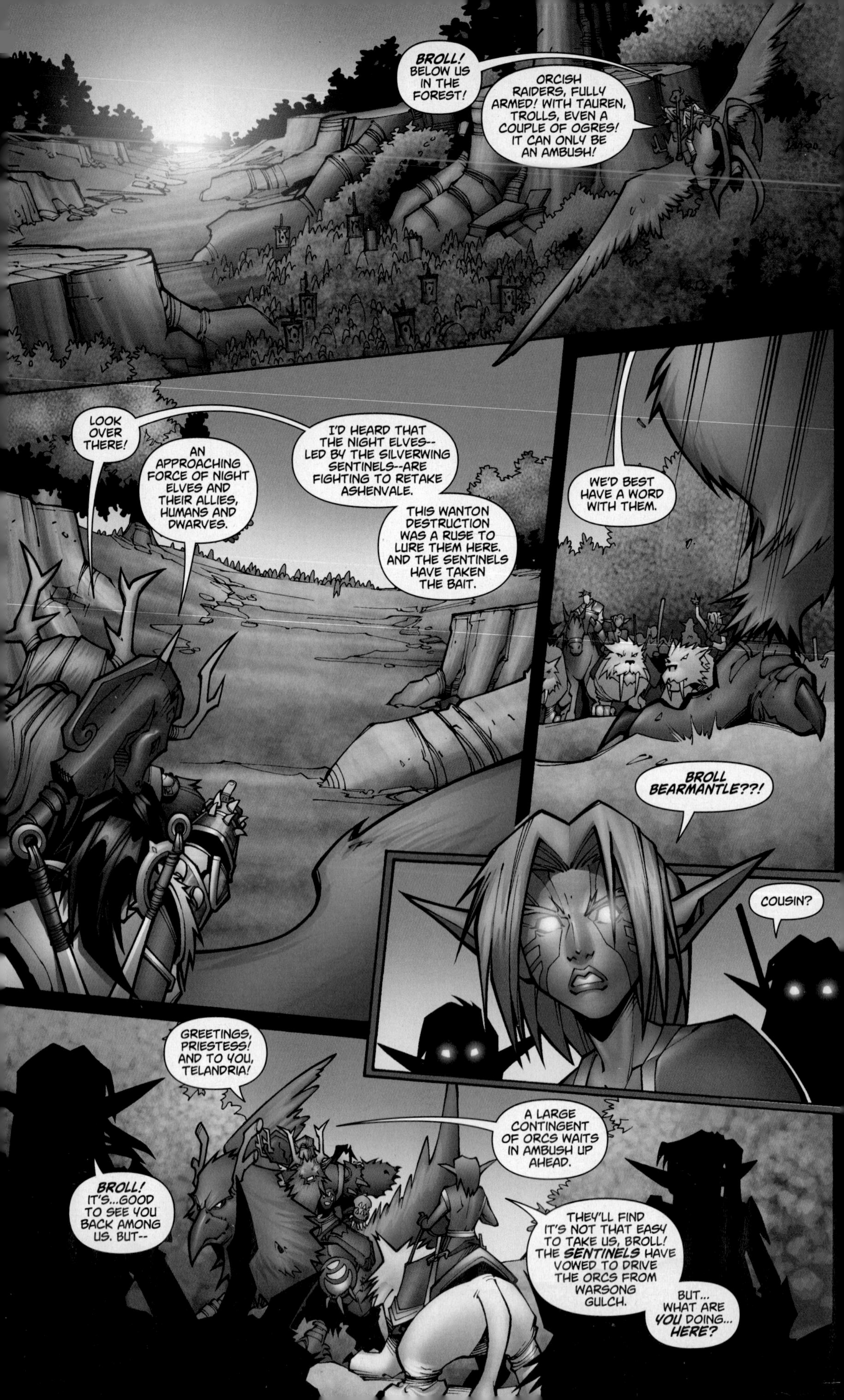
BROLL! BELOW US IN THE FOREST!
ORCISH RAIDERS, FULLY ARMED! WITH TAUREN, TROLLS, EVEN A COUPLE OF OGRES! IT CAN ONLY BE AN AMBUSH!
LOOK OVER THERE!
AN APPROACHING FORCE OF NIGHT ELVES AND THEIR ALLIES, HUMANS AND DWARVES.
I'D HEARD THAT THE NIGHT ELVES--LED BY THE SILVERWING SENTINELS--ARE FIGHTING TO RETAKE ASHENVALE.
THIS WANTON DESTRUCTION WAS A RUSE TO LURE THEM HERE. AND THE SENTINELS HAVE TAKEN THE BAIT.
WE'D BEST HAVE A WORD WITH THEM.
BROLL BEARMANTLE??!
COUSIN?
GREETINGS, PRIESTESS! AND TO YOU, TELANDRIA!
A LARGE CONTINGENT OF ORCS WAITS IN AMBUSH UP AHEAD.
BROLL! IT'S...GOOD TO SEE YOU BACK AMONG US. BUT--
THEY'LL FIND IT'S NOT THAT EASY TO TAKE US, BROLL! THE SENTINELS HAVE VOWED TO DRIVE THE ORCS FROM WARSONG GULCH.
BUT... WHAT ARE YOU DOING... HERE?

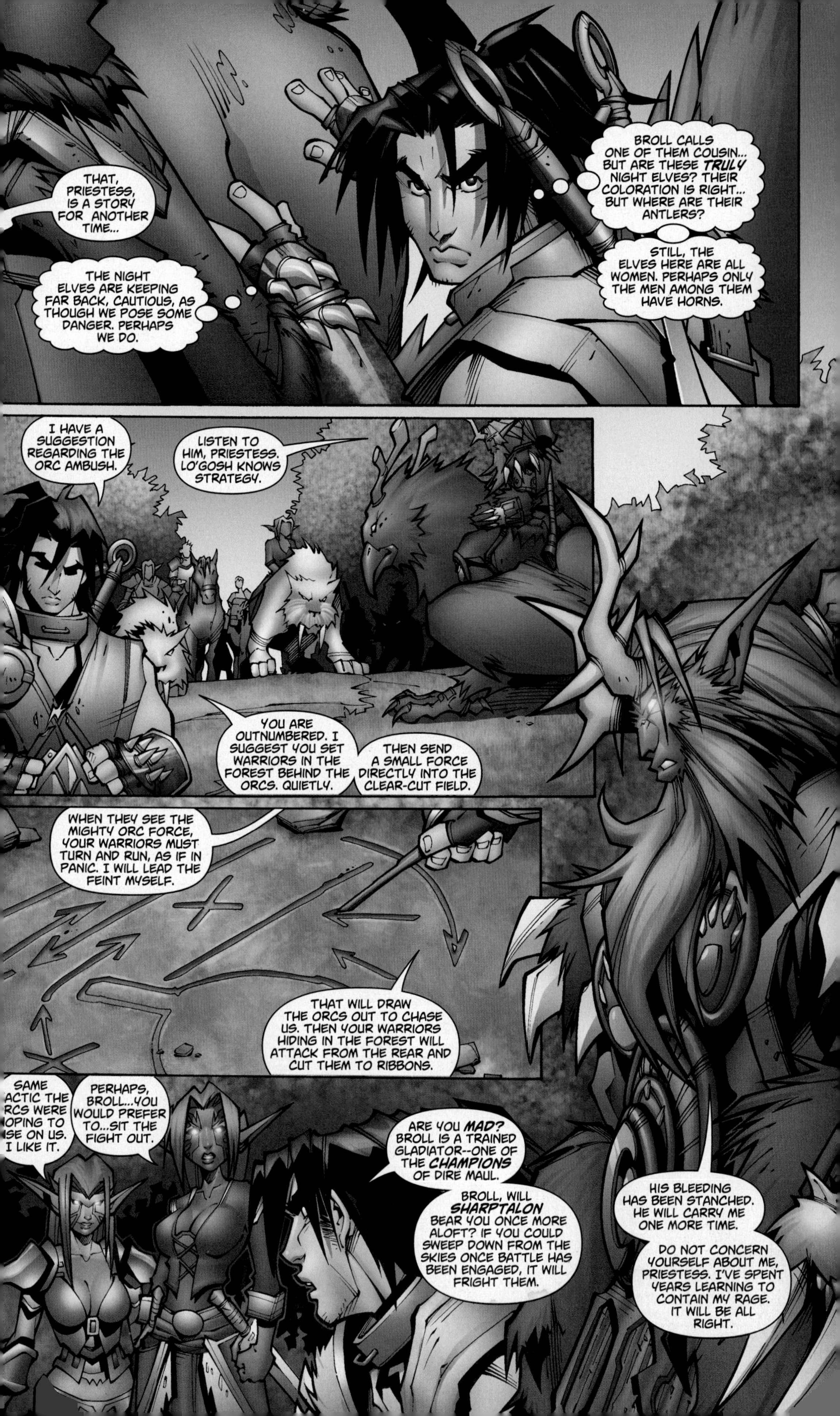
THAT, PRIESTESS, IS A STORY FOR ANOTHER TIME...
THE NIGHT ELVES ARE KEEPING FAR BACK, CAUTIOUS, AS THOUGH WE POSE SOME DANGER. PERHAPS WE DO.
BROLL CALLS ONE OF THEM COUSIN... BUT ARE THESE TRULY NIGHT ELVES? THEIR COLORATION IS RIGHT... BUT WHERE ARE THEIR ANTLERS?
STILL, THE ELVES HERE ARE ALL WOMEN. PERHAPS ONLY THE MEN AMONG THEM HAVE HORNS.
I HAVE A SUGGESTION REGARDING THE ORC AMBUSH.
LISTEN TO HIM, PRIESTESS. LO'GOSH KNOWS STRATEGY.
YOU ARE OUTNUMBERED. I SUGGEST YOU SET WARRIORS IN THE FOREST BEHIND THE ORCS. QUIETLY.
THEN SEND A SMALL FORCE DIRECTLY INTO THE CLEAR-CUT FIELD.
WHEN THEY SEE THE MIGHTY ORC FORCE, YOUR WARRIORS MUST TURN AND RUN, AS IF IN PANIC. I WILL LEAD THE FEINT MYSELF.
THAT WILL DRAW THE ORCS OUT TO CHASE US. THEN YOUR WARRIORS HIDING IN THE FOREST WILL ATTACK FROM THE REAR AND CUT THEM TO RIBBONS.
SAME ACTIC THE RCS WERE OPING TO SE ON US. I LIKE IT.
PERHAPS, BROLL...YOU WOULD PREFER TO...SIT THE FIGHT OUT.
ARE YOU MAD? BROLL IS A TRAINED GLADIATOR--ONE OF THE CHAMPIONS OF DIRE MAUL.
BROLL, WILL SHARPTALON BEAR YOU ONCE MORE ALOFT? IF YOU COULD SWEEP DOWN FROM THE SKIES ONCE BATTLE HAS BEEN ENGAGED, IT WILL FRIGHT THEM.
HIS BLEEDING HAS BEEN STANCHED. HE WILL CARRY ME ONE MORE TIME.
DO NOT CONCERN YOURSELF ABOUT ME, PRIESTESS. I'VE SPENT YEARS LEARNING TO CONTAIN MY RAGE. IT WILL BE ALL RIGHT.

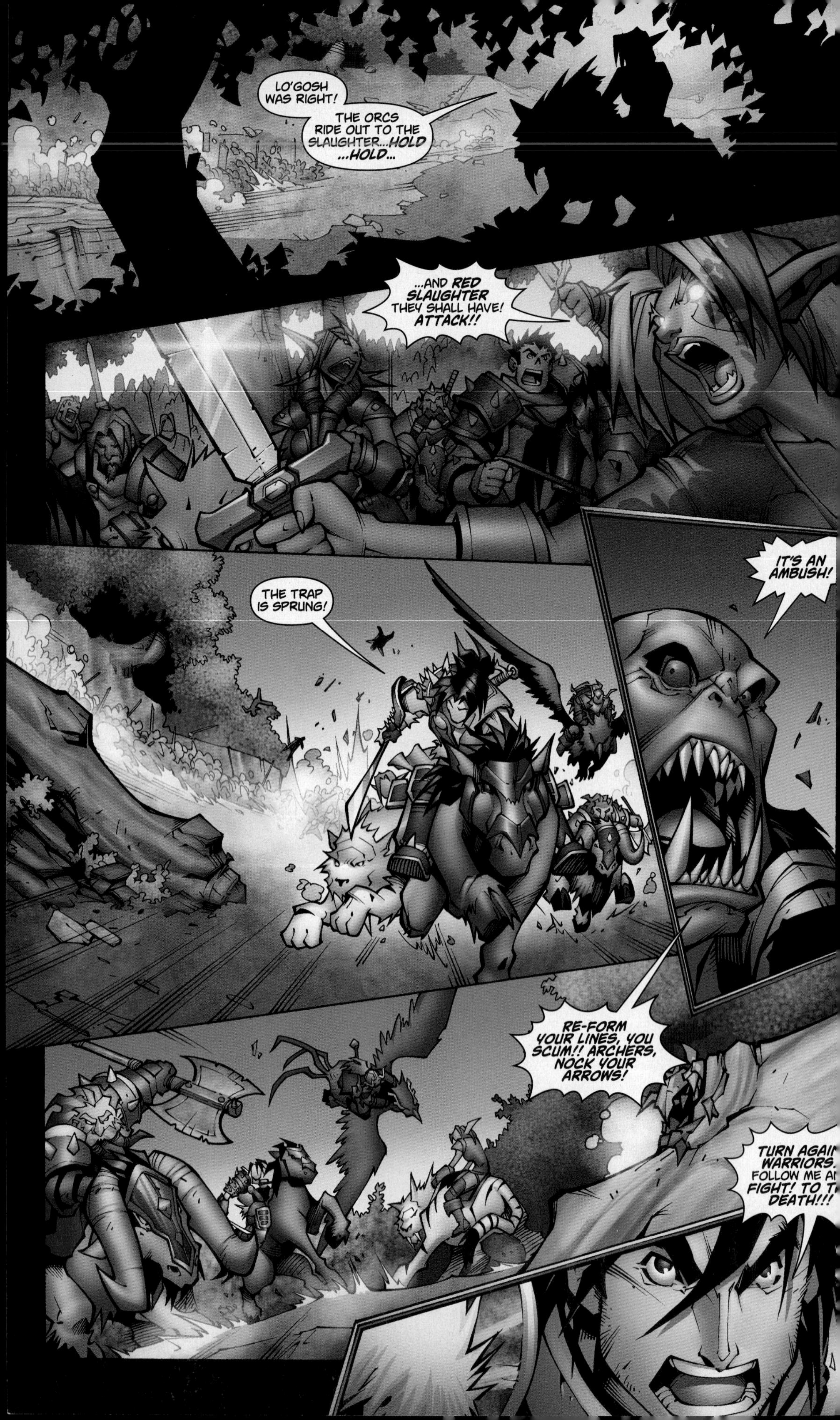
LO'GOSH WAS RIGHT!
THE ORCS RIDE OUT TO THE SLAUGHTER...HOLD ...HOLD...
...AND RED SLAUGHTER THEY SHALL HAVE! ATTACK!!
THE TRAP IS SPRUNG!
IT'S AN AMBUSH!
RE-FORM YOUR LINES, YOU SCUM!! ARCHERS, NOCK YOUR ARROWS!

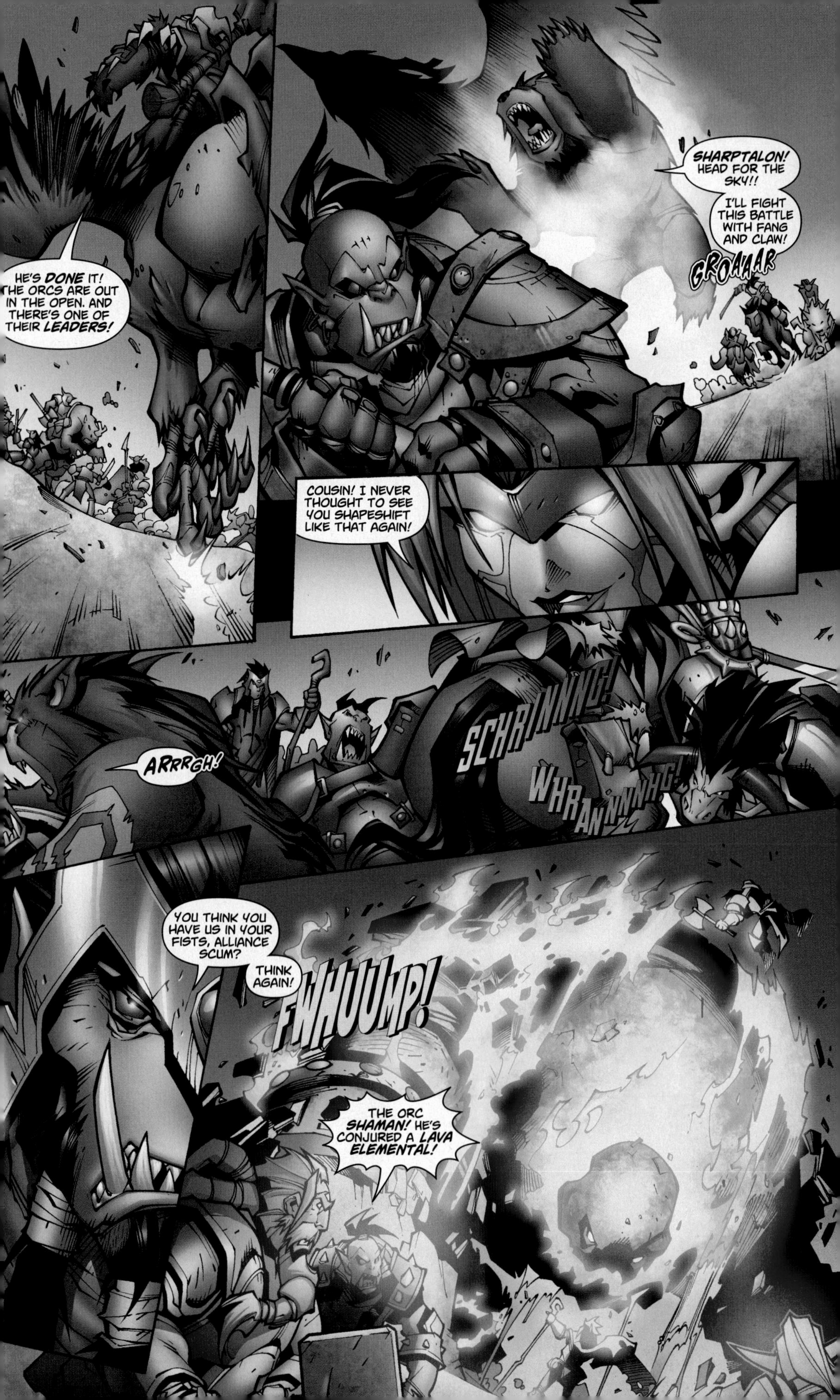
HE'S DONE IT! THE ORCS ARE OUT IN THE OPEN. AND THERE'S ONE OF THEIR LEADERS!
SHARPTALON! HEAD FOR THE SKY!!
I'LL FIGHT THIS BATTLE WITH FANG AND CLAW!
GROAAAR
COUSIN! I NEVER THOUGHT TO SEE YOU SHAPESHIFT LIKE THAT AGAIN!
ARRRGH!
SCHRINNNG!
WHRANNNNHG!
YOU THINK YOU HAVE US IN YOUR FISTS, ALLIANCE SCUM?
THINK AGAIN!
FWHUUMP!
THE ORC SHAMAN! HE'S CONJURED A LAVA ELEMENTAL!

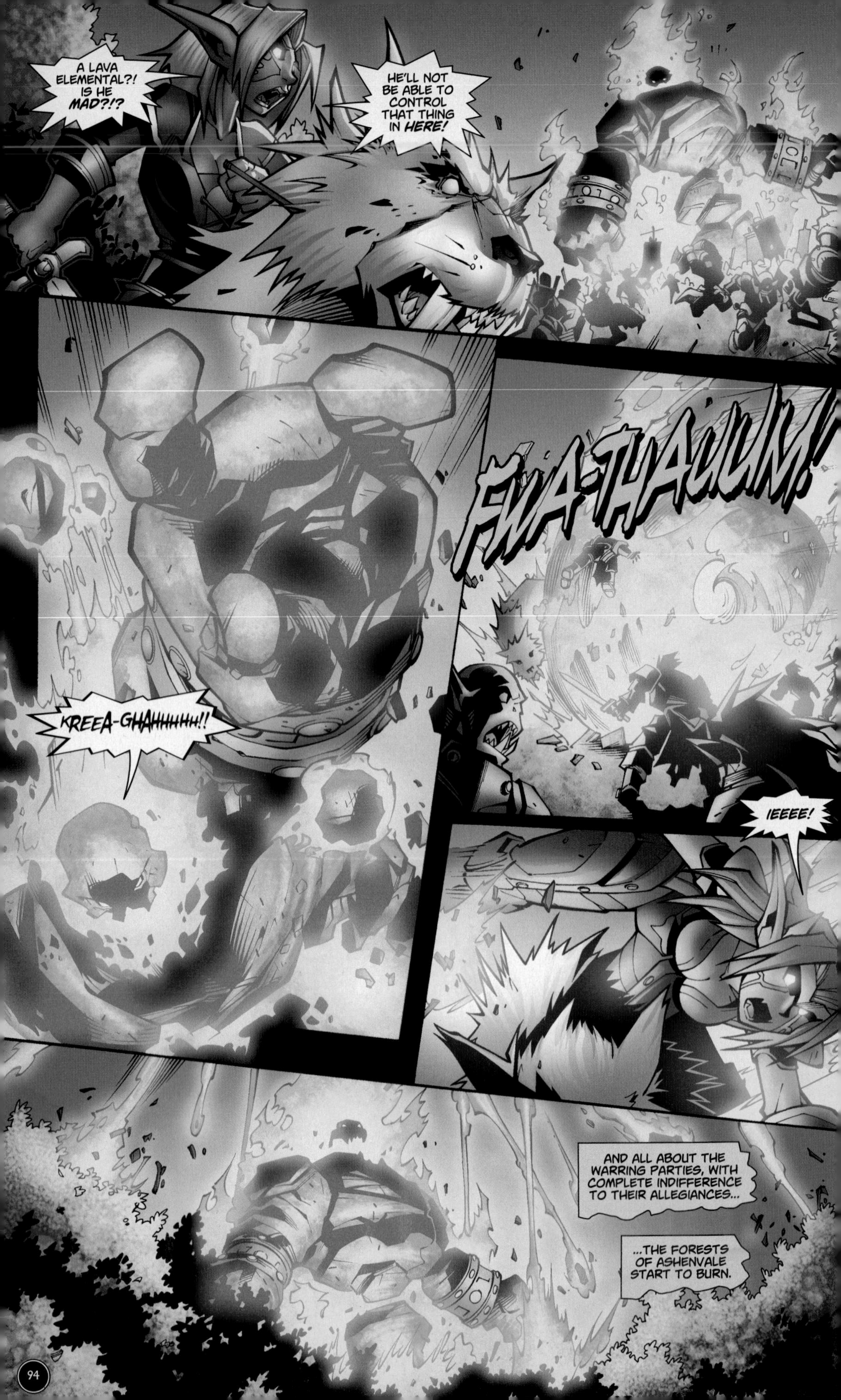
A LAVA ELEMENTAL?! IS HE MAD?!?
HE'LL NOT BE ABLE TO CONTROL THAT THING IN HERE!
FWA-THAUUM!
KREEA-GHAHHHHHH!!
IEEEE!
AND ALL ABOUT THE WARRING PARTIES, WITH COMPLETE INDIFFERENCE TO THEIR ALLEGIANCES...
...THE FORESTS OF ASHENVALE START TO BURN.

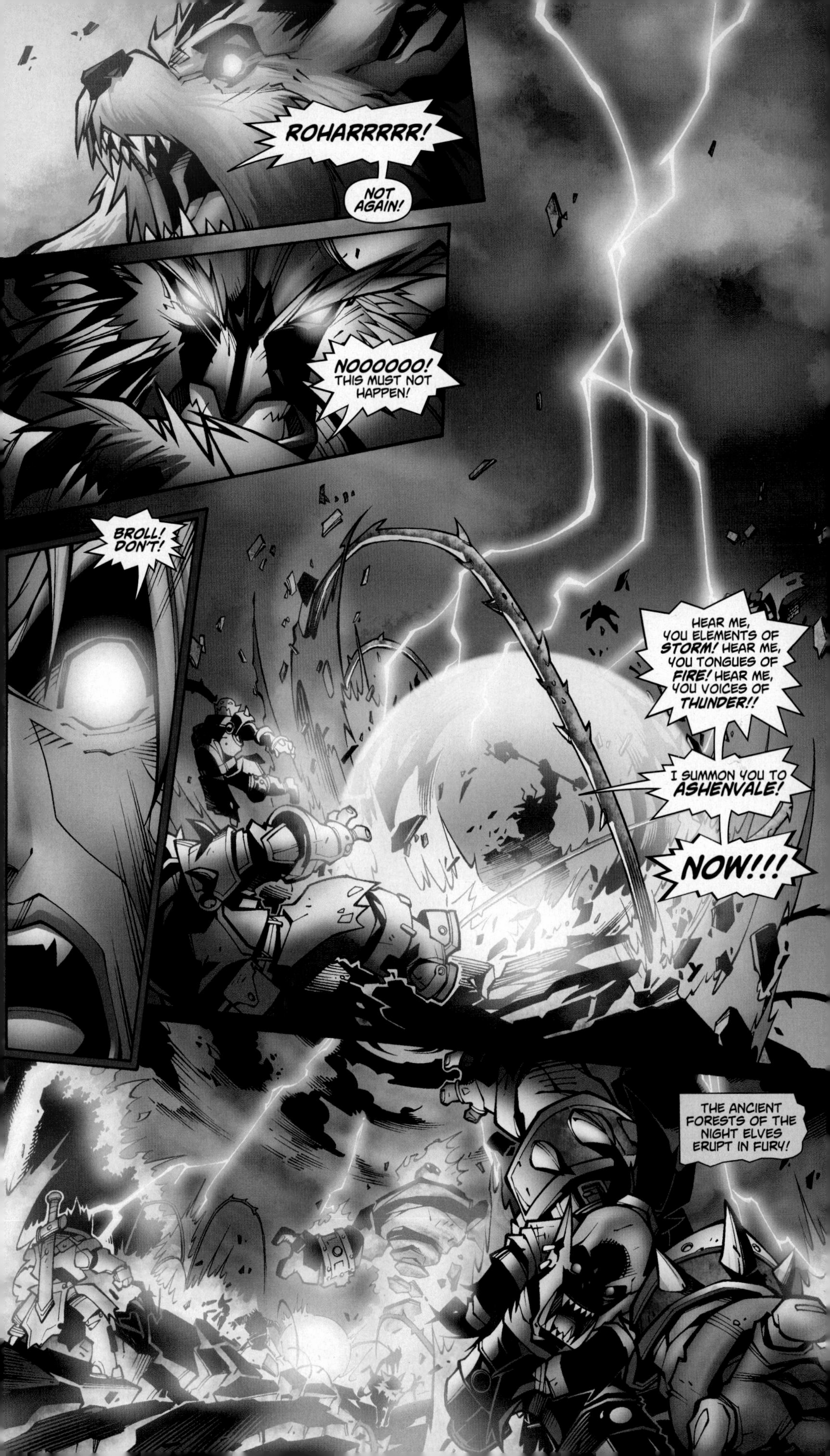
ROHARRRRR!
NOT AGAIN!
NOOOOOO! THIS MUST NOT HAPPEN!
BROLL! DON'T!
HEAR ME, YOU ELEMENTS OF STORM! HEAR ME, YOU TONGUES OF FIRE! HEAR ME, YOU VOICES OF THUNDER!!
I SUMMON YOU TO ASHENVALE!
NOW!!!
THE ANCIENT FORESTS OF THE NIGHT ELVES ERUPT IN FURY!

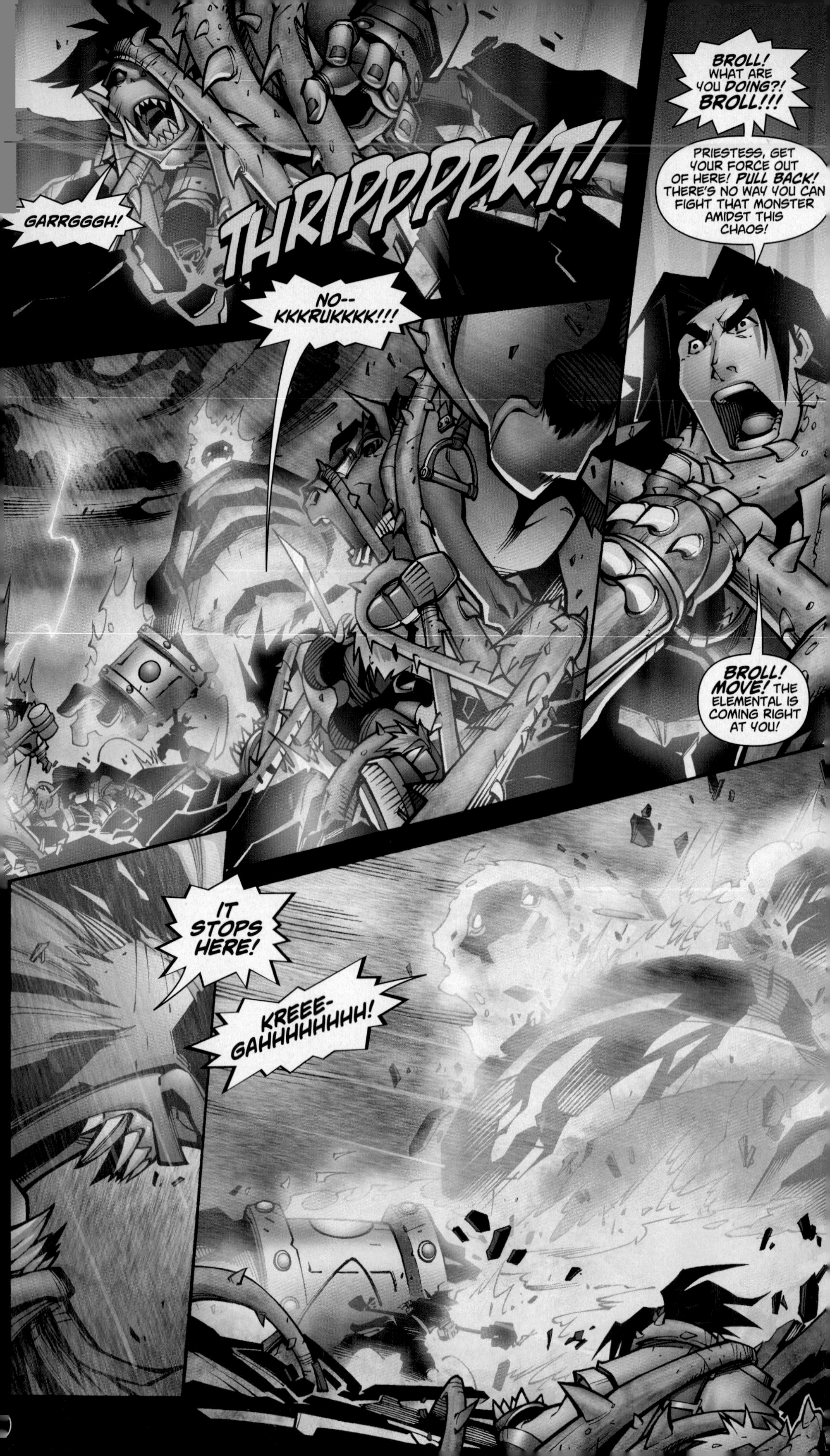
GARRGGGH!
THRIPPPPPKT!
BROLL! WHAT ARE YOU DOING?! BROLL!!!
PRIESTESS, GET YOUR FORCE OUT OF HERE! PULL BACK! THERE'S NO WAY YOU CAN FIGHT THAT MONSTER AMIDST THIS CHAOS!
NO-- KKKRUKKKK!!!
BROLL! MOVE! THE ELEMENTAL IS COMING RIGHT AT YOU!
IT STOPS HERE!
KREEE-GAHHHHHHHH!

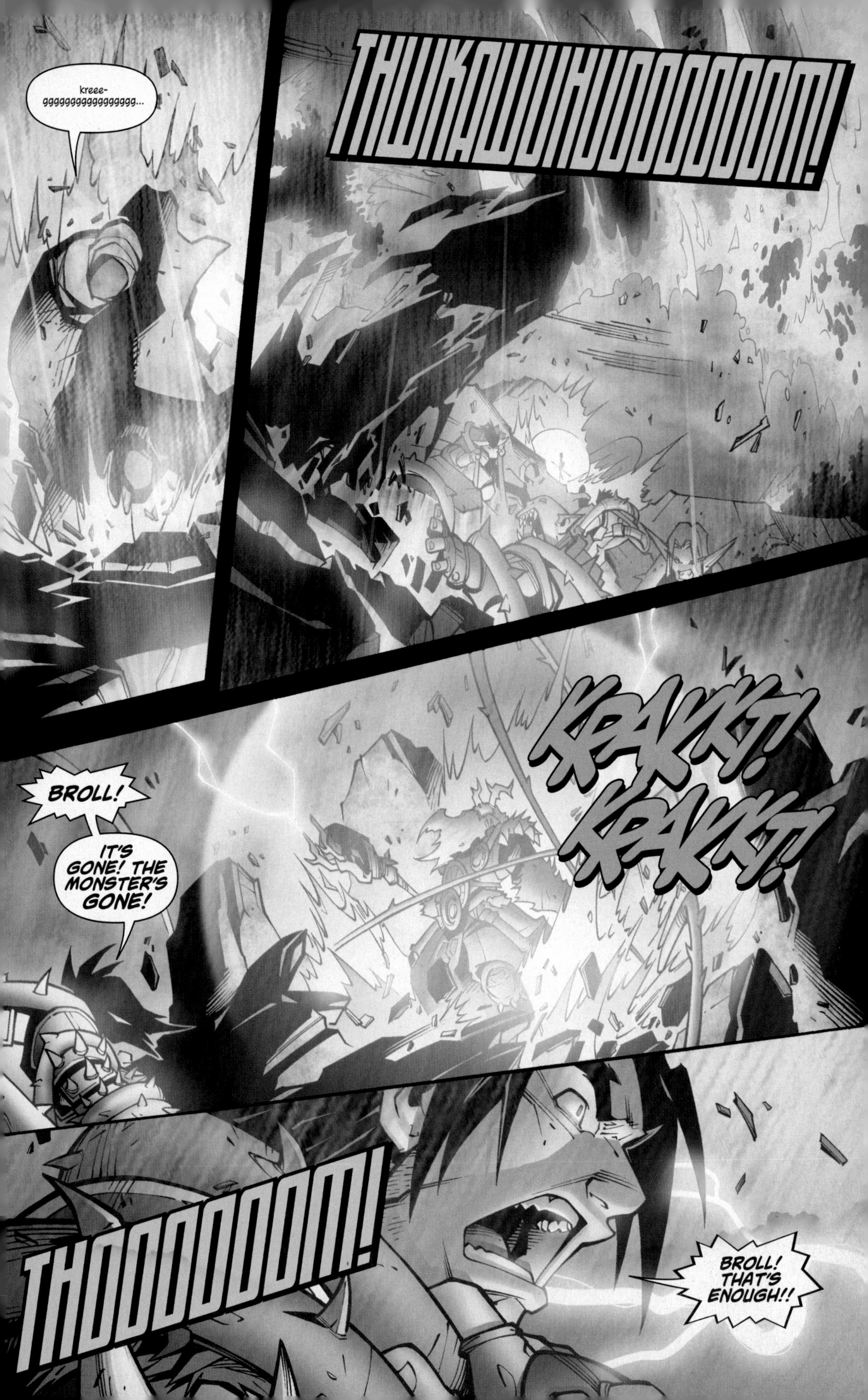

kreee-ggggggggggggggggg...
THWAKOWWHOOOOOOM!
BROLL!
IT'S GONE! THE MONSTER'S GONE!
KRAKKT! KRAKKT!
THOOOOOOM!
BROLL! THAT'S ENOUGH!!

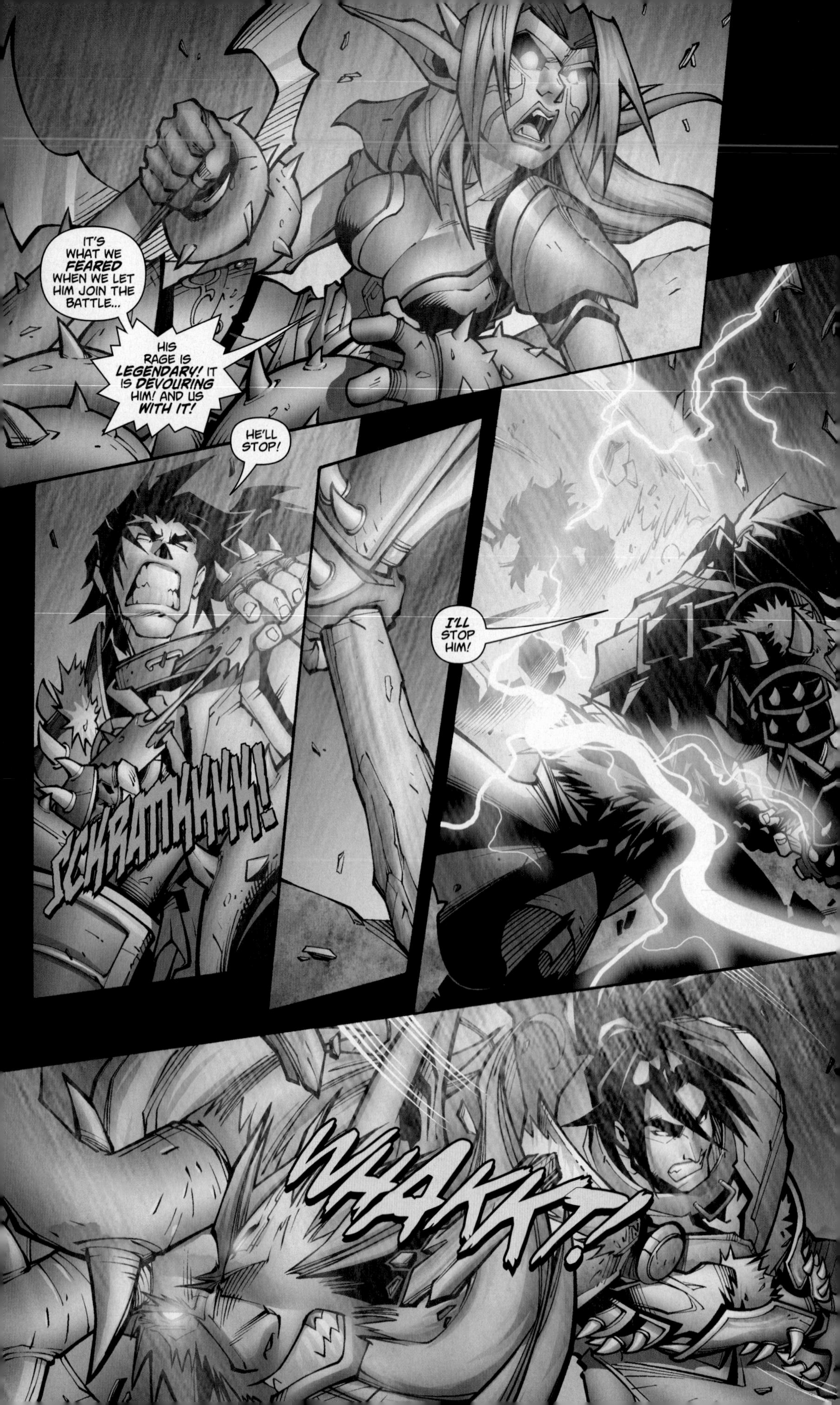
IT'S WHAT WE FEARED WHEN WE LET HIM JOIN THE BATTLE...
HIS RAGE IS LEGENDARY! IT IS DEVOURING HIM! AND US WITH IT!
HE'LL STOP!
SCHRAMKKKK!
I'LL STOP HIM!
WHAKKT!

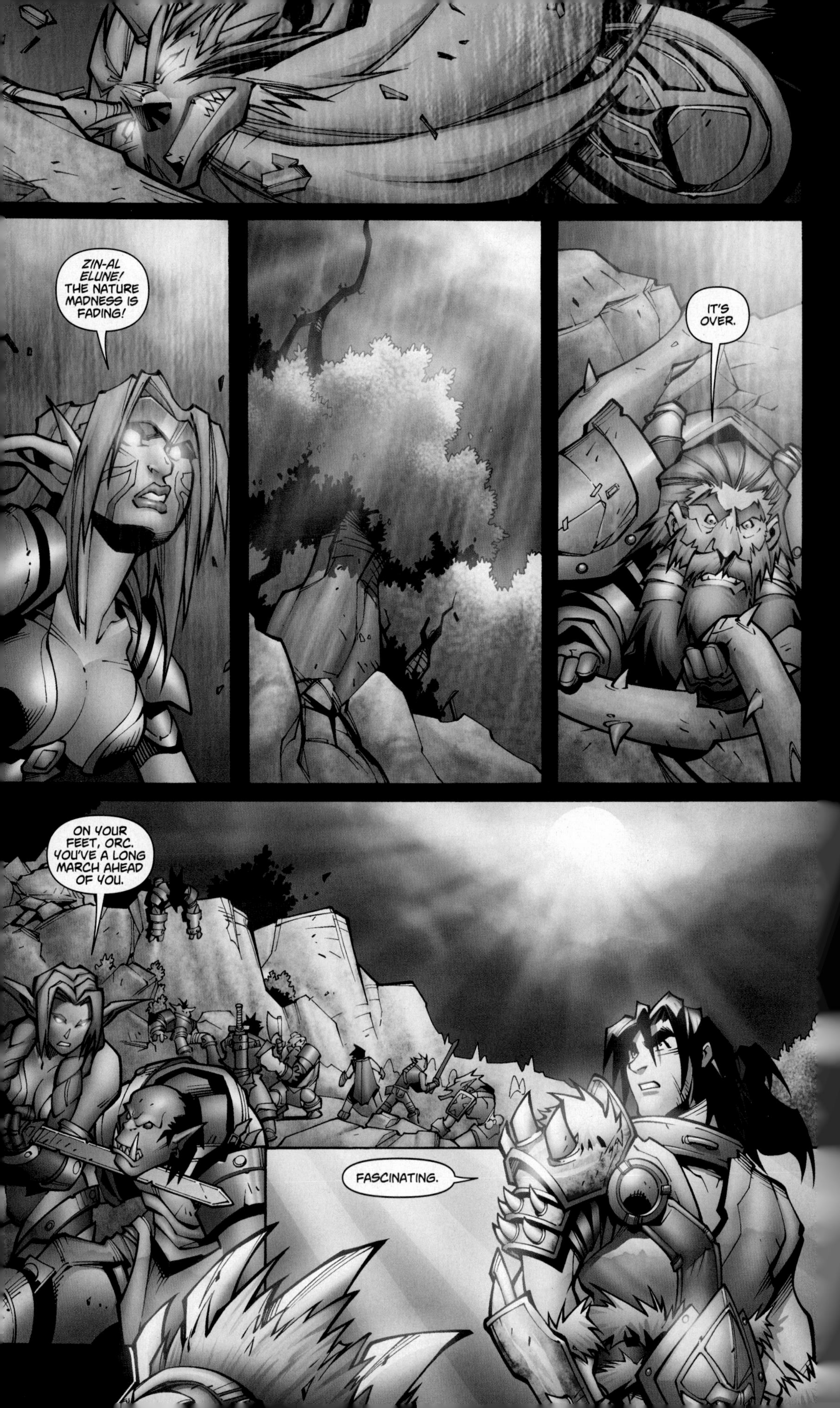
ZIN-AL ELUNE! THE NATURE MADNESS IS FADING!
IT'S OVER.
ON YOUR FEET, ORC. YOU'VE A LONG MARCH AHEAD OF YOU.
FASCINATING.

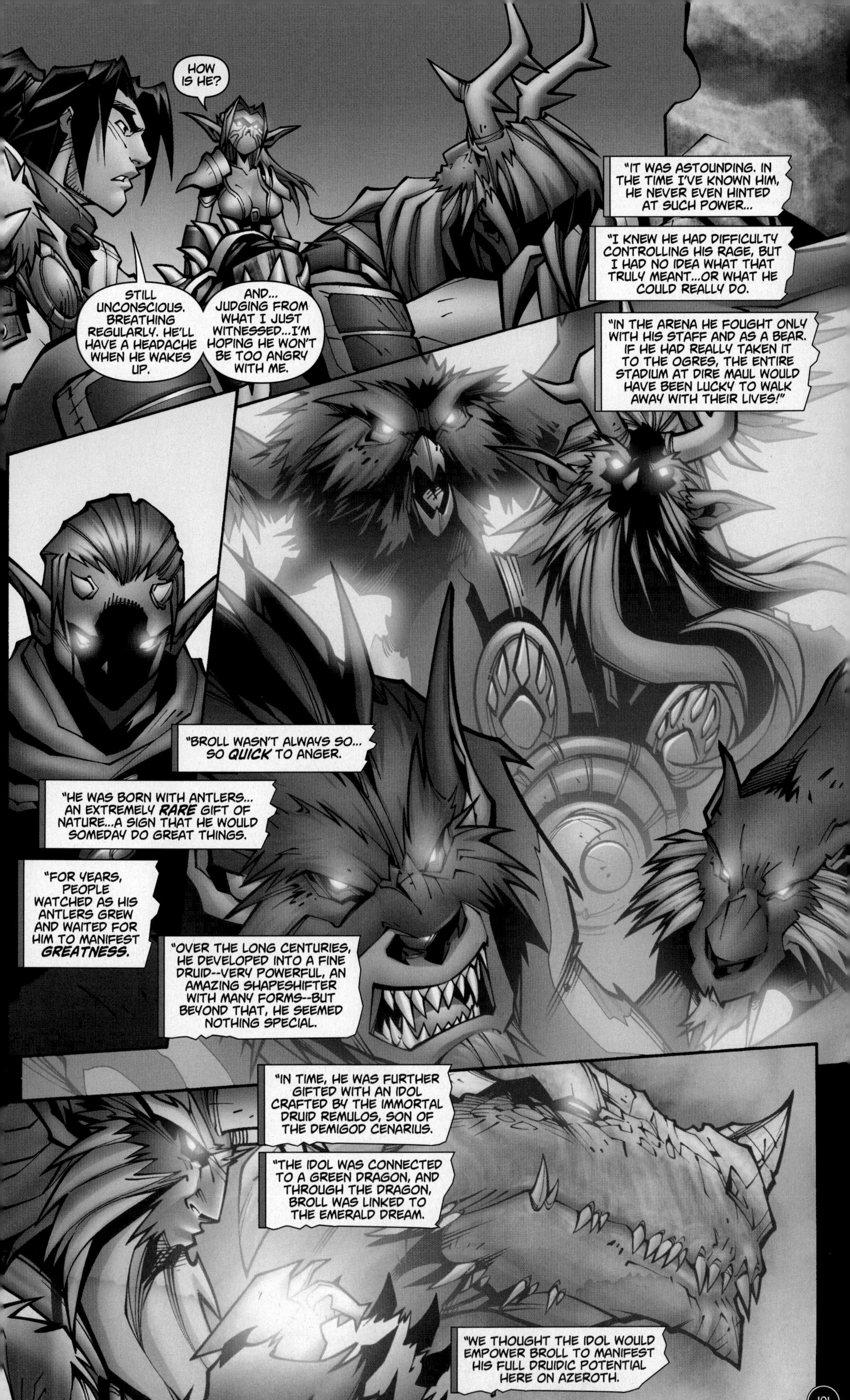
HOW IS HE?
STILL UNCONSCIOUS. BREATHING REGULARLY. HE'LL HAVE A HEADACHE WHEN HE WAKES UP.
AND... JUDGING FROM WHAT I JUST WITNESSED...I'M HOPING HE WON'T BE TOO ANGRY WITH ME.
"IT WAS ASTOUNDING. IN THE TIME I'VE KNOWN HIM, HE NEVER EVEN HINTED AT SUCH POWER...
"I KNEW HE HAD DIFFICULTY CONTROLLING HIS RAGE, BUT I HAD NO IDEA WHAT THAT TRULY MEANT...OR WHAT HE COULD REALLY DO.
"IN THE ARENA HE FOUGHT ONLY WITH HIS STAFF AND AS A BEAR. IF HE HAD REALLY TAKEN IT TO THE OGRES, THE ENTIRE STADIUM AT DIRE MAUL WOULD HAVE BEEN LUCKY TO WALK AWAY WITH THEIR LIVES!"
"BROLL WASN'T ALWAYS SO... SO QUICK TO ANGER.
"HE WAS BORN WITH ANTLERS... AN EXTREMELY RARE GIFT OF NATURE...A SIGN THAT HE WOULD SOMEDAY DO GREAT THINGS.
"FOR YEARS, PEOPLE WATCHED AS HIS ANTLERS GREW AND WAITED FOR HIM TO MANIFEST GREATNESS.
"OVER THE LONG CENTURIES, HE DEVELOPED INTO A FINE DRUID--VERY POWERFUL, AN AMAZING SHAPESHIFTER WITH MANY FORMS--BUT BEYOND THAT, HE SEEMED NOTHING SPECIAL.
"IN TIME, HE WAS FURTHER GIFTED WITH AN IDOL CRAFTED BY THE IMMORTAL DRUID REMULOS, SON OF THE DEMIGOD CENARIUS.
"THE IDOL WAS CONNECTED TO A GREEN DRAGON, AND THROUGH THE DRAGON, BROLL WAS LINKED TO THE EMERALD DREAM.
"WE THOUGHT THE IDOL WOULD EMPOWER BROLL TO MANIFEST HIS FULL DRUIDIC POTENTIAL HERE ON AZEROTH.

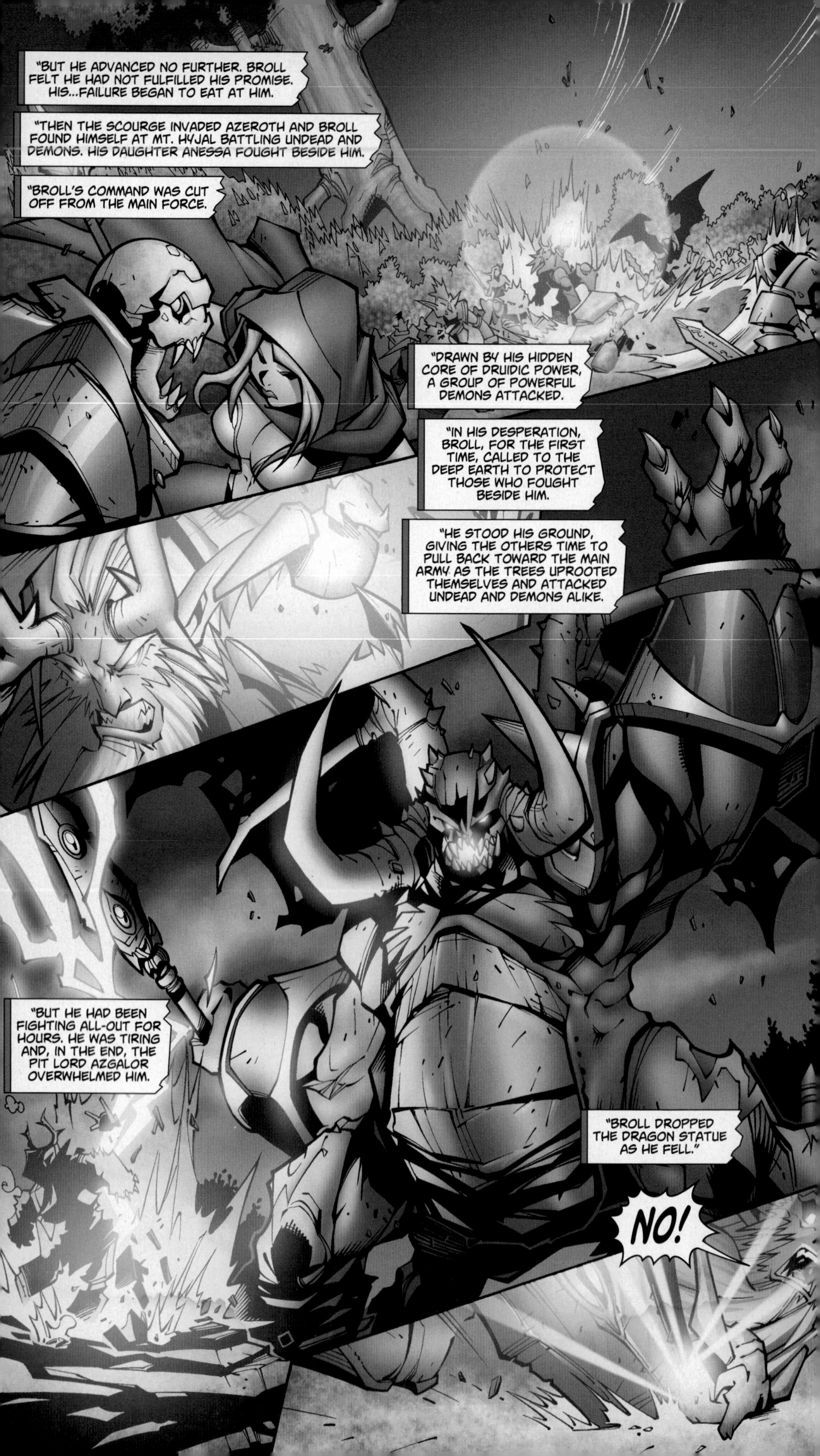
"BUT HE ADVANCED NO FURTHER. BROLL FELT HE HAD NOT FULFILLED HIS PROMISE. HIS...FAILURE BEGAN TO EAT AT HIM.
"THEN THE SCOURGE INVADED AZEROTH AND BROLL FOUND HIMSELF AT MT. HYJAL BATTLING UNDEAD AND DEMONS. HIS DAUGHTER ANESSA FOUGHT BESIDE HIM.
"BROLL'S COMMAND WAS CUT OFF FROM THE MAIN FORCE.
"DRAWN BY HIS HIDDEN CORE OF DRUIDIC POWER, A GROUP OF POWERFUL DEMONS ATTACKED.
"IN HIS DESPERATION, BROLL, FOR THE FIRST TIME, CALLED TO THE DEEP EARTH TO PROTECT THOSE WHO FOUGHT BESIDE HIM.
"HE STOOD HIS GROUND, GIVING THE OTHERS TIME TO PULL BACK TOWARD THE MAIN ARMY AS THE TREES UPROOTED THEMSELVES AND ATTACKED UNDEAD AND DEMONS ALIKE.
"BUT HE HAD BEEN FIGHTING ALL-OUT FOR HOURS. HE WAS TIRING AND, IN THE END, THE PIT LORD AZGALOR OVERWHELMED HIM.
"BROLL DROPPED THE DRAGON STATUE AS HE FELL."
NO!

"THE MYSTICS SAY THAT AS AZGALOR'S BLADE, SPITE, STRUCK THE IDOL...

"...THE DRAGON ROARED IN PAIN AND RAGE."

FATHER!

ANESSA! GET BACK!

"THE EXPLOSION OF FEL ENERGY FROM THE CORRUPTED STATUE KILLED HER INSTANTLY.

"...BUT BROLL'S VALIANT SACRIFICE SAVED MANY OTHER LIVES AND CONTRIBUTED GREATLY TO OUR VICTORY.

"HIS...MANIFESTATIONS BEGAN TO ENDANGER OTHERS.

"WHERE ONCE HE HAD JOYED IN ASSUMING THE SHAPES OF ANIMALS, HIS TRANSFORMATIONS BECAME...MONSTROUS. AND THEN CEASED ALTOGETHER.

"ONLY THE BEAR STOOD BY HIM AND ALLOWED HIM TO USE ITS FORM.

"THE FEL BLAST LEFT BROLL TRAUMATIZED AND TAINTED. HE BLAMED HIMSELF FOR THE LOSS OF THE IDOL AND THE DEATH OF HIS DAUGHTER, AND WAS UNABLE TO CONTAIN HIS SELF-LOATHING AND HIS RAGE.

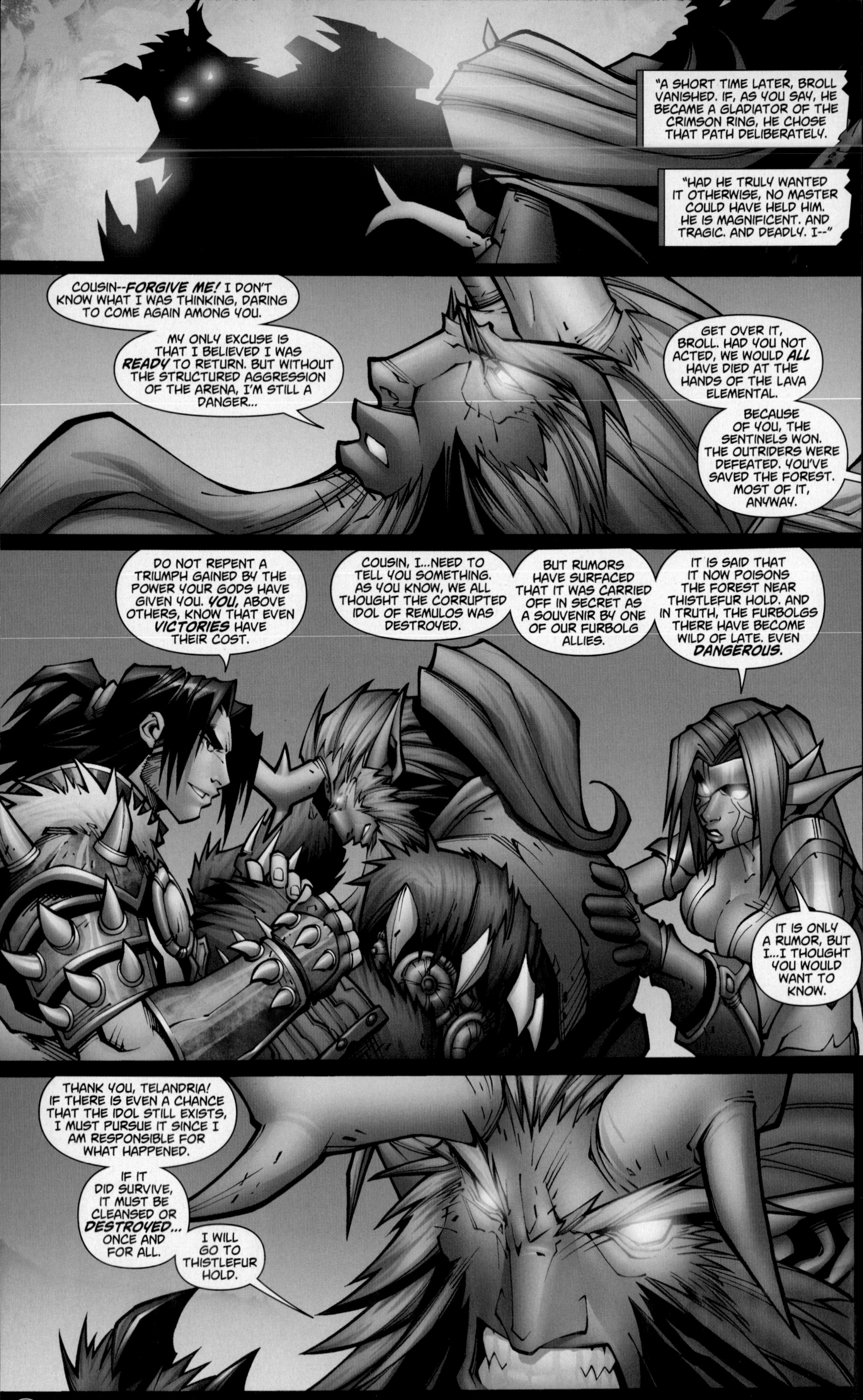
"A SHORT TIME LATER, BROLL VANISHED. IF, AS YOU SAY, HE BECAME A GLADIATOR OF THE CRIMSON RING, HE CHOSE THAT PATH DELIBERATELY.
"HAD HE TRULY WANTED IT OTHERWISE, NO MASTER COULD HAVE HELD HIM. HE IS MAGNIFICENT. AND TRAGIC. AND DEADLY. I--"
COUSIN--FORGIVE ME! I DON'T KNOW WHAT I WAS THINKING, DARING TO COME AGAIN AMONG YOU.
MY ONLY EXCUSE IS THAT I BELIEVED I WAS READY TO RETURN. BUT WITHOUT THE STRUCTURED AGGRESSION OF THE ARENA, I'M STILL A DANGER...
GET OVER IT, BROLL. HAD YOU NOT ACTED, WE WOULD ALL HAVE DIED AT THE HANDS OF THE LAVA ELEMENTAL.
BECAUSE OF YOU, THE SENTINELS WON. THE OUTRIDERS WERE DEFEATED. YOU'VE SAVED THE FOREST. MOST OF IT, ANYWAY.
DO NOT REPENT A TRIUMPH GAINED BY THE POWER YOUR GODS HAVE GIVEN YOU. YOU, ABOVE OTHERS, KNOW THAT EVEN VICTORIES HAVE THEIR COST.
COUSIN, I...NEED TO TELL YOU SOMETHING. AS YOU KNOW, WE ALL THOUGHT THE CORRUPTED IDOL OF REMULOS WAS DESTROYED.
BUT RUMORS HAVE SURFACED THAT IT WAS CARRIED OFF IN SECRET AS A SOUVENIR BY ONE OF OUR FURBOLG ALLIES.
IT IS SAID THAT IT NOW POISONS THE FOREST NEAR THISTLEFUR HOLD. AND IN TRUTH, THE FURBOLGS THERE HAVE BECOME WILD OF LATE. EVEN DANGEROUS.
IT IS ONLY A RUMOR, BUT I...I THOUGHT YOU WOULD WANT TO KNOW.
THANK YOU, TELANDRIA! IF THERE IS EVEN A CHANCE THAT THE IDOL STILL EXISTS, I MUST PURSUE IT SINCE I AM RESPONSIBLE FOR WHAT HAPPENED.
IF IT DID SURVIVE, IT MUST BE CLEANSED OR DESTROYED... ONCE AND FOR ALL.
I WILL GO TO THISTLEFUR HOLD.

CHAPTER 5

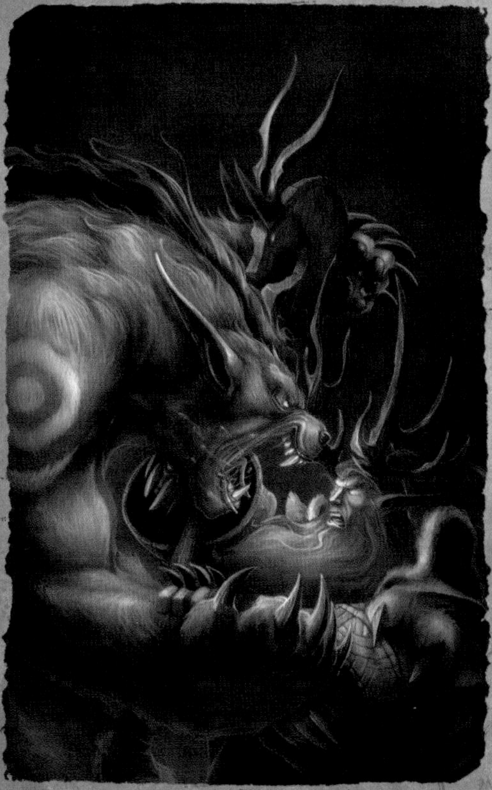

Issue #5 Cover
by Samwise Didier

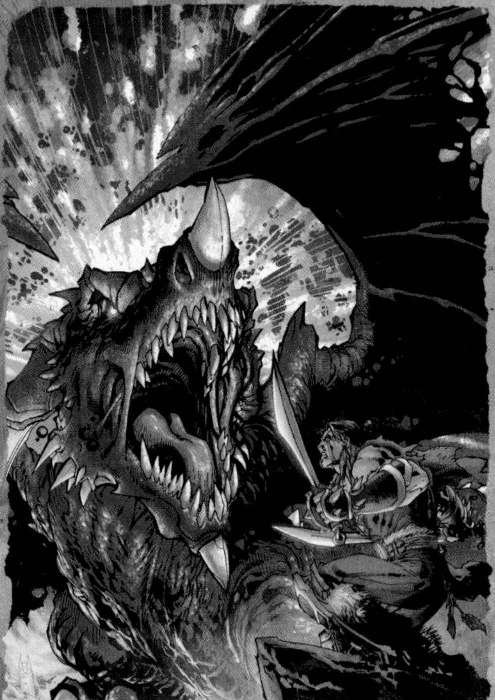

Issue #5 Cover
by Jim Lee and Alex Sinclair

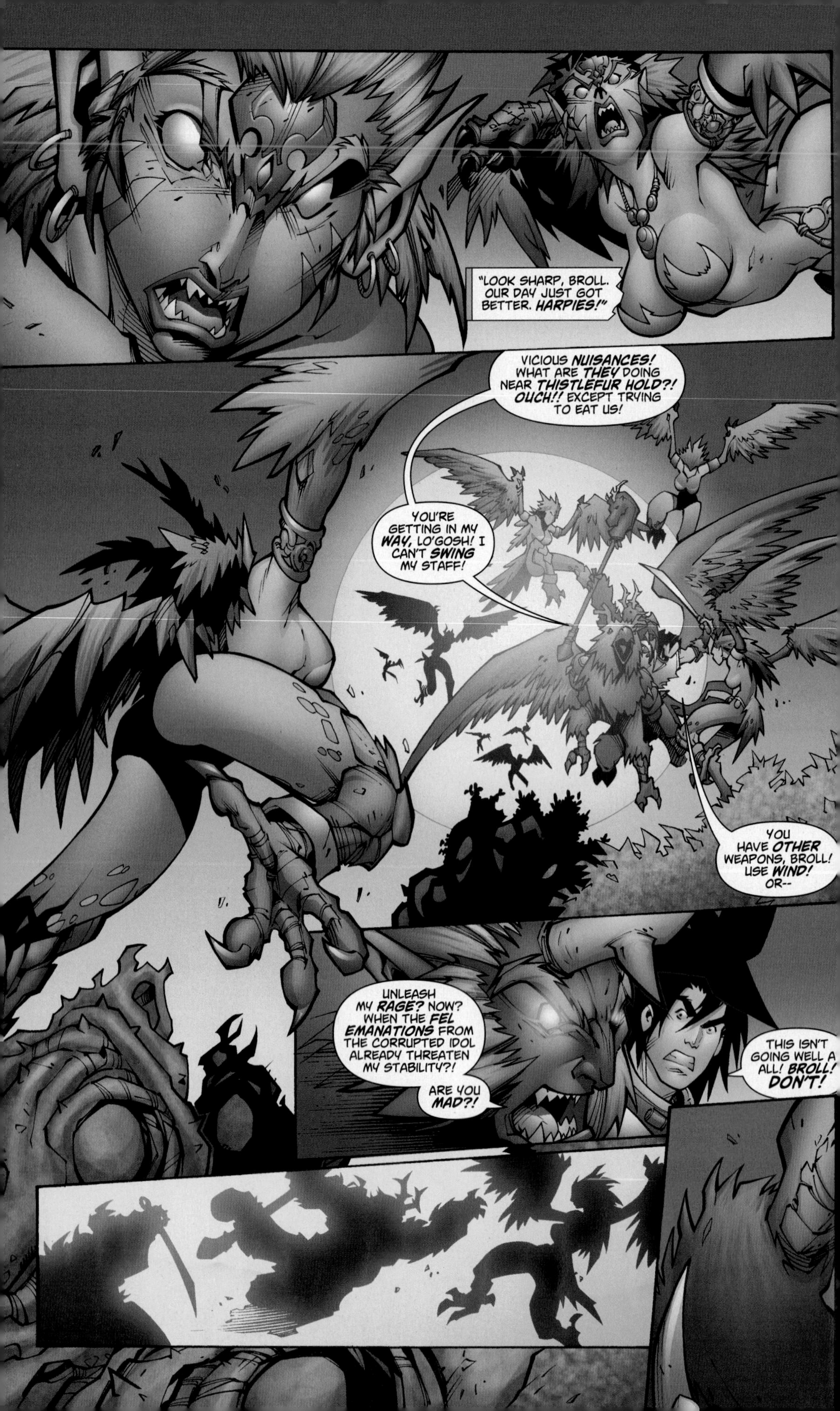
"LOOK SHARP, BROLL. OUR DAY JUST GOT BETTER. HARPIES!"
VICIOUS NUISANCES! WHAT ARE THEY DOING NEAR THISTLEFUR HOLD?! OUCH!! EXCEPT TRYING TO EAT US!
YOU'RE GETTING IN MY WAY, LO'GOSH! I CAN'T SWING MY STAFF!
YOU HAVE OTHER WEAPONS, BROLL! USE WIND! OR--
UNLEASH MY RAGE? NOW? WHEN THE FEL EMANATIONS FROM THE CORRUPTED IDOL ALREADY THREATEN MY STABILITY?!
ARE YOU MAD?!
THIS ISN'T GOING WELL A ALL! BROLL! DON'T!

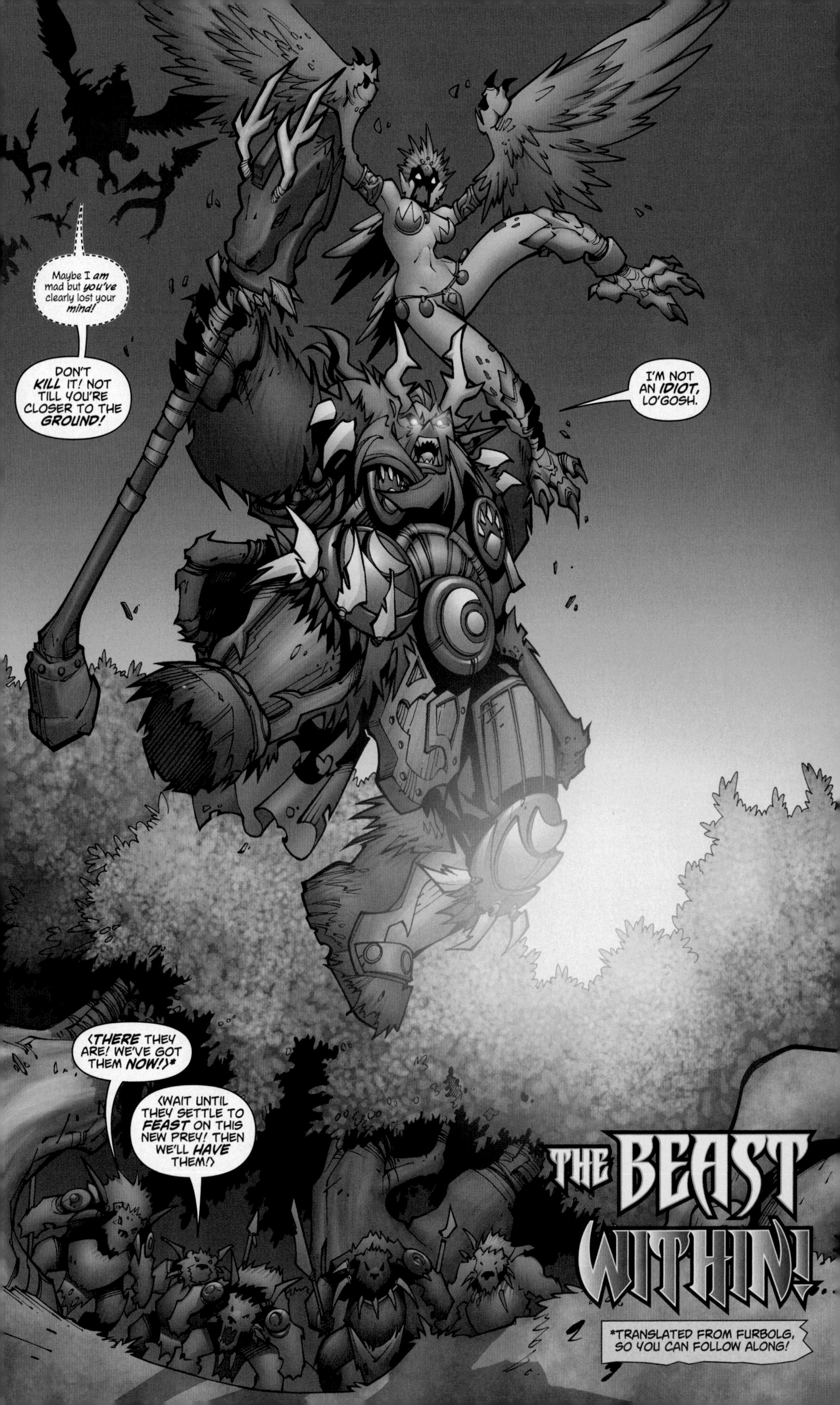
Maybe I *am* mad but *you've* clearly lost your *mind!*
DON'T *KILL* IT! NOT TILL YOU'RE CLOSER TO THE *GROUND!*
I'M NOT AN *IDIOT*, LO'GOSH.
‹*THERE* THEY ARE! WE'VE GOT THEM *NOW!*›*
‹WAIT UNTIL THEY SETTLE TO *FEAST* ON THIS NEW PREY! THEN WE'LL *HAVE* THEM!›
THE BEAST WITHIN!
*TRANSLATED FROM FURBOLG, SO YOU CAN FOLLOW ALONG!

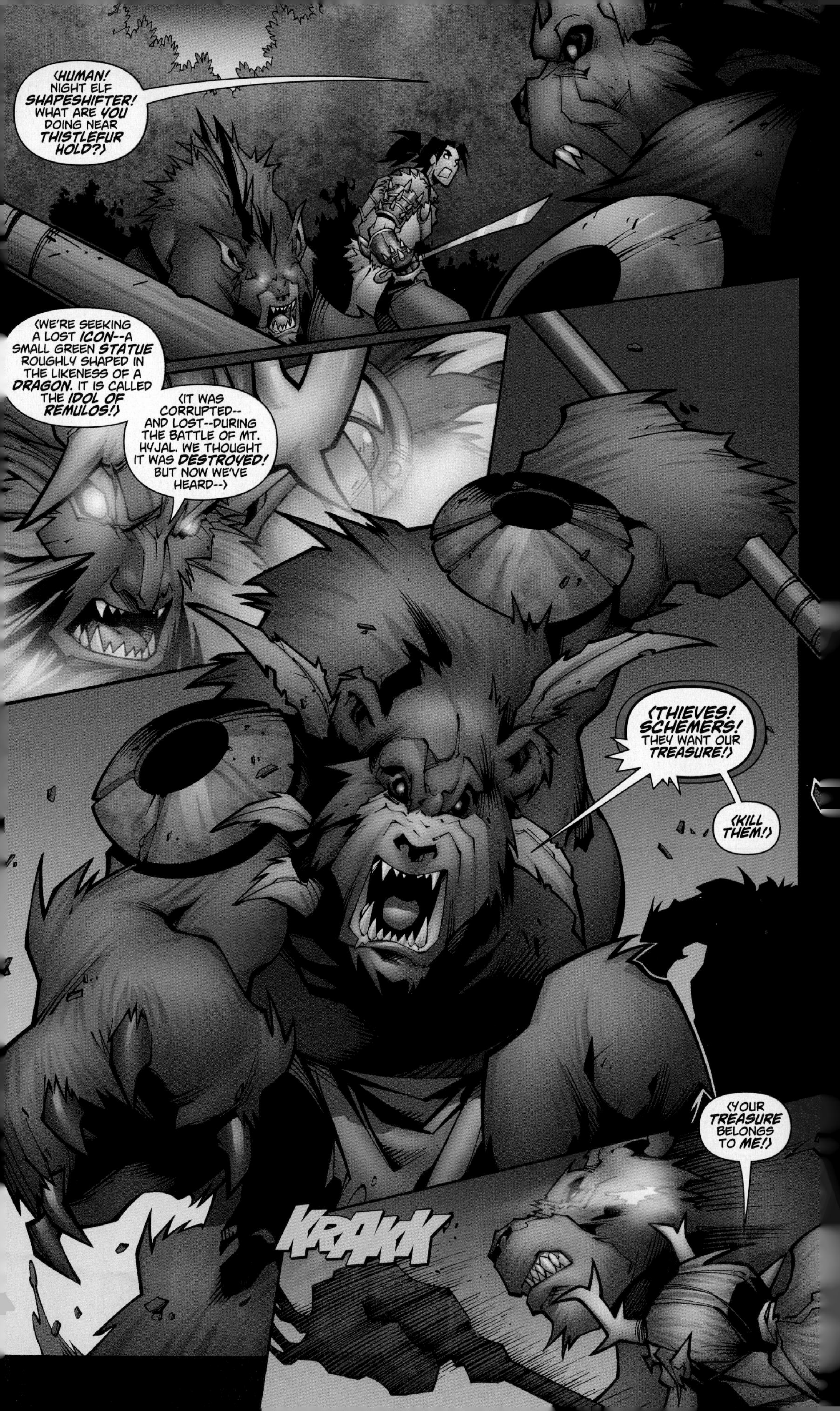
‹HUMAN! NIGHT ELF SHAPESHIFTER! WHAT ARE YOU DOING NEAR THISTLEFUR HOLD?›
‹WE'RE SEEKING A LOST ICON--A SMALL GREEN STATUE ROUGHLY SHAPED IN THE LIKENESS OF A DRAGON. IT IS CALLED THE IDOL OF REMULOS!›
‹IT WAS CORRUPTED-- AND LOST--DURING THE BATTLE OF MT. HYJAL. WE THOUGHT IT WAS DESTROYED! BUT NOW WE'VE HEARD--›
‹THIEVES! SCHEMERS! THEY WANT OUR TREASURE!›
‹KILL THEM!›
‹YOUR TREASURE BELONGS TO ME!›
KRAKK

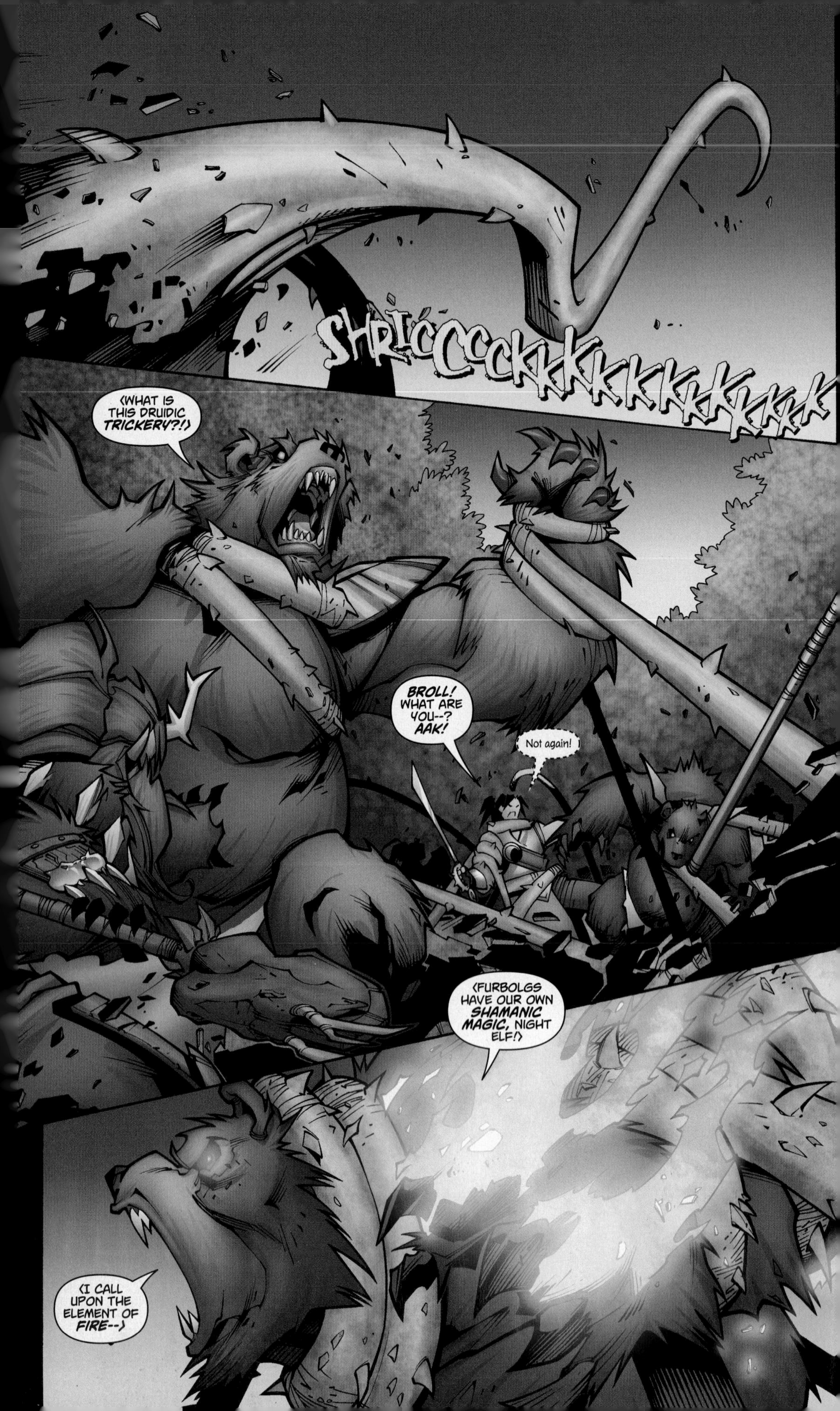
SHRICCCCKKKKKKKKKKK
‹WHAT IS THIS DRUIDIC TRICKERY?!›
BROLL! WHAT ARE YOU--? AAK!
Not again!
‹FURBOLGS HAVE OUR OWN SHAMANIC MAGIC, NIGHT ELF!›
‹I CALL UPON THE ELEMENT OF FIRE--›

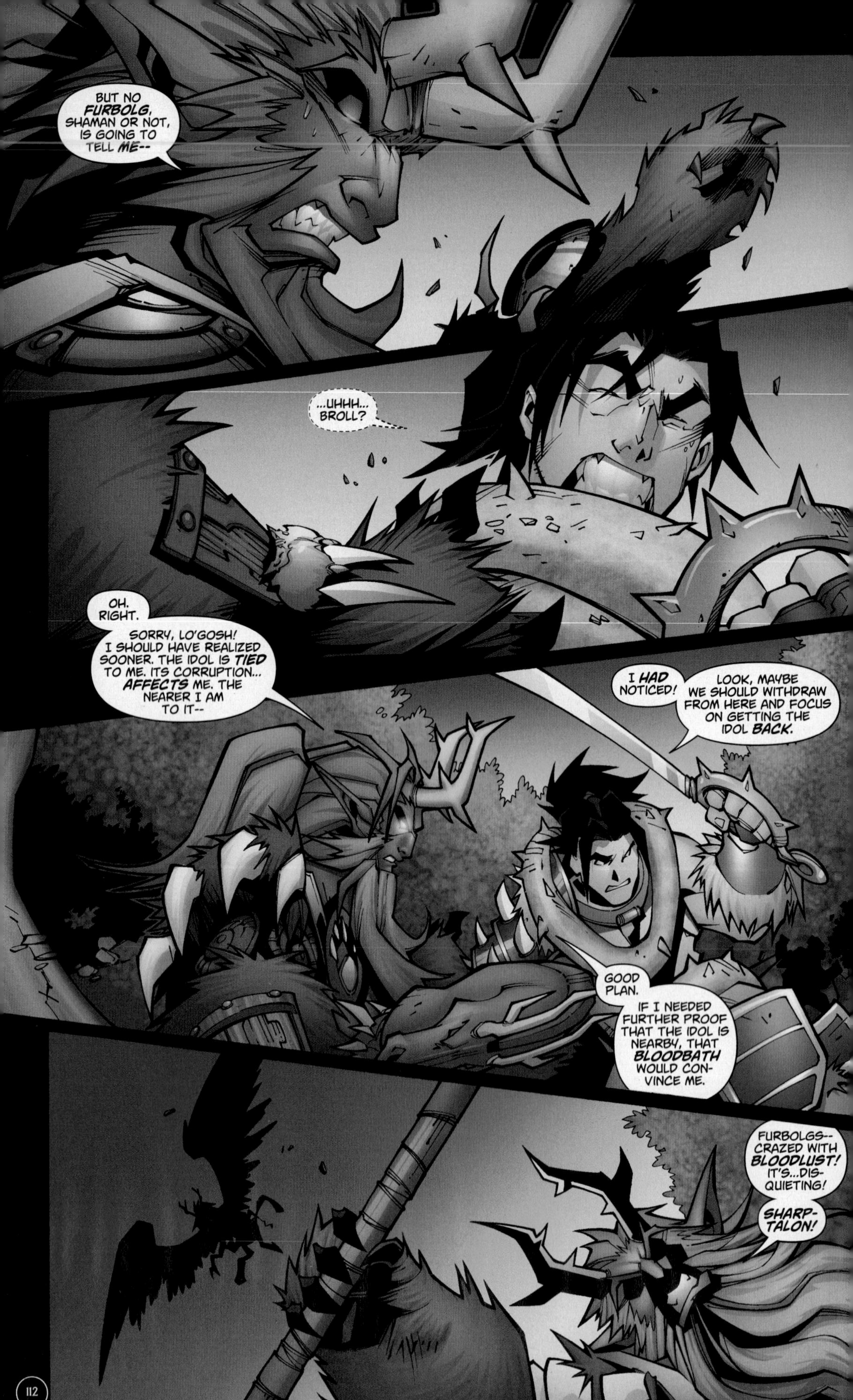

BUT NO FURBOLG, SHAMAN OR NOT, IS GOING TO TELL ME--
...UHHH... BROLL?
OH. RIGHT.
SORRY, LO'GOSH! I SHOULD HAVE REALIZED SOONER. THE IDOL IS TIED TO ME. ITS CORRUPTION... AFFECTS ME. THE NEARER I AM TO IT--
I HAD NOTICED!
LOOK, MAYBE WE SHOULD WITHDRAW FROM HERE AND FOCUS ON GETTING THE IDOL BACK.
GOOD PLAN.
IF I NEEDED FURTHER PROOF THAT THE IDOL IS NEARBY, THAT BLOODBATH WOULD CONVINCE ME.
FURBOLGS--CRAZED WITH BLOODLUST! IT'S...DISQUIETING!
SHARP-TALON!

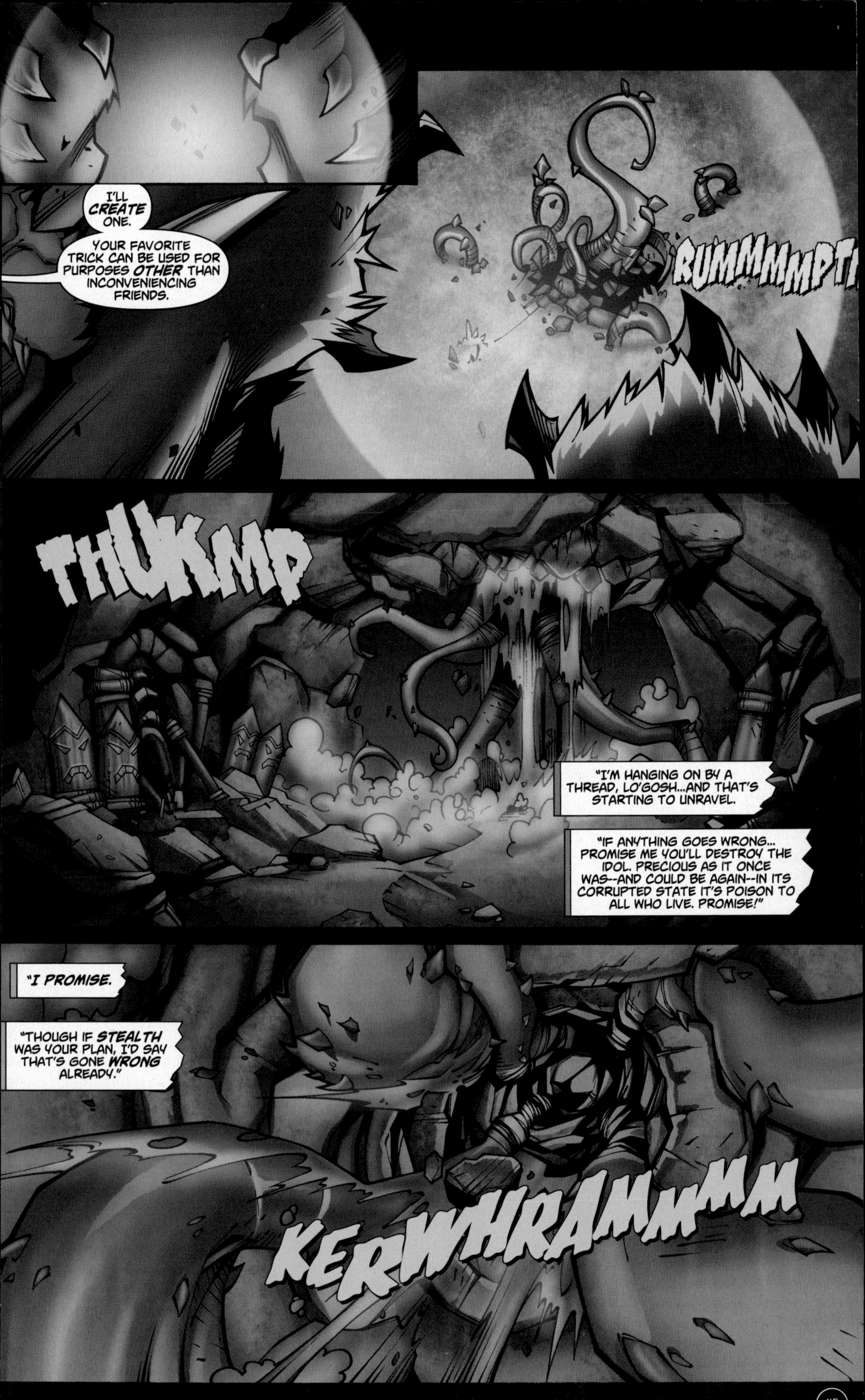

I'LL CREATE ONE.
YOUR FAVORITE TRICK CAN BE USED FOR PURPOSES OTHER THAN INCONVENIENCING FRIENDS.
RUMMMMPT!
THUKMP
"I'M HANGING ON BY A THREAD, LO'GOSH...AND THAT'S STARTING TO UNRAVEL.
"IF ANYTHING GOES WRONG... PROMISE ME YOU'LL DESTROY THE IDOL. PRECIOUS AS IT ONCE WAS--AND COULD BE AGAIN--IN ITS CORRUPTED STATE IT'S POISON TO ALL WHO LIVE. PROMISE!"
"I PROMISE.
"THOUGH IF STEALTH WAS YOUR PLAN, I'D SAY THAT'S GONE WRONG ALREADY."
KERWHRAMMMMM

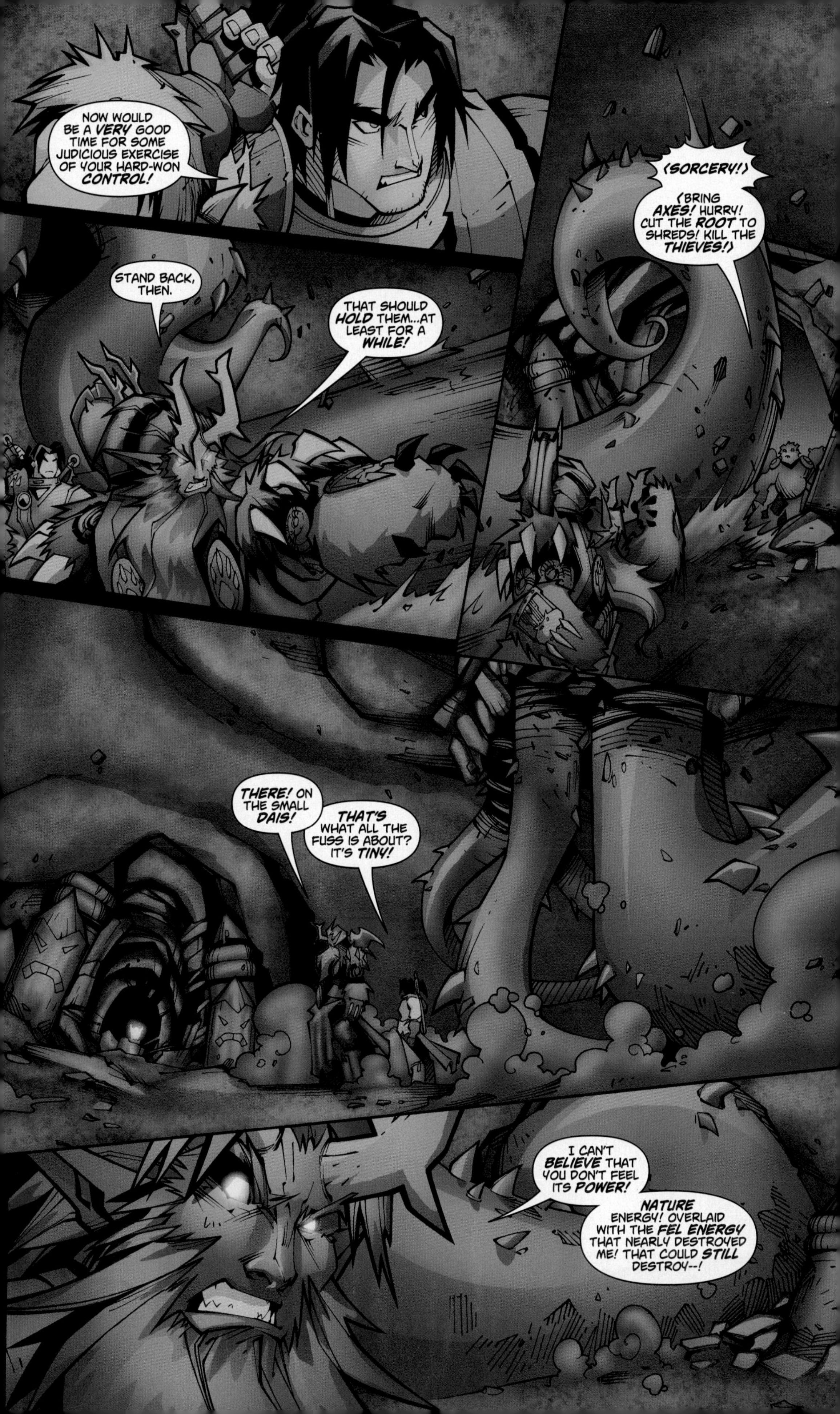
NOW WOULD BE A VERY GOOD TIME FOR SOME JUDICIOUS EXERCISE OF YOUR HARD-WON CONTROL!
STAND BACK, THEN.
THAT SHOULD HOLD THEM...AT LEAST FOR A WHILE!
(SORCERY!)
(BRING AXES! HURRY! CUT THE ROOT TO SHREDS! KILL THE THIEVES!)
THERE! ON THE SMALL DAIS!
THAT'S WHAT ALL THE FUSS IS ABOUT? IT'S TINY!
I CAN'T BELIEVE THAT YOU DON'T FEEL ITS POWER!
NATURE ENERGY! OVERLAID WITH THE FEL ENERGY THAT NEARLY DESTROYED ME! THAT COULD STILL DESTROY--!

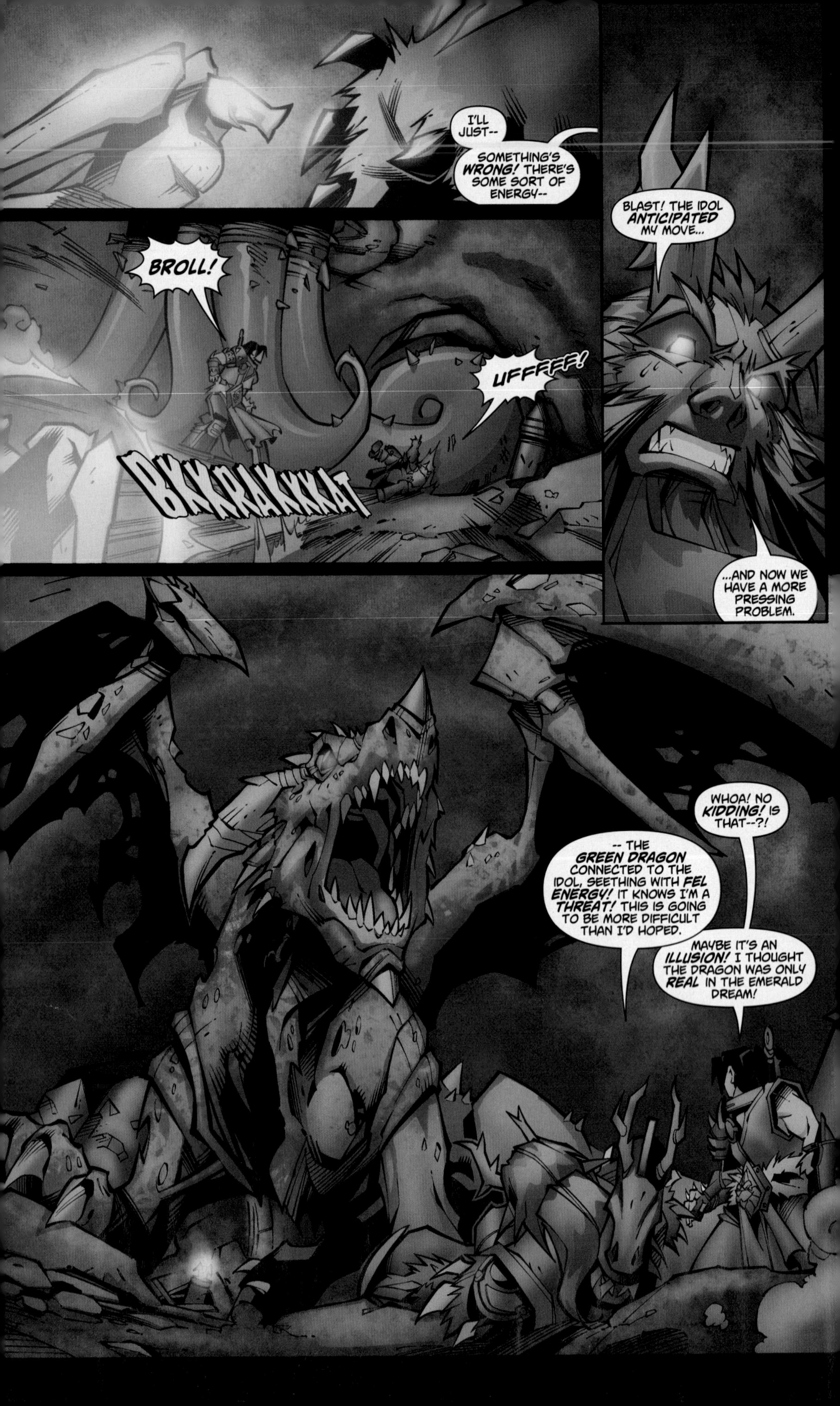
I'LL JUST--
SOMETHING'S WRONG! THERE'S SOME SORT OF ENERGY--
BLAST! THE IDOL ANTICIPATED MY MOVE...
BROLL!
UFFFFFF!
BKKRAKKKAT
...AND NOW WE HAVE A MORE PRESSING PROBLEM.
WHOA! NO KIDDING! IS THAT--?!
-- THE GREEN DRAGON CONNECTED TO THE IDOL, SEETHING WITH FEL ENERGY! IT KNOWS I'M A THREAT! THIS IS GOING TO BE MORE DIFFICULT THAN I'D HOPED.
MAYBE IT'S AN ILLUSION! I THOUGHT THE DRAGON WAS ONLY REAL IN THE EMERALD DREAM!

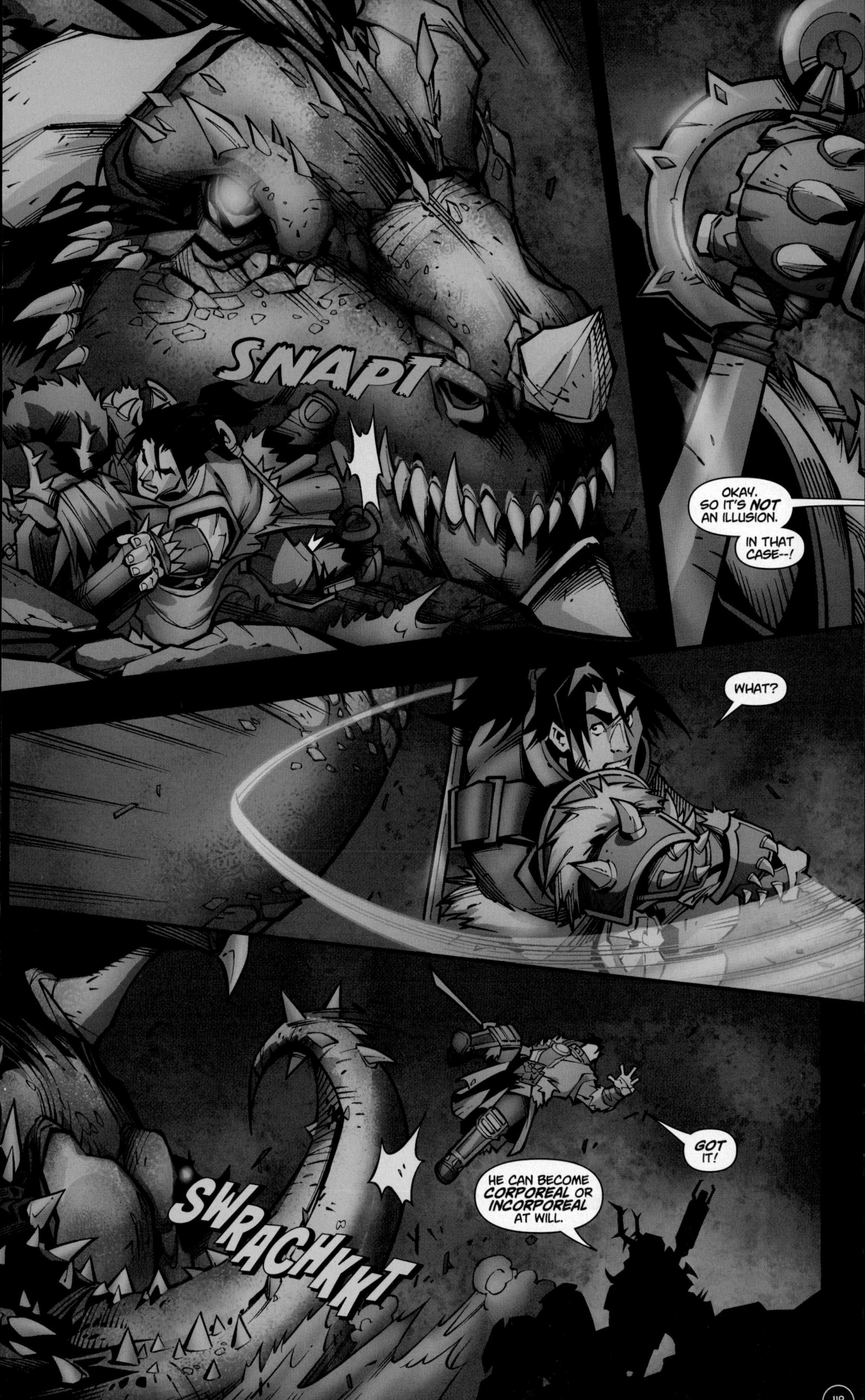
SNAPT
OKAY. SO IT'S NOT AN ILLUSION.
IN THAT CASE--!
WHAT?
SWRACHKKT
GOT IT!
HE CAN BECOME CORPOREAL OR INCORPOREAL AT WILL.

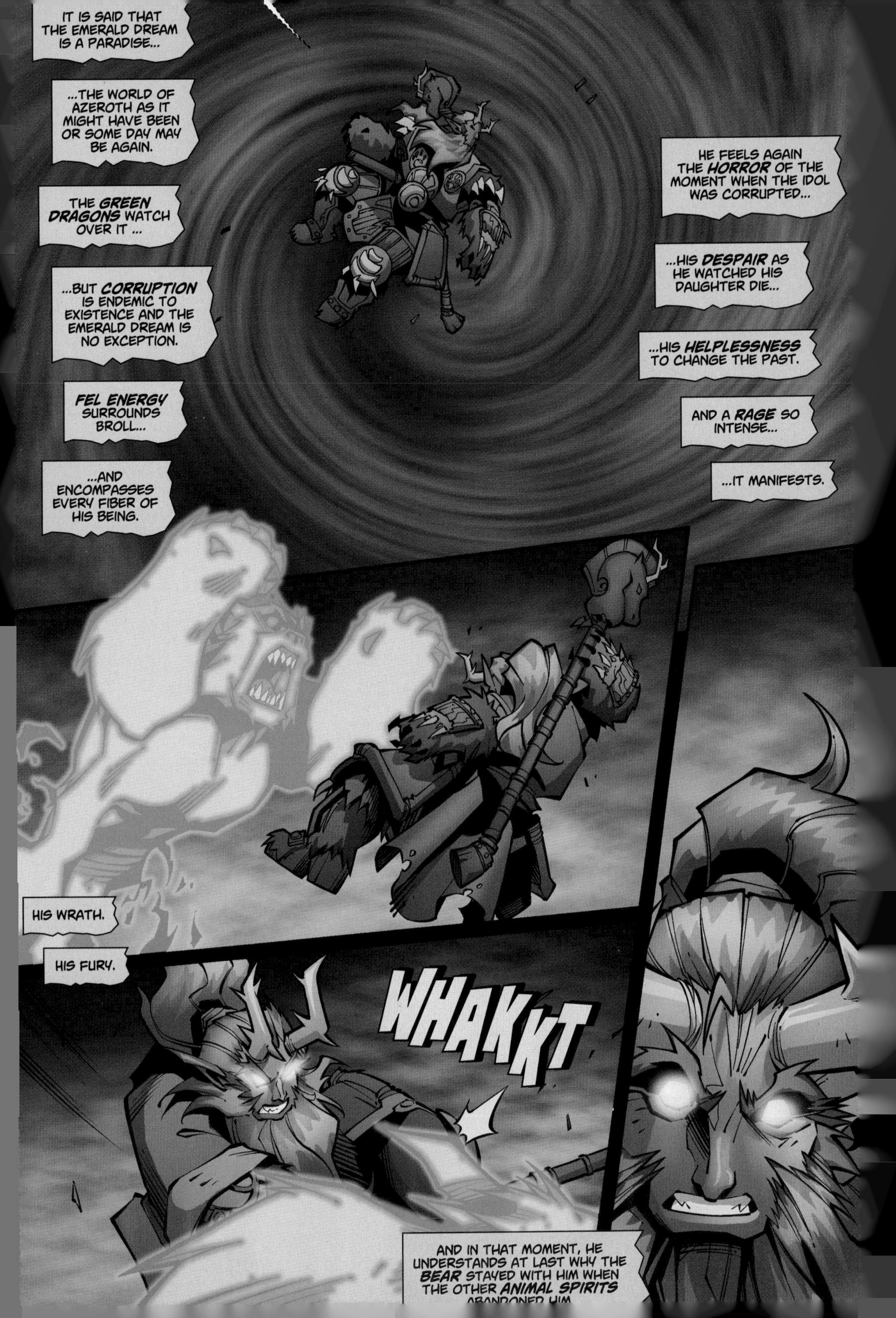
IT IS SAID THAT THE EMERALD DREAM IS A PARADISE...
...THE WORLD OF AZEROTH AS IT MIGHT HAVE BEEN OR SOME DAY MAY BE AGAIN.
THE GREEN DRAGONS WATCH OVER IT ...
...BUT CORRUPTION IS ENDEMIC TO EXISTENCE AND THE EMERALD DREAM IS NO EXCEPTION.
FEL ENERGY SURROUNDS BROLL...
...AND ENCOMPASSES EVERY FIBER OF HIS BEING.
HE FEELS AGAIN THE HORROR OF THE MOMENT WHEN THE IDOL WAS CORRUPTED...
...HIS DESPAIR AS HE WATCHED HIS DAUGHTER DIE...
...HIS HELPLESSNESS TO CHANGE THE PAST.
AND A RAGE SO INTENSE...
...IT MANIFESTS.
HIS WRATH.
HIS FURY.
WHAKKT
AND IN THAT MOMENT, HE UNDERSTANDS AT LAST WHY THE BEAR STAYED WITH HIM WHEN THE OTHER ANIMAL SPIRITS ABANDONED HIM.

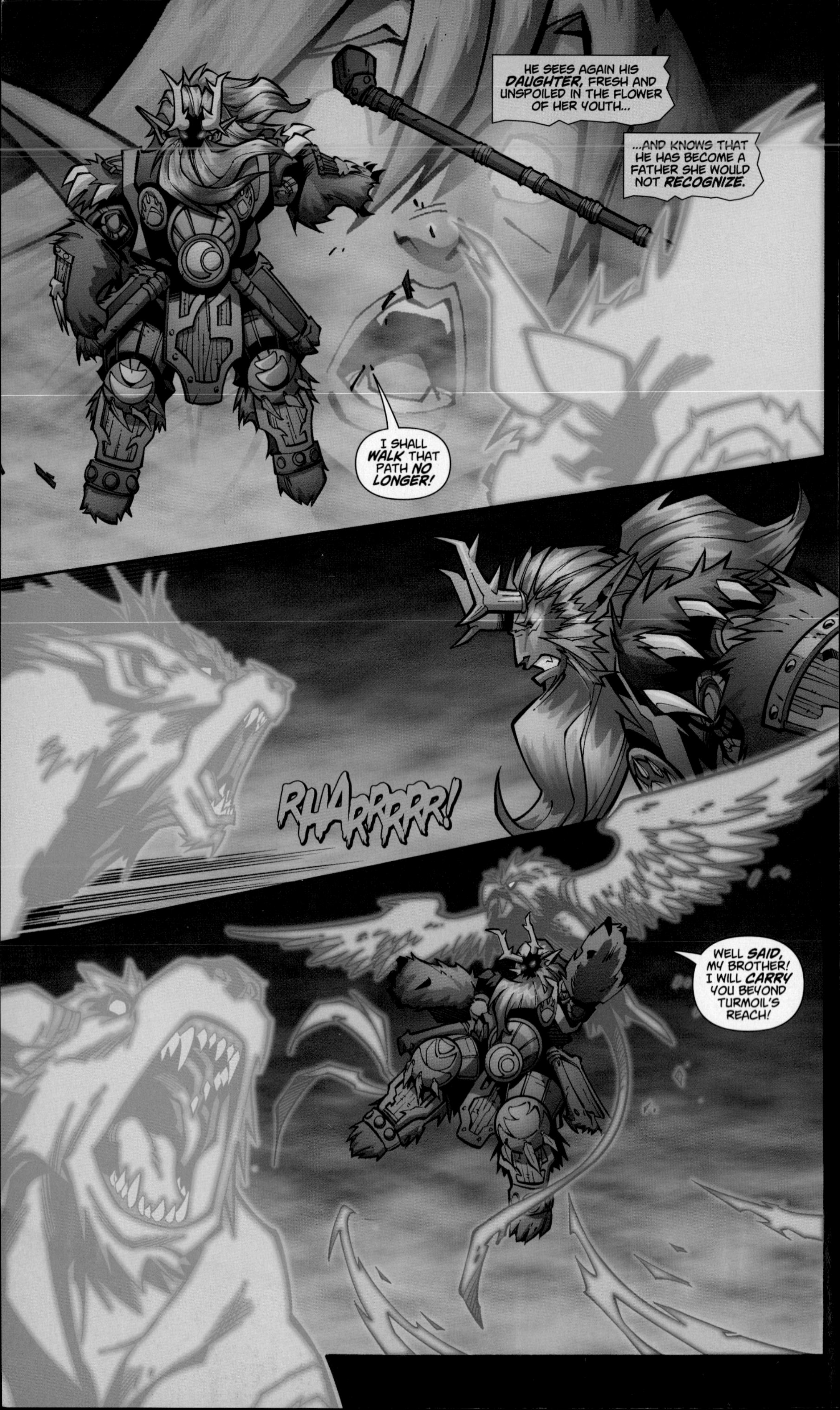
HE SEES AGAIN HIS DAUGHTER, FRESH AND UNSPOILED IN THE FLOWER OF HER YOUTH...
...AND KNOWS THAT HE HAS BECOME A FATHER SHE WOULD NOT RECOGNIZE.
I SHALL WALK THAT PATH NO LONGER!
RHARRRRR!
WELL SAID, MY BROTHER! I WILL CARRY YOU BEYOND TURMOIL'S REACH!

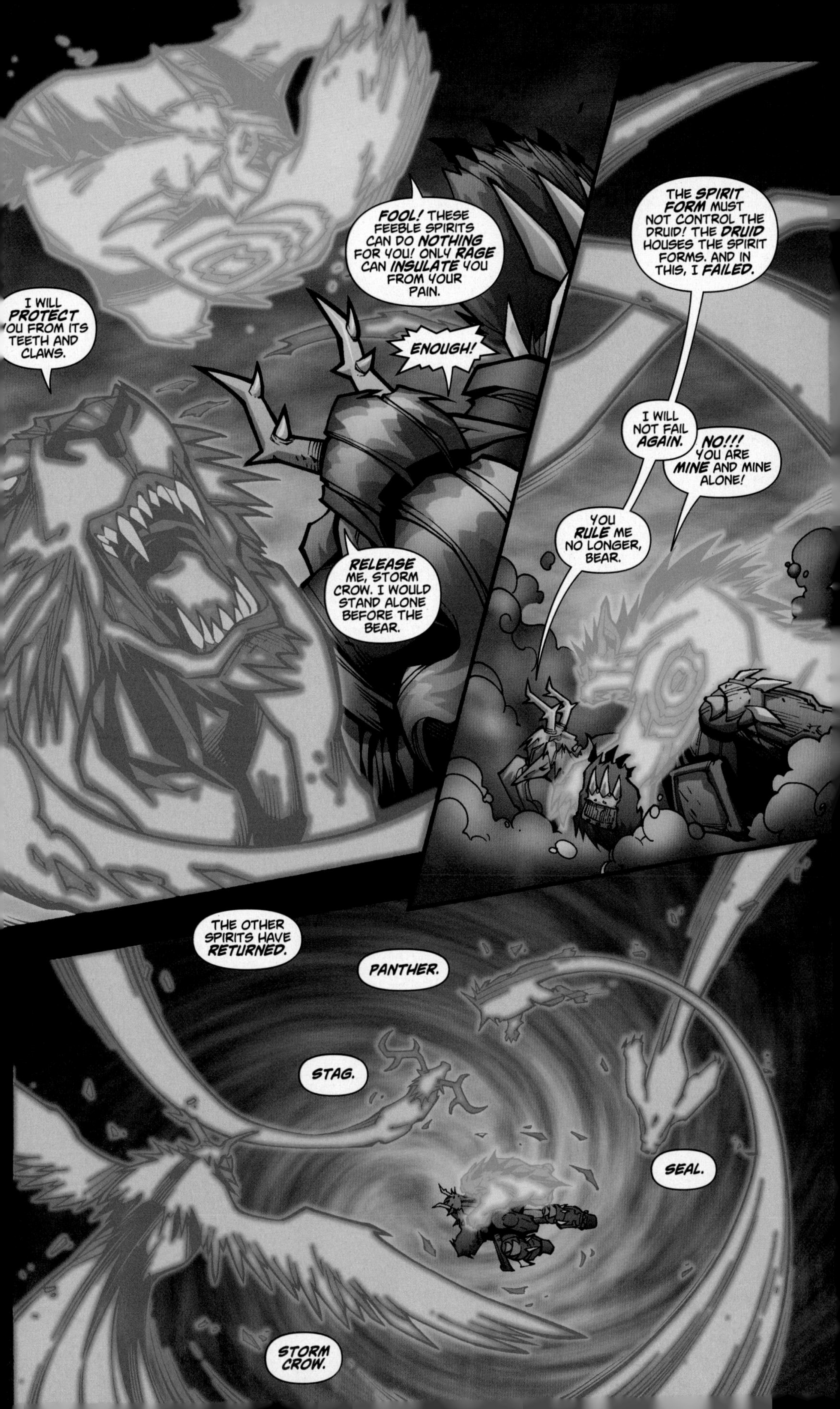

I WILL PROTECT YOU FROM ITS TEETH AND CLAWS.
FOOL! THESE FEEBLE SPIRITS CAN DO NOTHING FOR YOU! ONLY RAGE CAN INSULATE YOU FROM YOUR PAIN.
ENOUGH!
RELEASE ME, STORM CROW. I WOULD STAND ALONE BEFORE THE BEAR.
THE SPIRIT FORM MUST NOT CONTROL THE DRUID! THE DRUID HOUSES THE SPIRIT FORMS. AND IN THIS, I FAILED.
I WILL NOT FAIL AGAIN.
NO!!! YOU ARE MINE AND MINE ALONE!
YOU RULE ME NO LONGER, BEAR.
THE OTHER SPIRITS HAVE RETURNED.
PANTHER.
STAG.
SEAL.
STORM CROW.

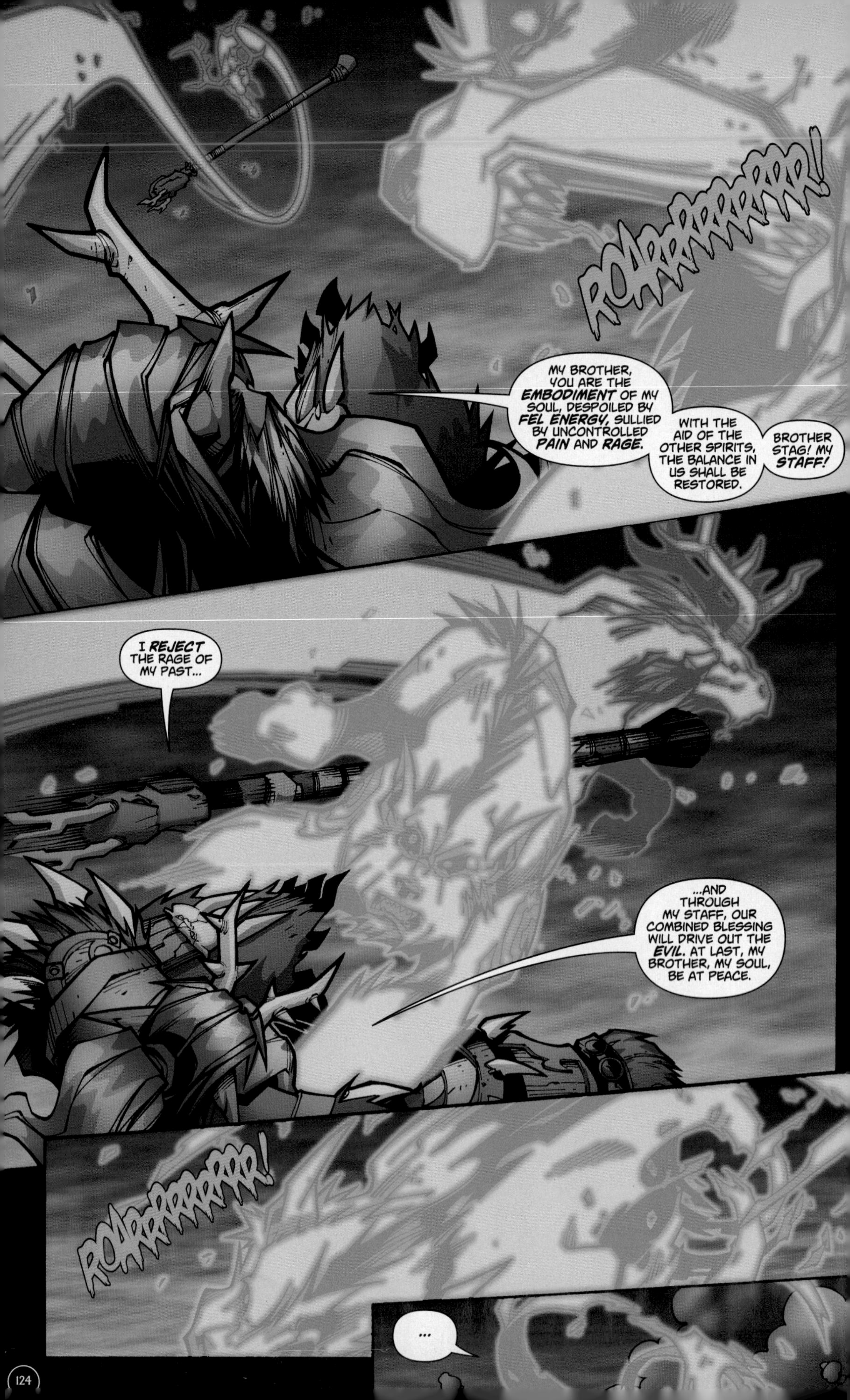
ROARRRRRRRRR!
MY BROTHER, YOU ARE THE EMBODIMENT OF MY SOUL, DESPOILED BY FEL ENERGY, SULLIED BY UNCONTROLLED PAIN AND RAGE.
WITH THE AID OF THE OTHER SPIRITS, THE BALANCE IN US SHALL BE RESTORED.
BROTHER STAG! MY STAFF!
I REJECT THE RAGE OF MY PAST...
...AND THROUGH MY STAFF, OUR COMBINED BLESSING WILL DRIVE OUT THE EVIL. AT LAST, MY BROTHER, MY SOUL, BE AT PEACE.
ROARRRRRRRR!
...

CHAPTER 6

Issue #6 Cover
by Samwise Didier

Issue #6 Cover
by Jim Lee and Alex Sinclair

RECENTLY, THE LIFE OF VALEERA SANGUINAR HAS BEEN COMPLEX.

SHE WAS *JAILED, SOLD,* FOUGHT AS A *GLADIATOR,* WON A *CHAMPIONSHIP, SOLD* AGAIN, *ESCAPED,* AND TRIED TO *FREE* HER OLD TEAMMATES, ONLY TO LEARN THAT THEY HAD FREED *THEMSELVES* AND DISAPPEARED.

NOW SHE HAS FOLLOWED AN *ASSASSIN,* WHO IS HOT ON THE TRAIL OF HER FRIENDS, TO *WARSONG GULCH...*

GREETINGS, SENTINELS! I SEE YOU'VE PUT SOME ORC CAPTIVES TO *HARD LABOR!*

WELCOME, HUMAN! HAVE YOU COME TO *JOIN* US IN OUR BATTLES?

...*ROUNDEYE,* HERE, TELLS ME *BROLL* HAS PURIFIED THE *IDOL OF REMULOS* AND HAS FREED HIMSELF OF ITS *CURSE!*

NOW HE AND LO'GOSH ARE TAKING IT TO *DARNASSUS--*

Silverwing sentinels! Led by a *Priestess of the Moon--*

PRRRT?

Hush, *Bristlefur!* A *blood elf* in these parts won't get as warm a welcome as the human!

IDOL?! WHAT IDOL?! WHAT CURSE?!!

Wait *here.* I need to get closer to listen to what they're saying.

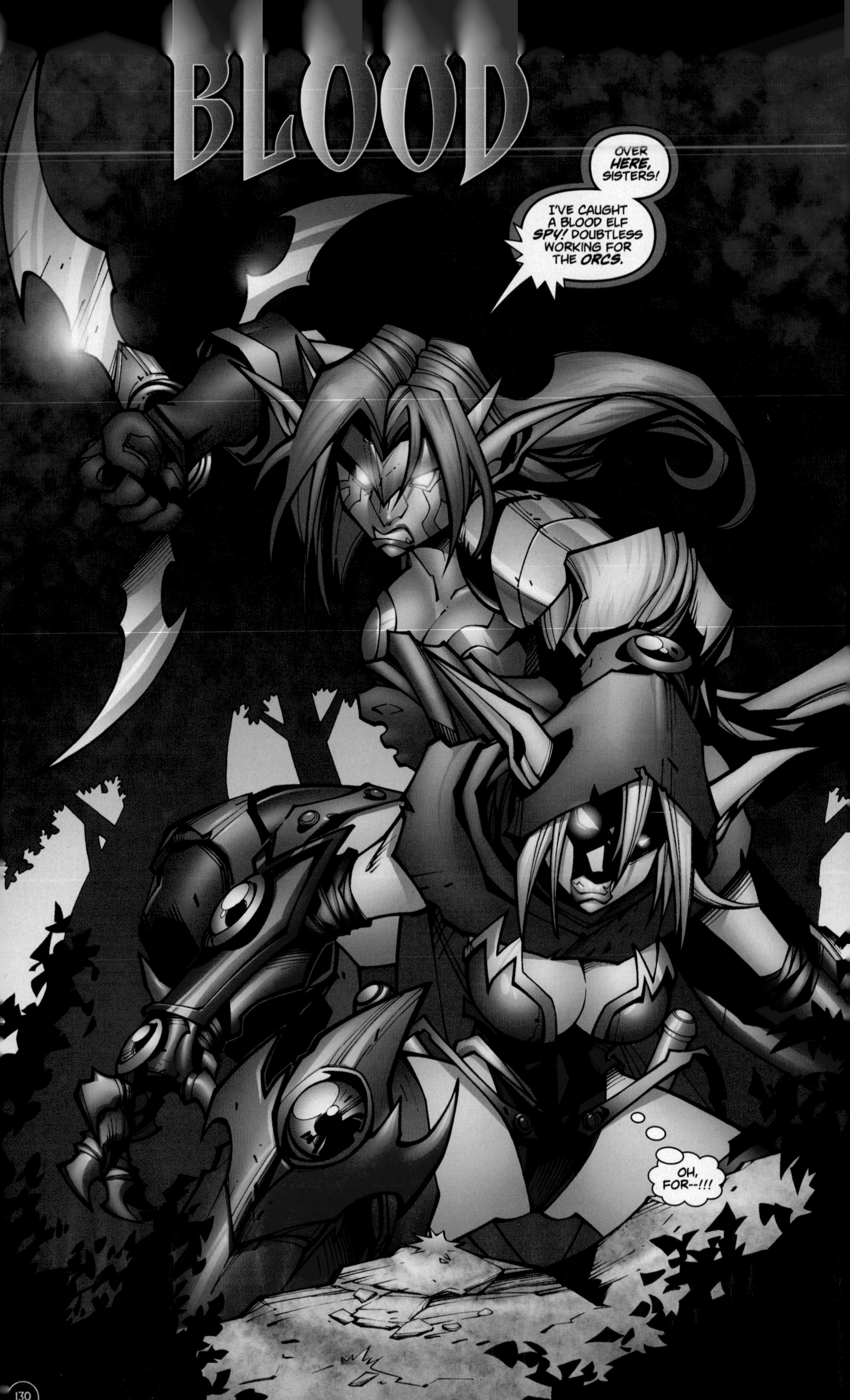
BLOOD
OVER HERE, SISTERS!
I'VE CAUGHT A BLOOD ELF SPY! DOUBTLESS WORKING FOR THE ORCS.
OH, FOR--!!!

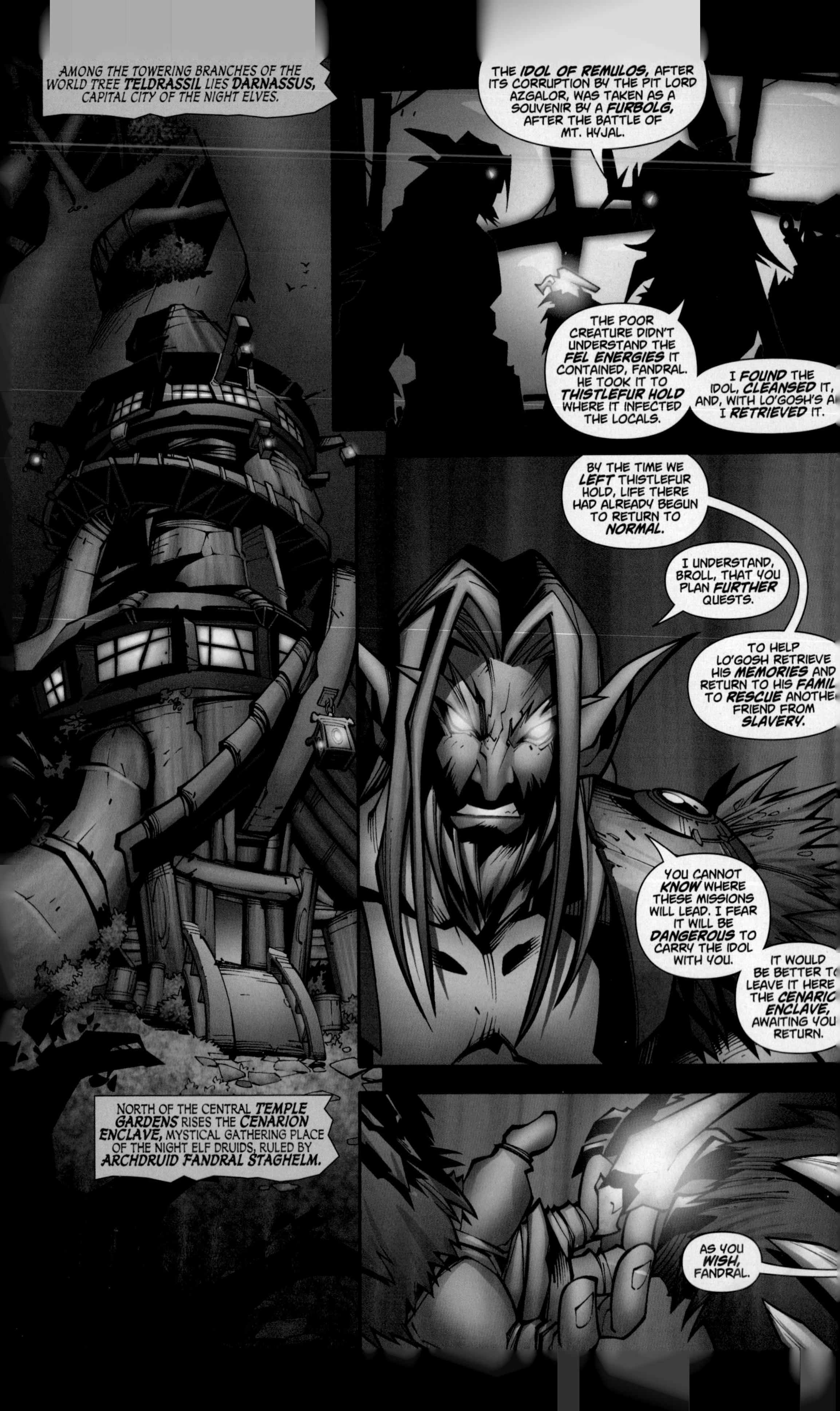
AMONG THE TOWERING BRANCHES OF THE WORLD TREE TELDRASSIL LIES DARNASSUS, CAPITAL CITY OF THE NIGHT ELVES.
NORTH OF THE CENTRAL TEMPLE GARDENS RISES THE CENARION ENCLAVE, MYSTICAL GATHERING PLACE OF THE NIGHT ELF DRUIDS, RULED BY ARCHDRUID FANDRAL STAGHELM.
THE IDOL OF REMULOS, AFTER ITS CORRUPTION BY THE PIT LORD AZGALOR, WAS TAKEN AS A SOUVENIR BY A FURBOLG, AFTER THE BATTLE OF MT. HYJAL.
THE POOR CREATURE DIDN'T UNDERSTAND THE FEL ENERGIES IT CONTAINED, FANDRAL. HE TOOK IT TO THISTLEFUR HOLD WHERE IT INFECTED THE LOCALS.
I FOUND THE IDOL, CLEANSED IT, AND, WITH LO'GOSH'S A I RETRIEVED IT.
BY THE TIME WE LEFT THISTLEFUR HOLD, LIFE THERE HAD ALREADY BEGUN TO RETURN TO NORMAL.
I UNDERSTAND, BROLL, THAT YOU PLAN FURTHER QUESTS.
TO HELP LO'GOSH RETRIEVE HIS MEMORIES AND RETURN TO HIS FAMIL TO RESCUE ANOTHE FRIEND FROM SLAVERY.
YOU CANNOT KNOW WHERE THESE MISSIONS WILL LEAD. I FEAR IT WILL BE DANGEROUS TO CARRY THE IDOL WITH YOU.
IT WOULD BE BETTER TO LEAVE IT HERE THE CENARIC ENCLAVE, AWAITING YOU RETURN.
AS YOU WISH, FANDRAL.

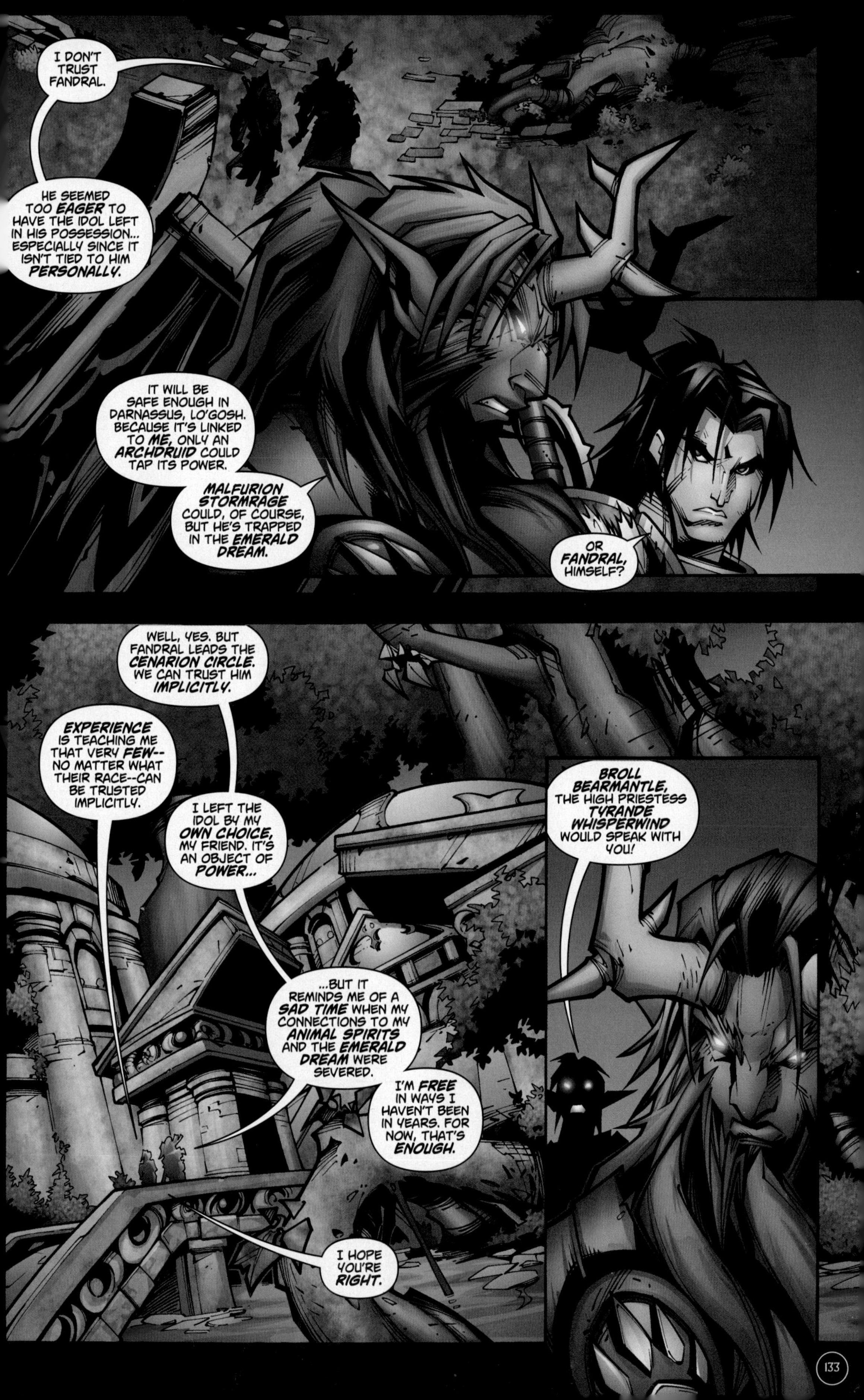

I DON'T TRUST FANDRAL.
HE SEEMED TOO EAGER TO HAVE THE IDOL LEFT IN HIS POSSESSION... ESPECIALLY SINCE IT ISN'T TIED TO HIM PERSONALLY.
IT WILL BE SAFE ENOUGH IN DARNASSUS, LO'GOSH. BECAUSE IT'S LINKED TO ME, ONLY AN ARCHDRUID COULD TAP ITS POWER.
MALFURION STORMRAGE COULD, OF COURSE, BUT HE'S TRAPPED IN THE EMERALD DREAM.
OR FANDRAL, HIMSELF?
WELL, YES. BUT FANDRAL LEADS THE CENARION CIRCLE. WE CAN TRUST HIM IMPLICITLY.
EXPERIENCE IS TEACHING ME THAT VERY FEW-- NO MATTER WHAT THEIR RACE--CAN BE TRUSTED IMPLICITLY.
I LEFT THE IDOL BY MY OWN CHOICE, MY FRIEND. IT'S AN OBJECT OF POWER...
...BUT IT REMINDS ME OF A SAD TIME WHEN MY CONNECTIONS TO MY ANIMAL SPIRITS AND THE EMERALD DREAM WERE SEVERED.
I'M FREE IN WAYS I HAVEN'T BEEN IN YEARS. FOR NOW, THAT'S ENOUGH.
I HOPE YOU'RE RIGHT.
BROLL BEARMANTLE, THE HIGH PRIESTESS TYRANDE WHISPERWIND WOULD SPEAK WITH YOU!

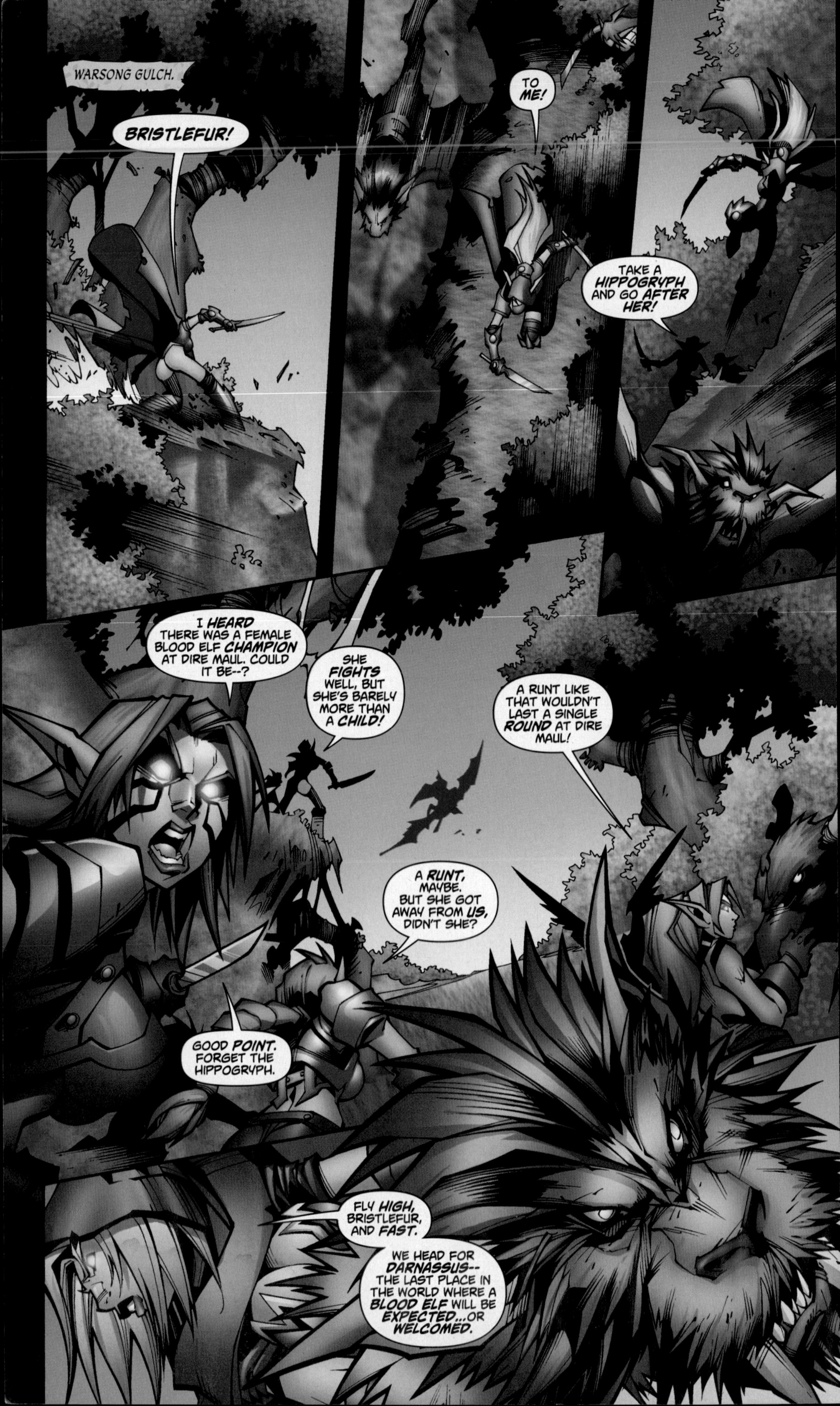
WARSONG GULCH.
BRISTLEFUR!
TO ME!
TAKE A HIPPOGRYPH AND GO AFTER HER!
I HEARD THERE WAS A FEMALE BLOOD ELF CHAMPION AT DIRE MAUL. COULD IT BE--?
SHE FIGHTS WELL, BUT SHE'S BARELY MORE THAN A CHILD!
A RUNT LIKE THAT WOULDN'T LAST A SINGLE ROUND AT DIRE MAUL!
A RUNT, MAYBE. BUT SHE GOT AWAY FROM US, DIDN'T SHE?
GOOD POINT. FORGET THE HIPPOGRYPH.
FLY HIGH, BRISTLEFUR, AND FAST.
WE HEAD FOR DARNASSUS-- THE LAST PLACE IN THE WORLD WHERE A BLOOD ELF WILL BE EXPECTED...OR WELCOMED.

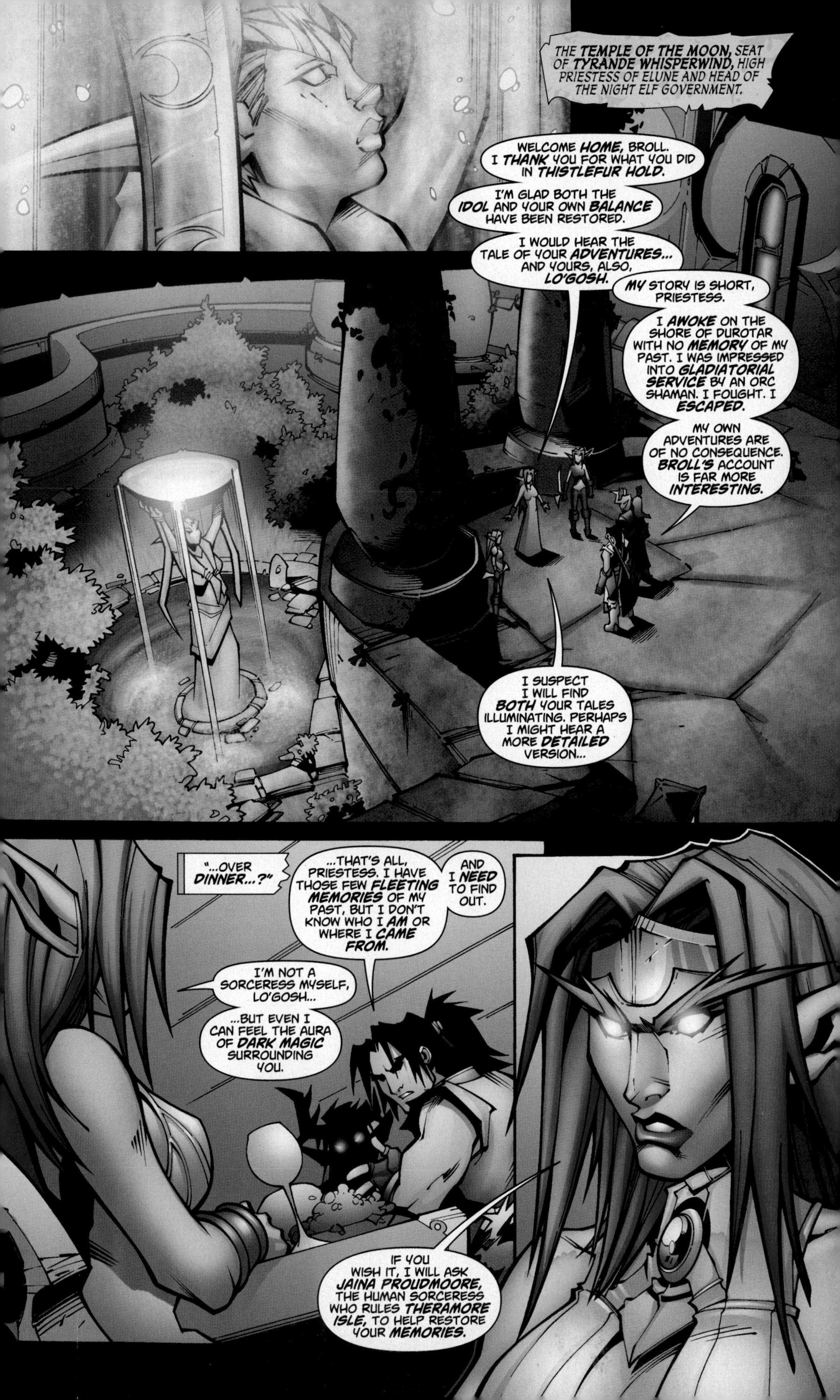
THE TEMPLE OF THE MOON, SEAT OF TYRANDE WHISPERWIND, HIGH PRIESTESS OF ELUNE AND HEAD OF THE NIGHT ELF GOVERNMENT.
WELCOME HOME, BROLL. I THANK YOU FOR WHAT YOU DID IN THISTLEFUR HOLD.
I'M GLAD BOTH THE IDOL AND YOUR OWN BALANCE HAVE BEEN RESTORED.
I WOULD HEAR THE TALE OF YOUR ADVENTURES... AND YOURS, ALSO, LO'GOSH.
MY STORY IS SHORT, PRIESTESS.
I AWOKE ON THE SHORE OF DUROTAR WITH NO MEMORY OF MY PAST. I WAS IMPRESSED INTO GLADIATORIAL SERVICE BY AN ORC SHAMAN. I FOUGHT. I ESCAPED.
MY OWN ADVENTURES ARE OF NO CONSEQUENCE. BROLL'S ACCOUNT IS FAR MORE INTERESTING.
I SUSPECT I WILL FIND BOTH YOUR TALES ILLUMINATING. PERHAPS I MIGHT HEAR A MORE DETAILED VERSION...
"...OVER DINNER...?"
...THAT'S ALL, PRIESTESS. I HAVE THOSE FEW FLEETING MEMORIES OF MY PAST, BUT I DON'T KNOW WHO I AM OR WHERE I CAME FROM.
AND I NEED TO FIND OUT.
I'M NOT A SORCERESS MYSELF, LO'GOSH...
...BUT EVEN I CAN FEEL THE AURA OF DARK MAGIC SURROUNDING YOU.
IF YOU WISH IT, I WILL ASK JAINA PROUDMOORE, THE HUMAN SORCERESS WHO RULES THERAMORE ISLE, TO HELP RESTORE YOUR MEMORIES.

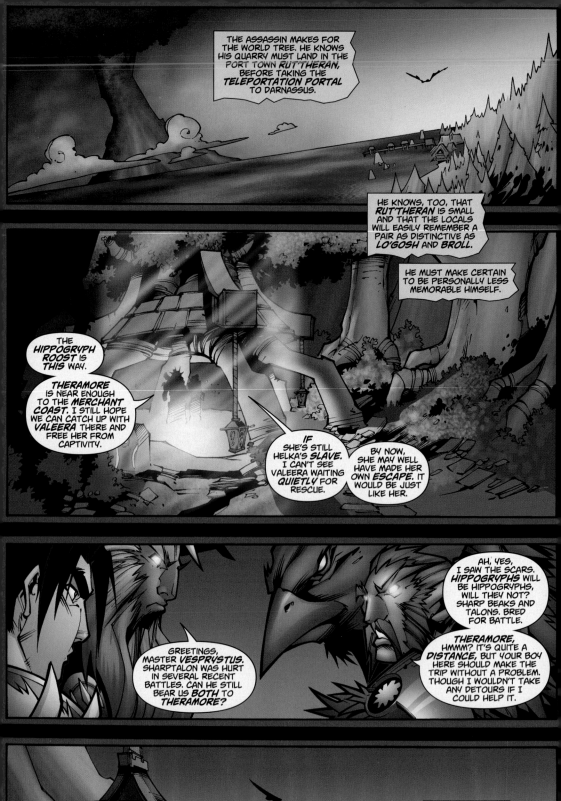

THE ASSASSIN MAKES FOR THE WORLD TREE. HE KNOWS HIS QUARRY MUST LAND IN THE PORT TOWN *RUT'THERAN*, BEFORE TAKING THE *TELEPORTATION PORTAL* TO DARNASSUS.

HE KNOWS, TOO, THAT *RUT'THERAN* IS SMALL AND THAT THE LOCALS WILL EASILY REMEMBER A PAIR AS DISTINCTIVE AS *LO'GOSH* AND *BROLL*.

HE MUST MAKE CERTAIN TO BE PERSONALLY LESS MEMORABLE HIMSELF.

THE *HIPPOGRYPH ROOST* IS *THIS* WAY.

THERAMORE IS NEAR ENOUGH TO THE *MERCHANT COAST*. I STILL HOPE WE CAN CATCH UP WITH *VALEERA* THERE AND FREE HER FROM CAPTIVITY.

IF SHE'S STILL HELKA'S *SLAVE*. I CAN'T SEE VALEERA WAITING *QUIETLY* FOR RESCUE.

BY NOW, SHE MAY WELL HAVE MADE HER OWN *ESCAPE*. IT WOULD BE JUST LIKE HER.

GREETINGS, MASTER *VESPRYSTUS*. SHARPTALON WAS HURT IN SEVERAL RECENT BATTLES. CAN HE STILL BEAR US *BOTH* TO *THERAMORE*?

AH, YES, I SAW THE SCARS. *HIPPOGRYPHS* WILL BE HIPPOGRYPHS, WILL THEY NOT? SHARP BEAKS AND TALONS. BRED FOR BATTLE.

THERAMORE, HMMM? IT'S QUITE A *DISTANCE*, BUT YOUR BOY HERE SHOULD MAKE THE TRIP WITHOUT A PROBLEM. THOUGH I WOULDN'T TAKE ANY DETOURS IF I COULD HELP IT.

MOMENTS LATER, SHARPTALON IS AIRBORNE...

...AS SOMEWHERE BELOW IN RUT'THERAN, AN EBON GRYPHON TOUCHES DOWN IN THE MAIN SQUARE.

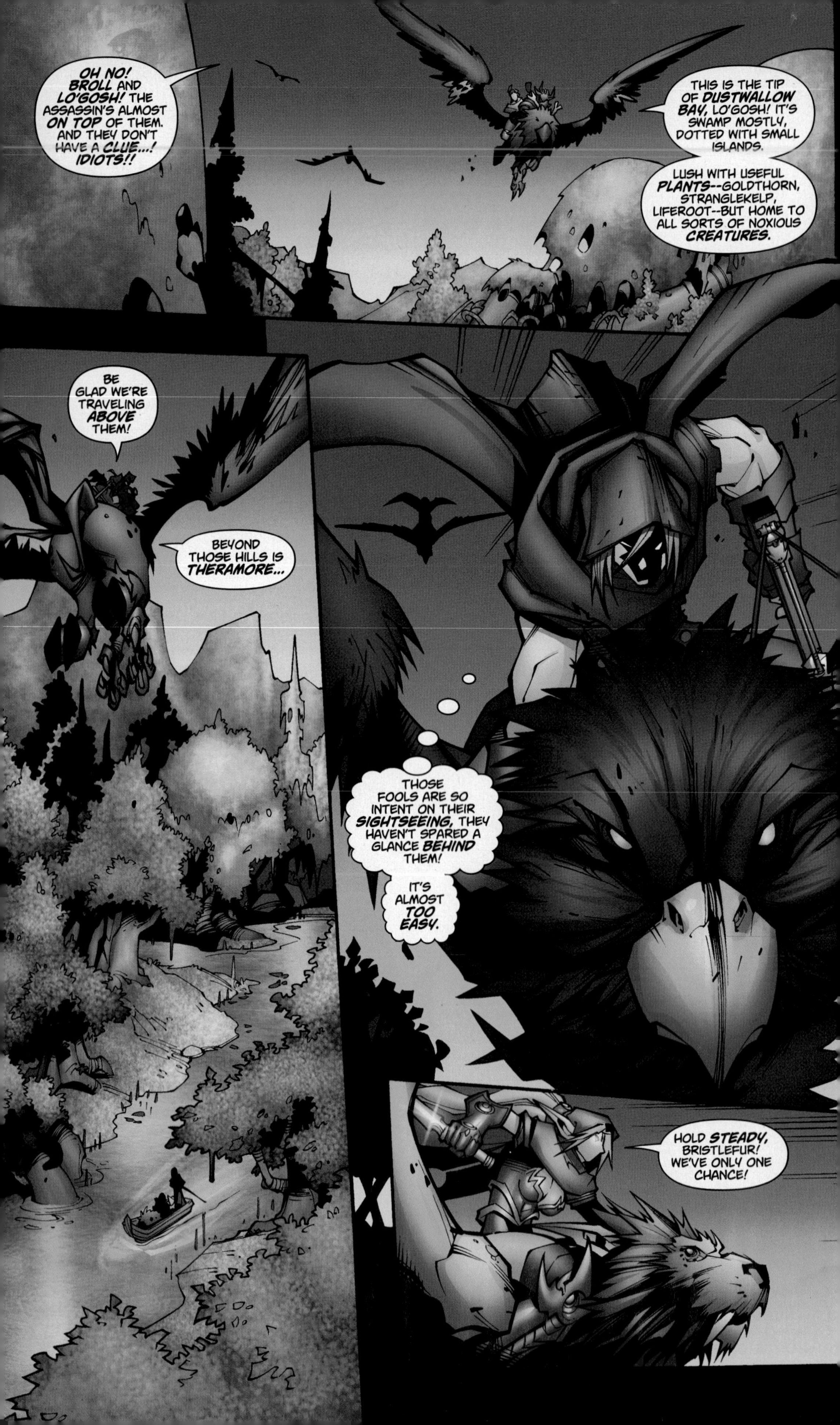
OH NO! BROLL AND LO'GOSH! THE ASSASSIN'S ALMOST ON TOP OF THEM. AND THEY DON'T HAVE A CLUE...! IDIOTS!!
THIS IS THE TIP OF DUSTWALLOW BAY, LO'GOSH! IT'S SWAMP MOSTLY, DOTTED WITH SMALL ISLANDS.
LUSH WITH USEFUL PLANTS--GOLDTHORN, STRANGLEKELP, LIFEROOT--BUT HOME TO ALL SORTS OF NOXIOUS CREATURES.
BE GLAD WE'RE TRAVELING ABOVE THEM!
BEYOND THOSE HILLS IS THERAMORE...
THOSE FOOLS ARE SO INTENT ON THEIR SIGHTSEEING, THEY HAVEN'T SPARED A GLANCE BEHIND THEM!
IT'S ALMOST TOO EASY.
HOLD STEADY, BRISTLEFUR! WE'VE ONLY ONE CHANCE!

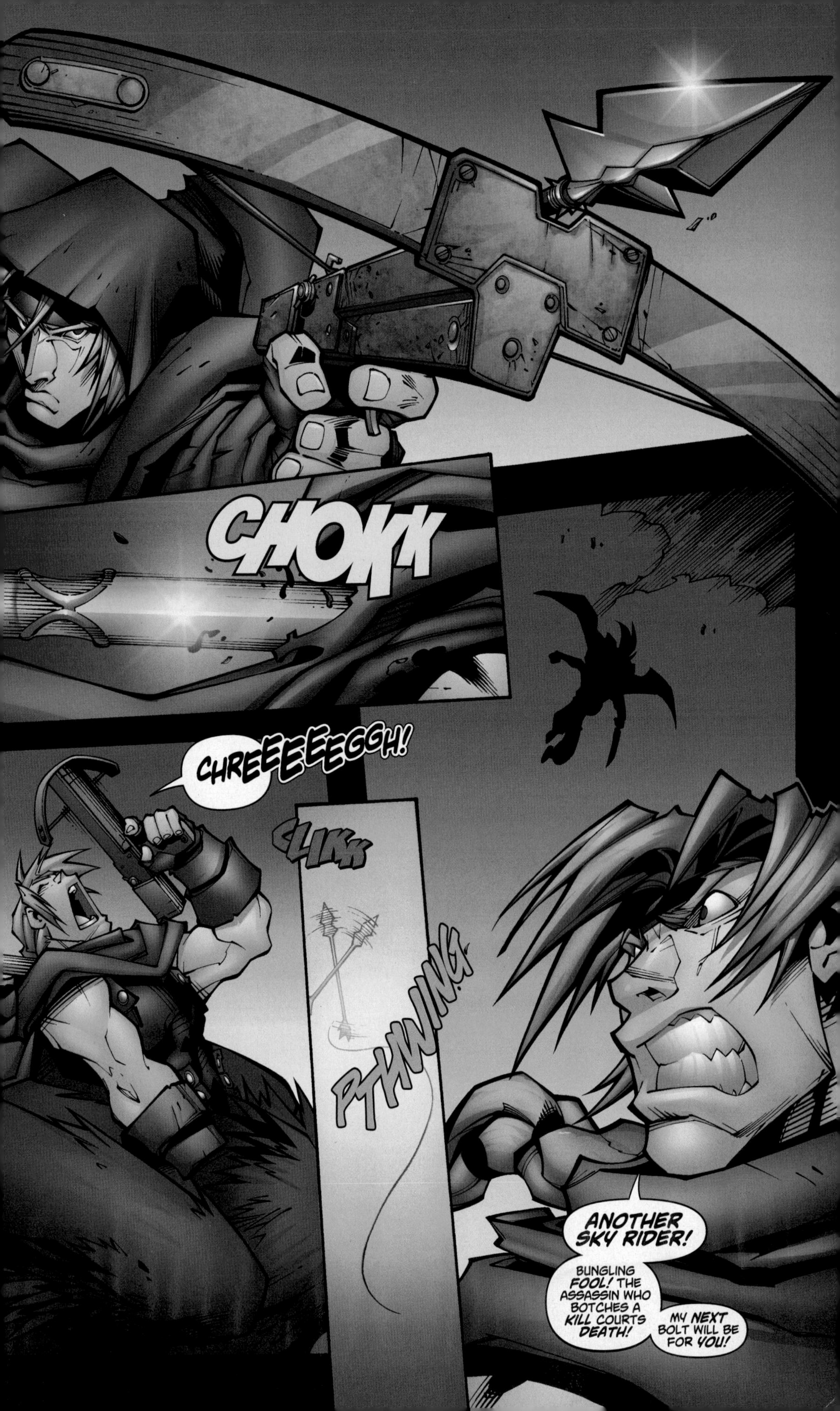
CHOKK
CHREEEEEEGGH!
CLIKK
PTHWING
ANOTHER SKY RIDER!
BUNGLING FOOL! THE ASSASSIN WHO BOTCHES A KILL COURTS DEATH!
MY NEXT BOLT WILL BE FOR YOU!

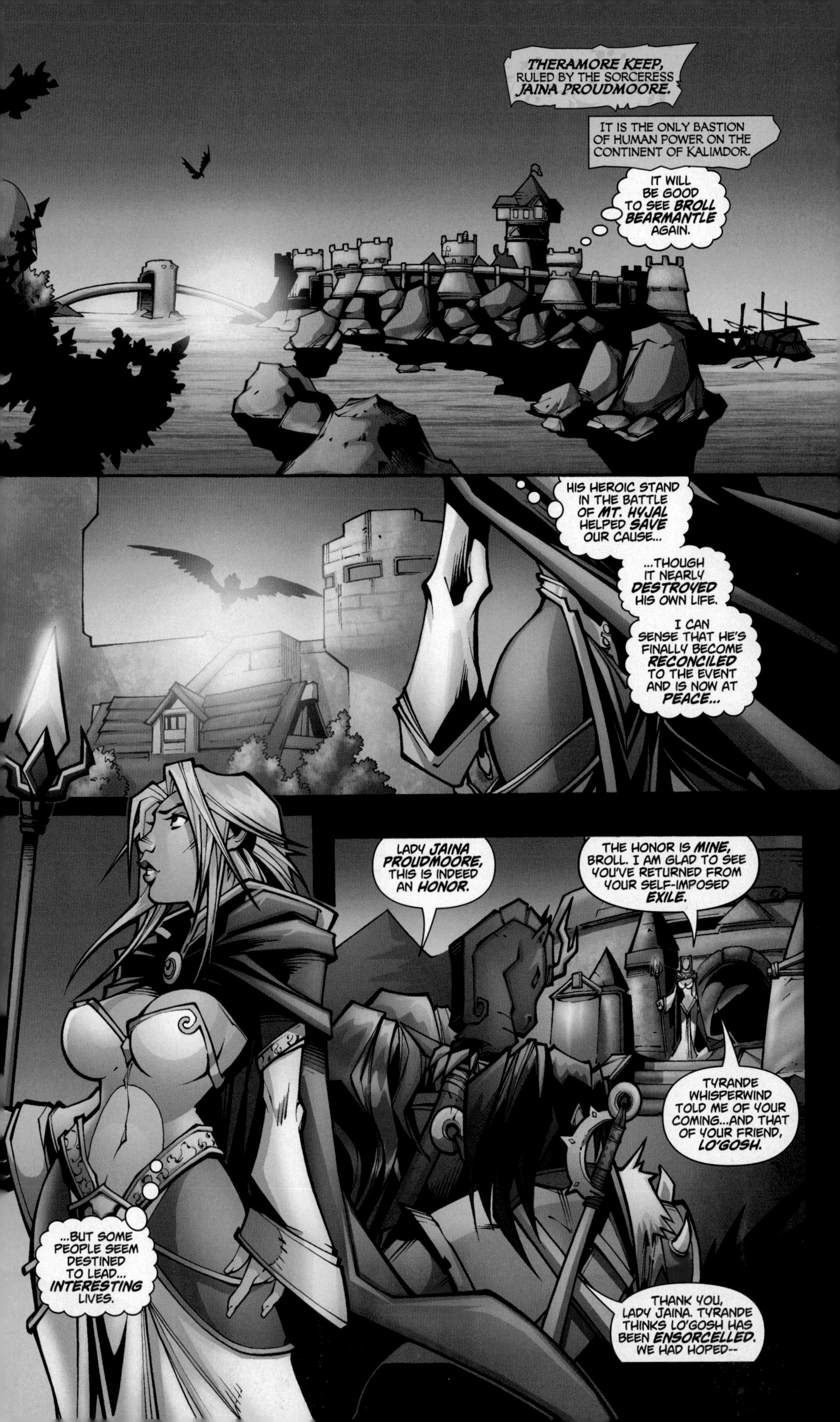
THERAMORE KEEP, RULED BY THE SORCERESS JAINA PROUDMOORE.
IT IS THE ONLY BASTION OF HUMAN POWER ON THE CONTINENT OF KALIMDOR.
IT WILL BE GOOD TO SEE BROLL BEARMANTLE AGAIN.
HIS HEROIC STAND IN THE BATTLE OF MT. HYJAL HELPED SAVE OUR CAUSE...
...THOUGH IT NEARLY DESTROYED HIS OWN LIFE.
I CAN SENSE THAT HE'S FINALLY BECOME RECONCILED TO THE EVENT AND IS NOW AT PEACE...
LADY JAINA PROUDMOORE, THIS IS INDEED AN HONOR.
THE HONOR IS MINE, BROLL. I AM GLAD TO SEE YOU'VE RETURNED FROM YOUR SELF-IMPOSED EXILE.
TYRANDE WHISPERWIND TOLD ME OF YOUR COMING...AND THAT OF YOUR FRIEND, LO'GOSH.
...BUT SOME PEOPLE SEEM DESTINED TO LEAD... INTERESTING LIVES.
THANK YOU, LADY JAINA. TYRANDE THINKS LO'GOSH HAS BEEN ENSORCELLED. WE HAD HOPED--

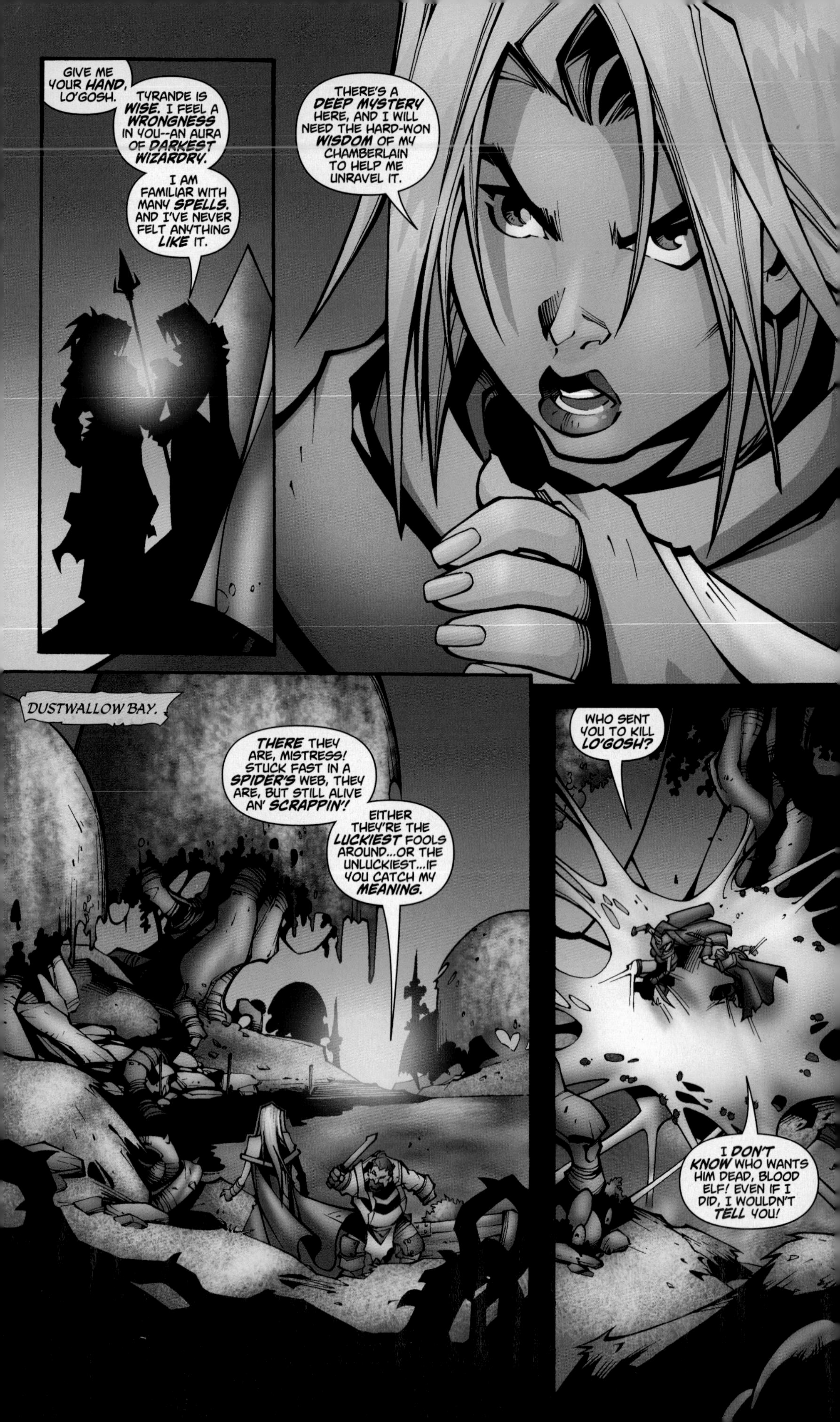
GIVE ME YOUR HAND, LO'GOSH.
TYRANDE IS WISE. I FEEL A WRONGNESS IN YOU--AN AURA OF DARKEST WIZARDRY.
I AM FAMILIAR WITH MANY SPELLS. AND I'VE NEVER FELT ANYTHING LIKE IT.
THERE'S A DEEP MYSTERY HERE, AND I WILL NEED THE HARD-WON WISDOM OF MY CHAMBERLAIN TO HELP ME UNRAVEL IT.
DUSTWALLOW BAY.
THERE THEY ARE, MISTRESS! STUCK FAST IN A SPIDER'S WEB, THEY ARE, BUT STILL ALIVE AN' SCRAPPIN'!
EITHER THEY'RE THE LUCKIEST FOOLS AROUND...OR THE UNLUCKIEST...IF YOU CATCH MY MEANING.
WHO SENT YOU TO KILL LO'GOSH?
I DON'T KNOW WHO WANTS HIM DEAD, BLOOD ELF! EVEN IF I DID, I WOULDN'T TELL YOU!

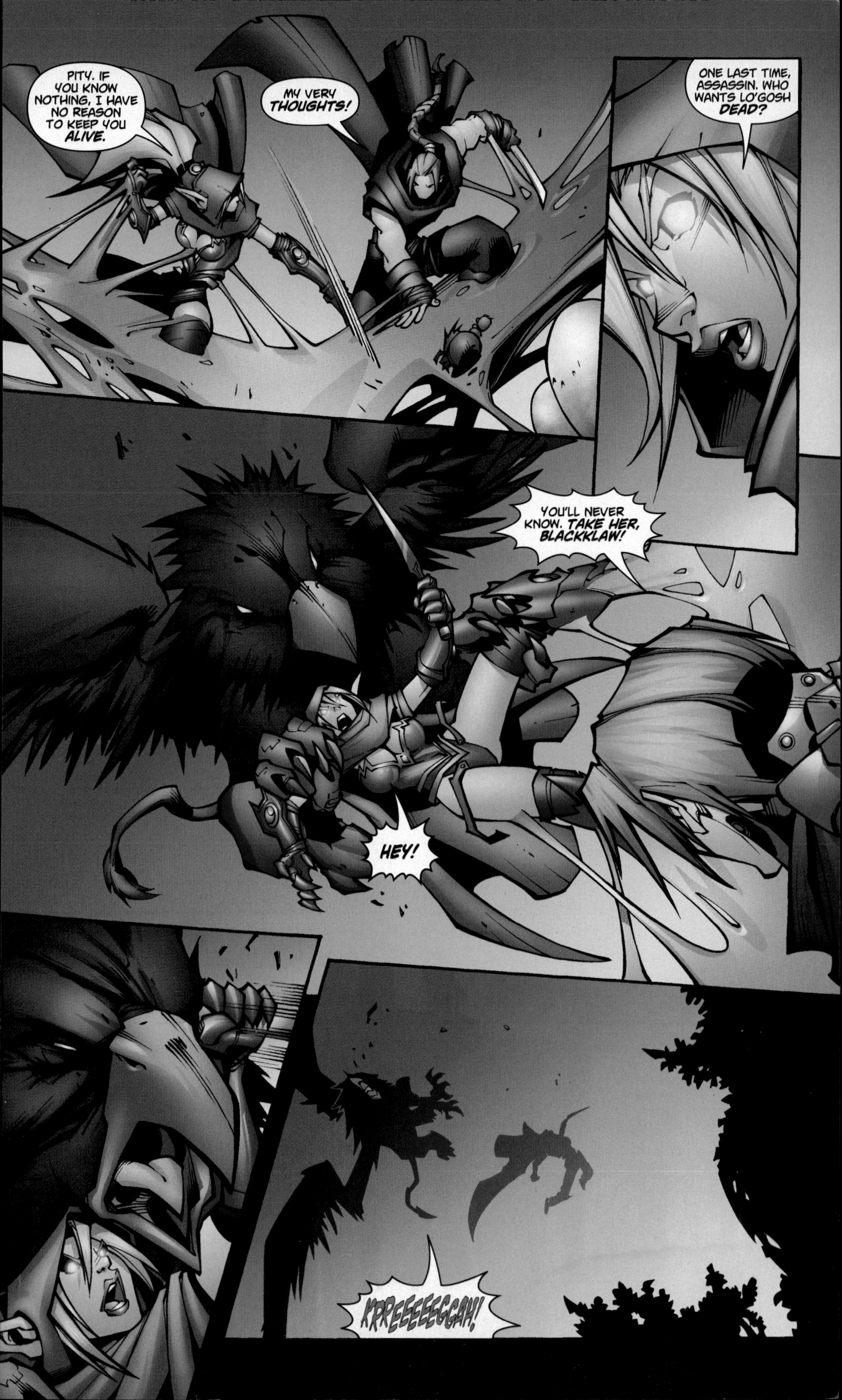
PITY. IF YOU KNOW NOTHING, I HAVE NO REASON TO KEEP YOU ALIVE.
MY VERY THOUGHTS!
ONE LAST TIME, ASSASSIN. WHO WANTS LO'GOSH DEAD?
YOU'LL NEVER KNOW. TAKE HER, BLACKKLAW!
HEY!
KRREEEEEEGGAH!

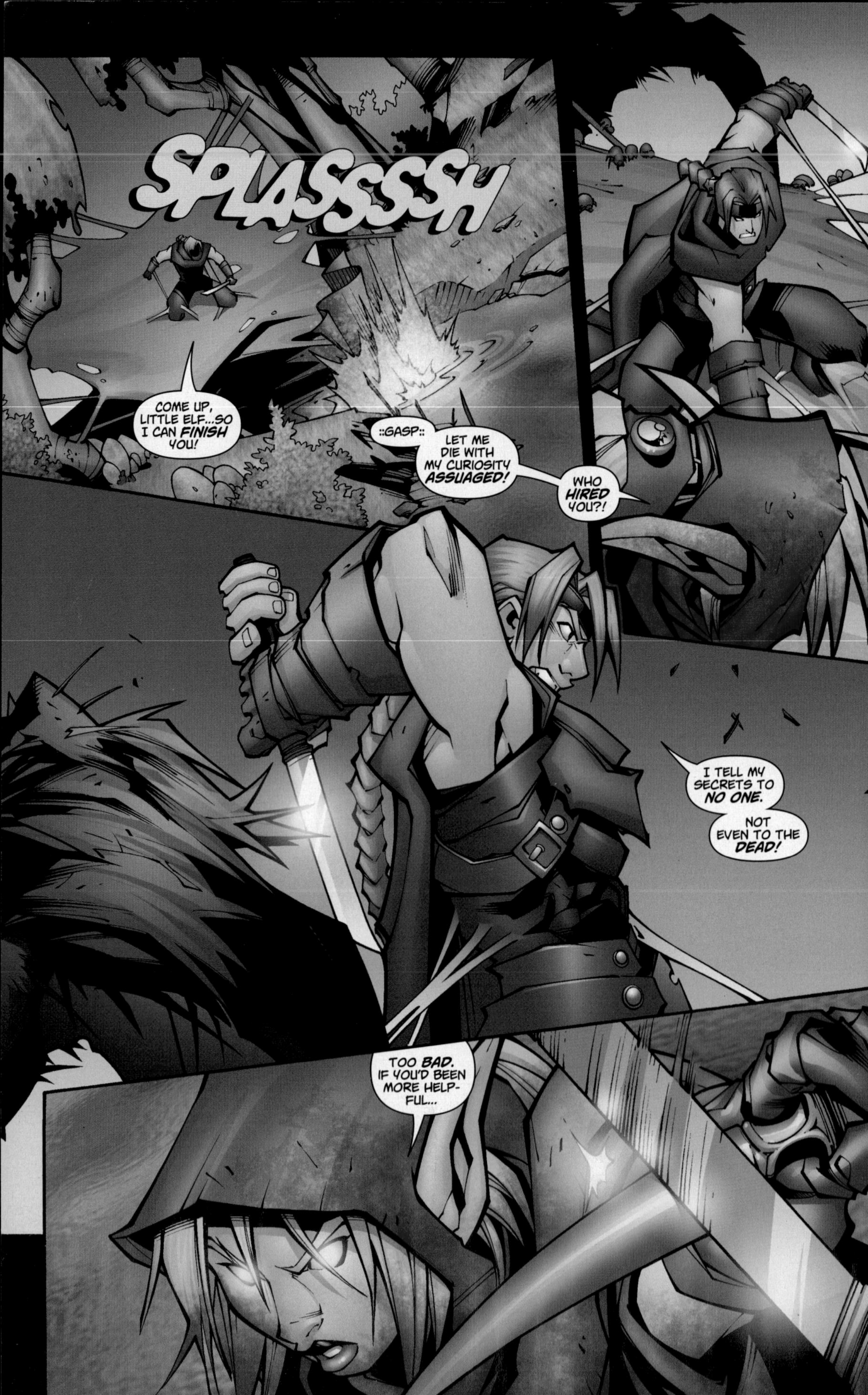
SPLASSSSH
COME UP, LITTLE ELF...SO I CAN FINISH YOU!
::GASP::
LET ME DIE WITH MY CURIOSITY ASSUAGED!
WHO HIRED YOU?!
I TELL MY SECRETS TO NO ONE.
NOT EVEN TO THE DEAD!
TOO BAD. IF YOU'D BEEN MORE HELP-FUL...

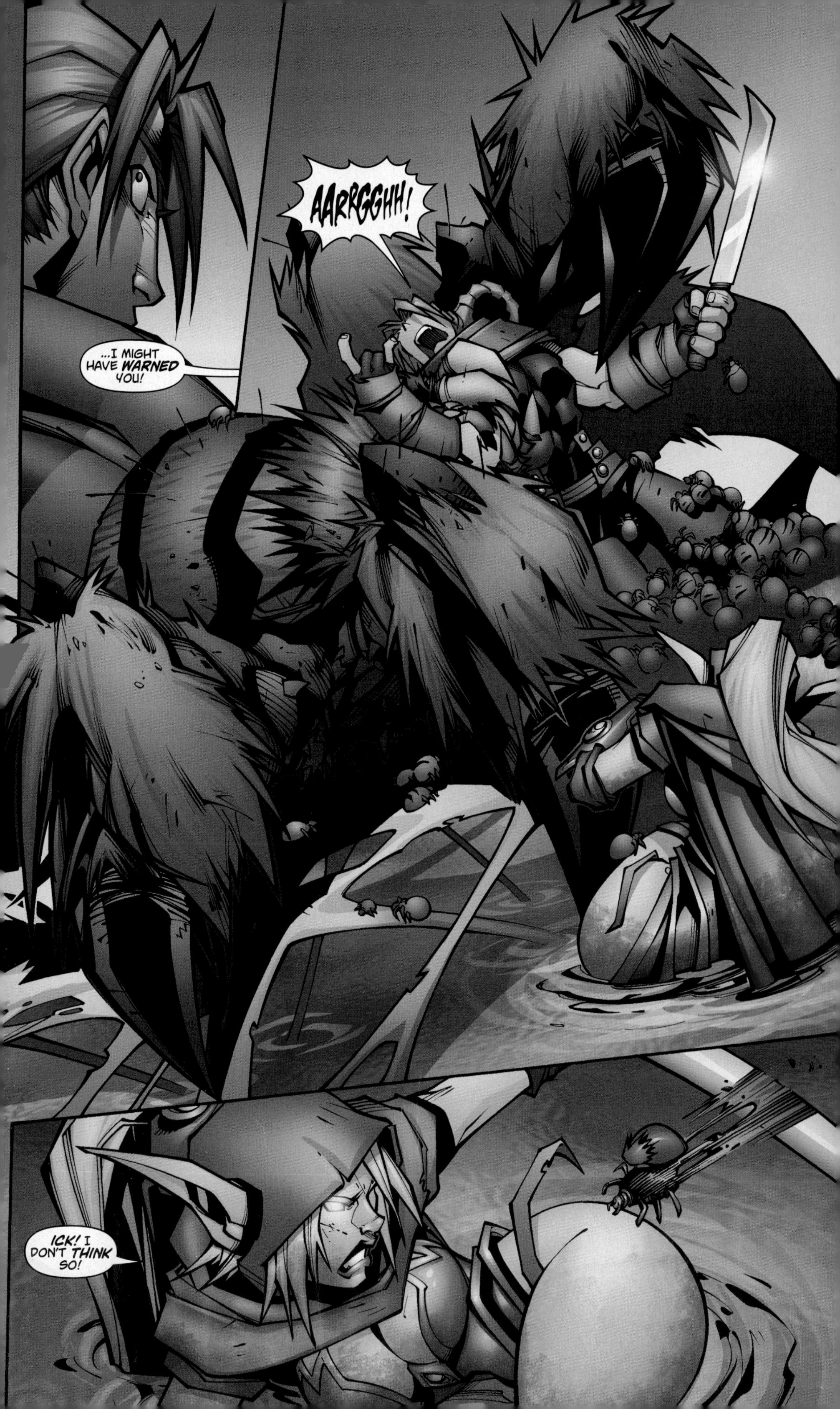
...I MIGHT HAVE WARNED YOU!
AARRGGHH!
ICK! I DON'T THINK SO!

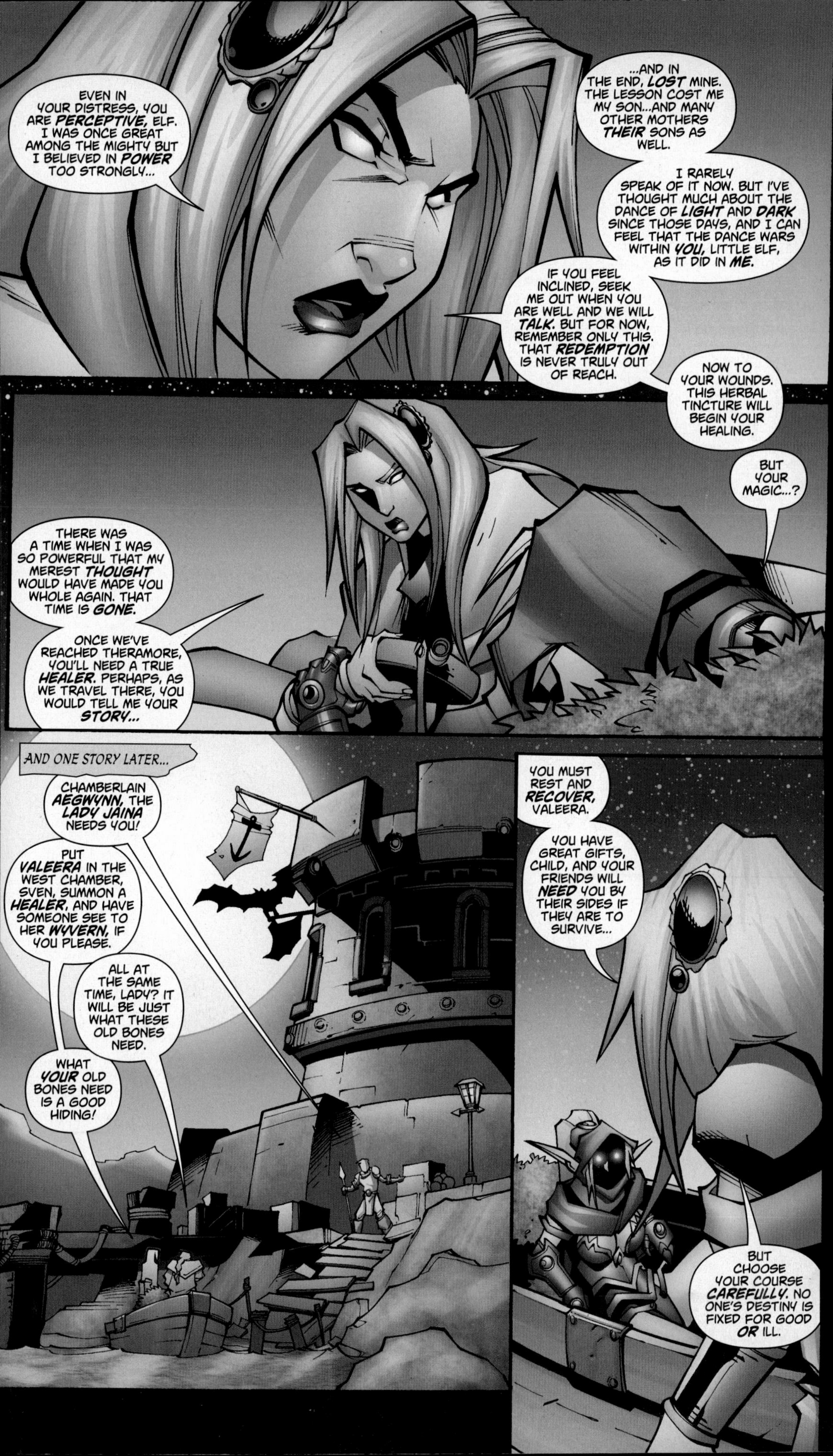
EVEN IN YOUR DISTRESS, YOU ARE PERCEPTIVE, ELF. I WAS ONCE GREAT AMONG THE MIGHTY BUT I BELIEVED IN POWER TOO STRONGLY...
...AND IN THE END, LOST MINE. THE LESSON COST ME MY SON...AND MANY OTHER MOTHERS THEIR SONS AS WELL.
I RARELY SPEAK OF IT NOW. BUT I'VE THOUGHT MUCH ABOUT THE DANCE OF LIGHT AND DARK SINCE THOSE DAYS, AND I CAN FEEL THAT THE DANCE WARS WITHIN YOU, LITTLE ELF, AS IT DID IN ME.
IF YOU FEEL INCLINED, SEEK ME OUT WHEN YOU ARE WELL AND WE WILL TALK. BUT FOR NOW, REMEMBER ONLY THIS. THAT REDEMPTION IS NEVER TRULY OUT OF REACH.
NOW TO YOUR WOUNDS. THIS HERBAL TINCTURE WILL BEGIN YOUR HEALING.
BUT YOUR MAGIC...?
THERE WAS A TIME WHEN I WAS SO POWERFUL THAT MY MEREST THOUGHT WOULD HAVE MADE YOU WHOLE AGAIN. THAT TIME IS GONE.
ONCE WE'VE REACHED THERAMORE, YOU'LL NEED A TRUE HEALER. PERHAPS, AS WE TRAVEL THERE, YOU WOULD TELL ME YOUR STORY...
AND ONE STORY LATER...
CHAMBERLAIN AEGWYNN, THE LADY JAINA NEEDS YOU!
PUT VALEERA IN THE WEST CHAMBER, SVEN, SUMMON A HEALER, AND HAVE SOMEONE SEE TO HER WYVERN, IF YOU PLEASE.
ALL AT THE SAME TIME, LADY? IT WILL BE JUST WHAT THESE OLD BONES NEED.
WHAT YOUR OLD BONES NEED IS A GOOD HIDING!
YOU MUST REST AND RECOVER, VALEERA.
YOU HAVE GREAT GIFTS, CHILD, AND YOUR FRIENDS WILL NEED YOU BY THEIR SIDES IF THEY ARE TO SURVIVE...
BUT CHOOSE YOUR COURSE CAREFULLY. NO ONE'S DESTINY IS FIXED FOR GOOD OR ILL.

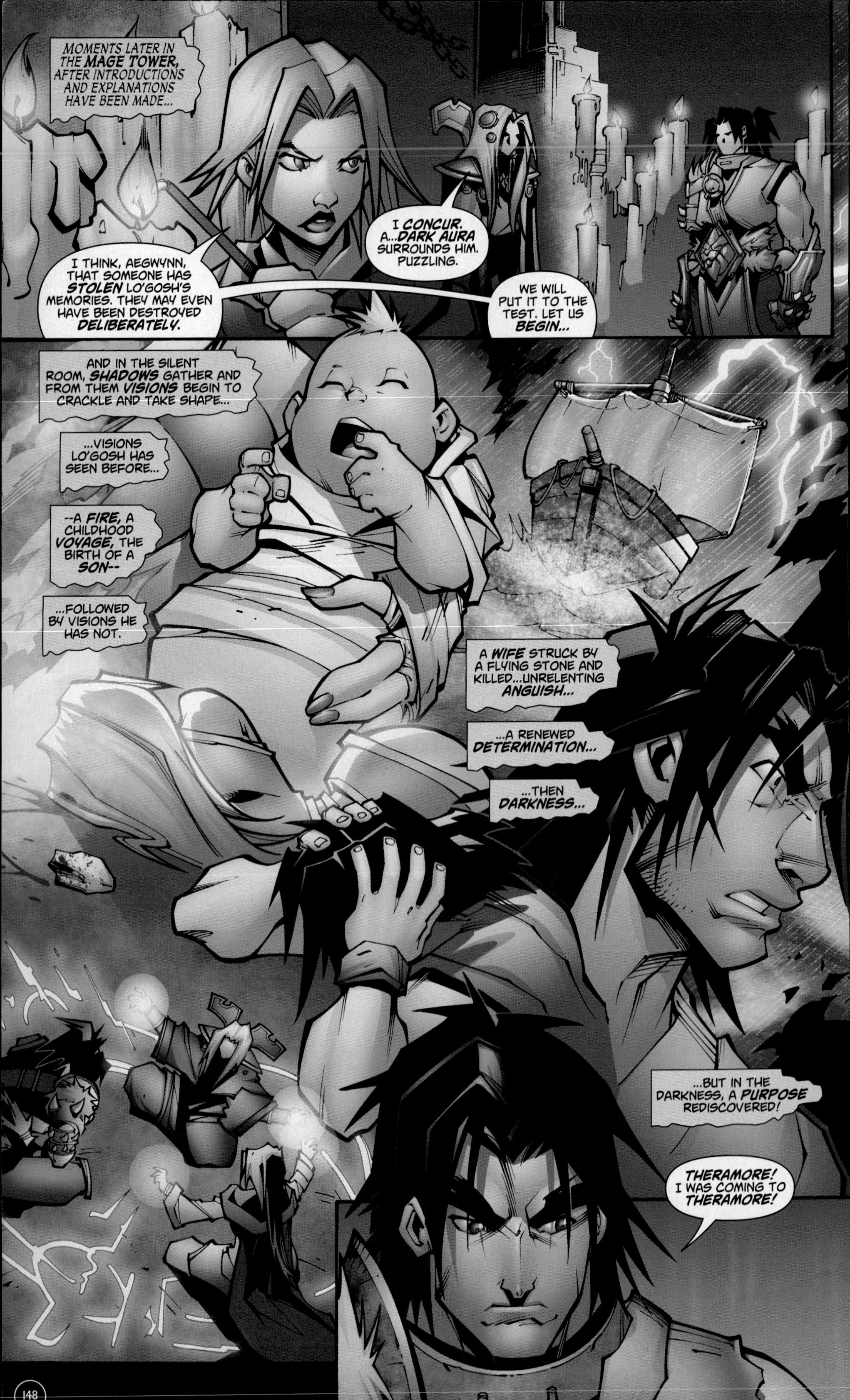

MOMENTS LATER IN THE MAGE TOWER, AFTER INTRODUCTIONS AND EXPLANATIONS HAVE BEEN MADE...
I THINK, AEGWYNN, THAT SOMEONE HAS STOLEN LO'GOSH'S MEMORIES. THEY MAY EVEN HAVE BEEN DESTROYED DELIBERATELY.
I CONCUR. A...DARK AURA SURROUNDS HIM. PUZZLING.
WE WILL PUT IT TO THE TEST. LET US BEGIN...
AND IN THE SILENT ROOM, SHADOWS GATHER AND FROM THEM VISIONS BEGIN TO CRACKLE AND TAKE SHAPE...
...VISIONS LO'GOSH HAS SEEN BEFORE...
--A FIRE, A CHILDHOOD VOYAGE, THE BIRTH OF A SON--
...FOLLOWED BY VISIONS HE HAS NOT.
A WIFE STRUCK BY A FLYING STONE AND KILLED...UNRELENTING ANGUISH...
...A RENEWED DETERMINATION...
...THEN DARKNESS...
...BUT IN THE DARKNESS, A PURPOSE REDISCOVERED!
THERAMORE! I WAS COMING TO THERAMORE!

CHAPTER 7

Issue #7 Cover
by Samwise Didier

Issue #7 Cover
by Ludo Lullabi, Sandra Hope
and Randy Mayor

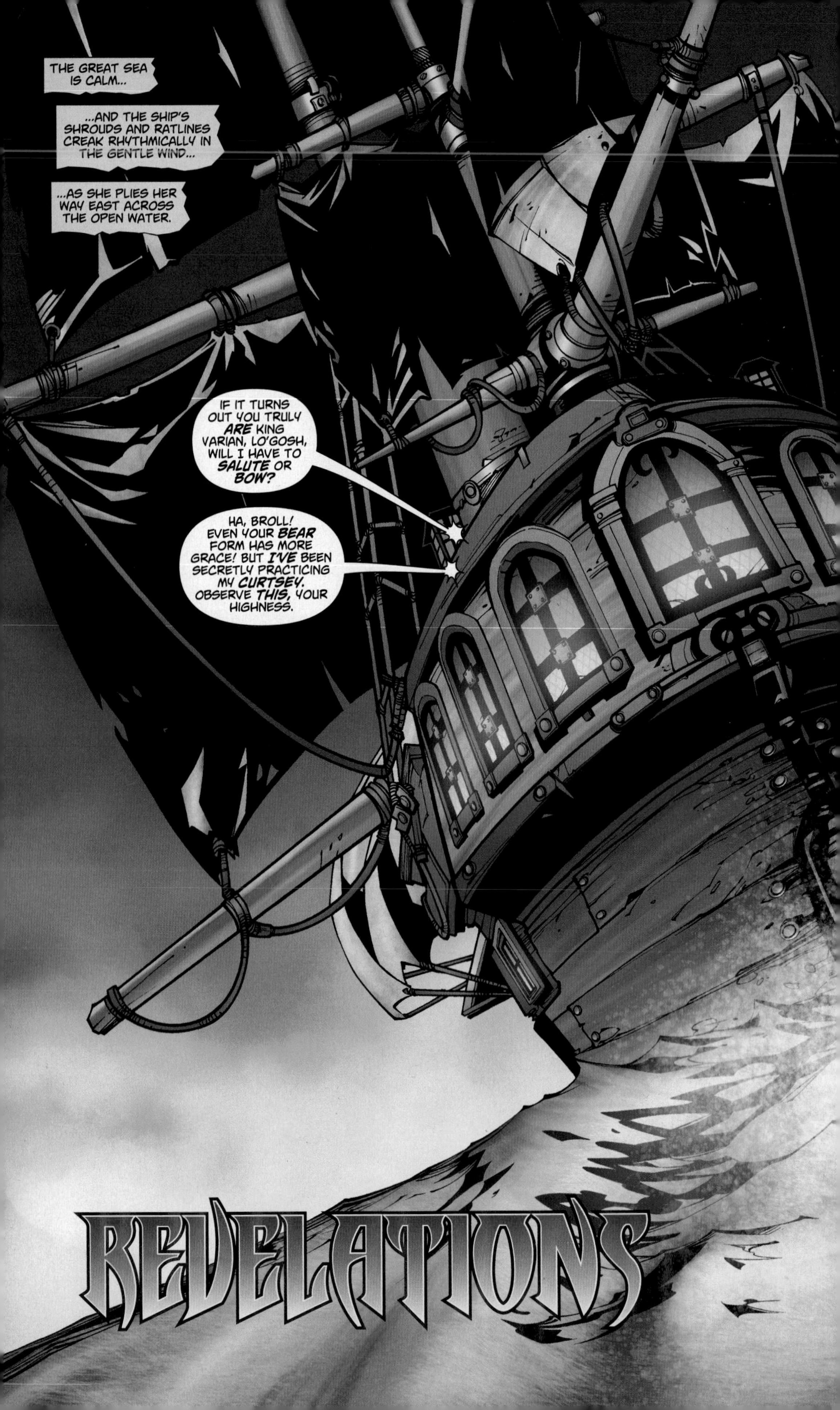

THE GREAT SEA IS CALM...
...AND THE SHIP'S SHROUDS AND RATLINES CREAK RHYTHMICALLY IN THE GENTLE WIND...
...AS SHE PLIES HER WAY EAST ACROSS THE OPEN WATER.
IF IT TURNS OUT YOU TRULY ARE KING VARIAN, LO'GOSH, WILL I HAVE TO SALUTE OR BOW?
HA, BROLL! EVEN YOUR BEAR FORM HAS MORE GRACE! BUT I'VE BEEN SECRETLY PRACTICING MY CURTSEY. OBSERVE THIS, YOUR HIGHNESS.
REVELATIONS

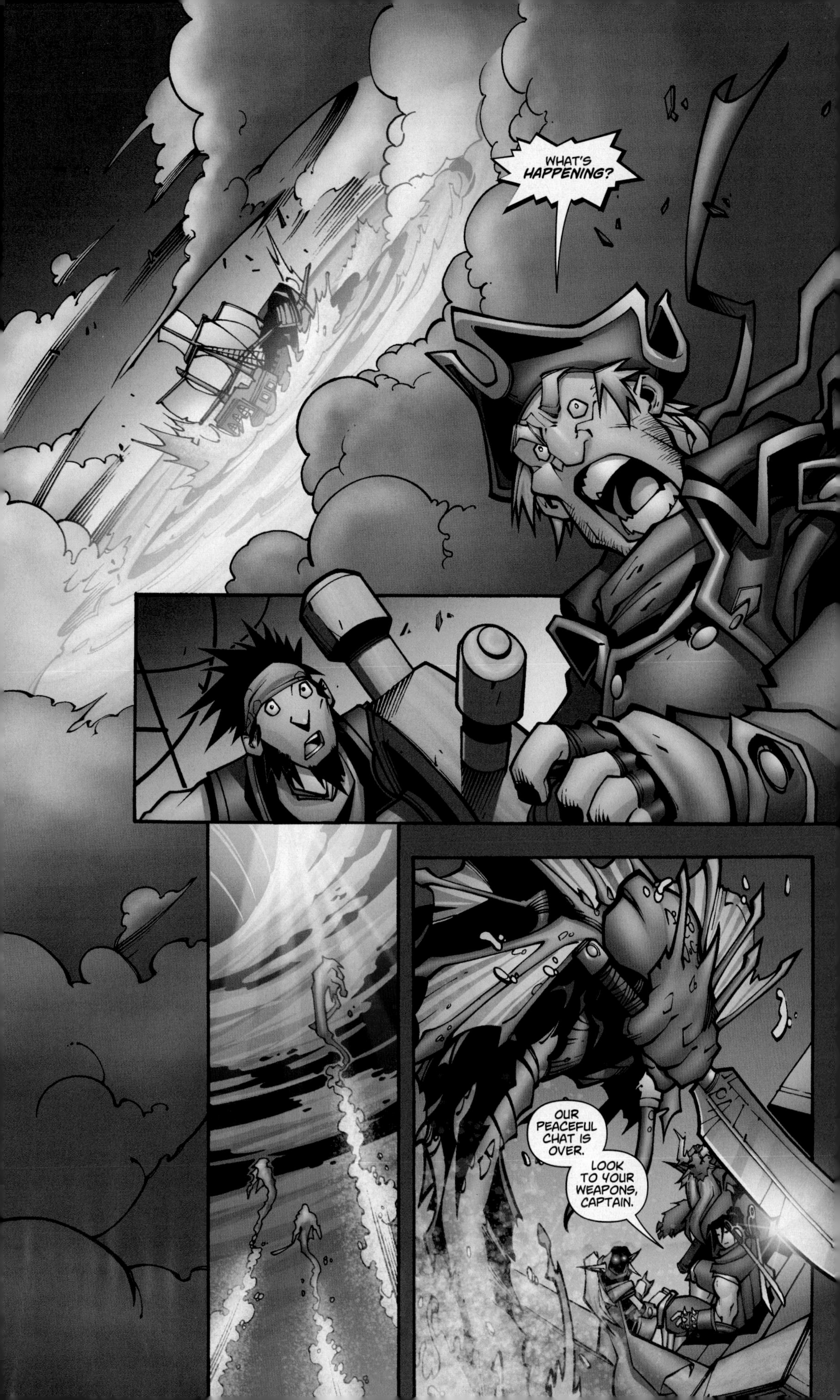
WHAT'S HAPPENING?
OUR PEACEFUL CHAT IS OVER.
LOOK TO YOUR WEAPONS, CAPTAIN.

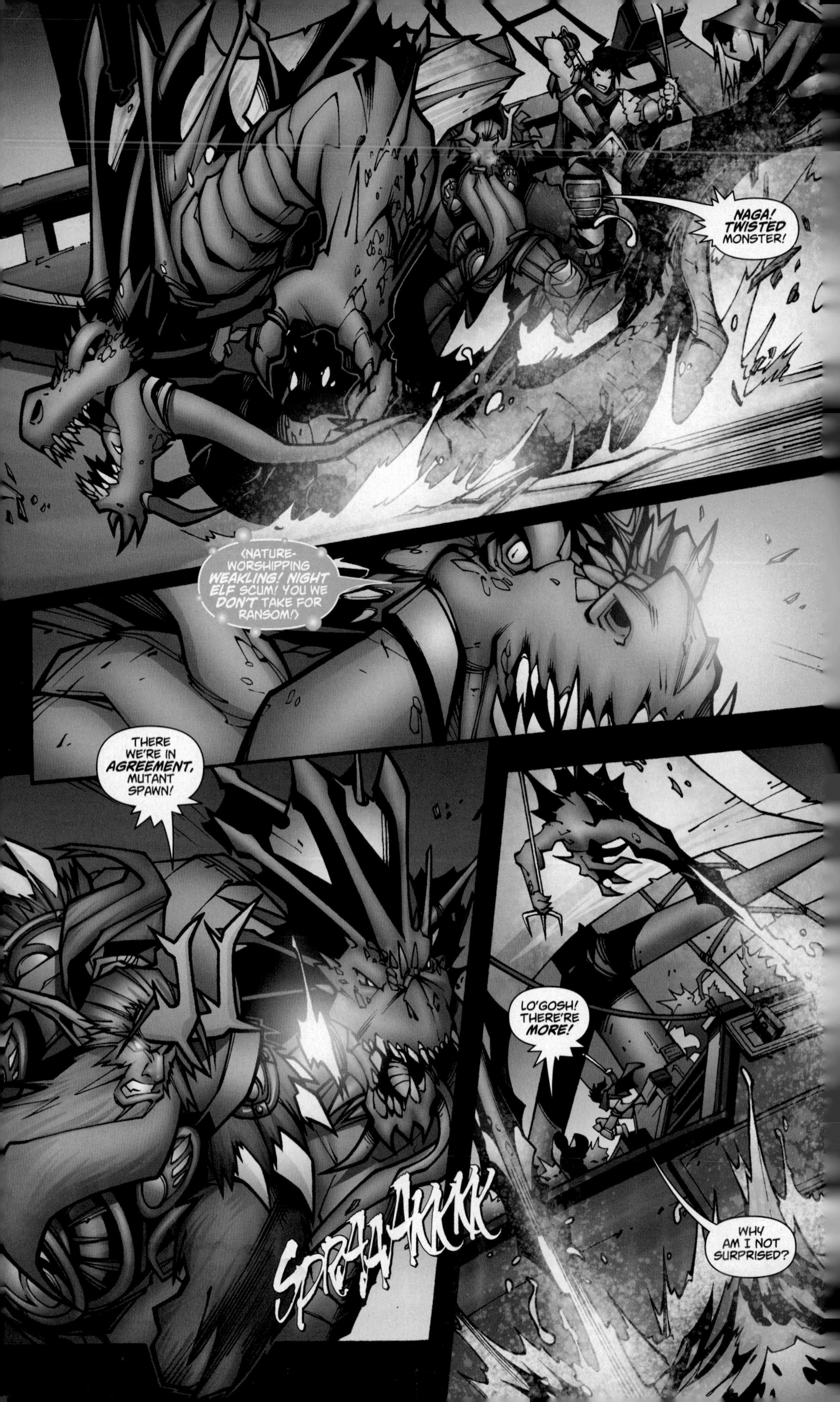
NAGA! TWISTED MONSTER!
‹NATURE-WORSHIPPING WEAKLING! NIGHT ELF SCUM! YOU WE DON'T TAKE FOR RANSOM!›
THERE WE'RE IN AGREEMENT, MUTANT SPAWN!
LO'GOSH! THERE'RE MORE!
WHY AM I NOT SURPRISED?
SPRAAAKKKK

ROARRARRR!!

SHWAK-DOOM

WHAT WAS *THAT!?*

THE *NAGA SIREN!* SHE'S TRYING TO DESTROY THE SHIP WITH *ARCANE ENERGY* BURSTS!

KEEP *AWAY* FROM HER, VALEERA!

ARCANE ENERGY IS *SINISTER*...A DANGEROUS *TEMPTATION* FOR YOU BECAUSE OF WHAT YOU *ARE.*

WE *BLOOD ELVES* AREN'T SO FEARFUL OF THE *ARCANE,* BROLL...OR SO CONVINCED OF ITS INNATE *EVIL.*

AND THAT'S THE PROBLEM! PROMISE ME, VALEERA! ABSORBING TOO MUCH ARCANE MAGIC WILL TEMPT YOU...

...TOWARDS EVEN DARKER MAGIC.

ALL RIGHT. I'LL DO AS YOU SAY, BUT--

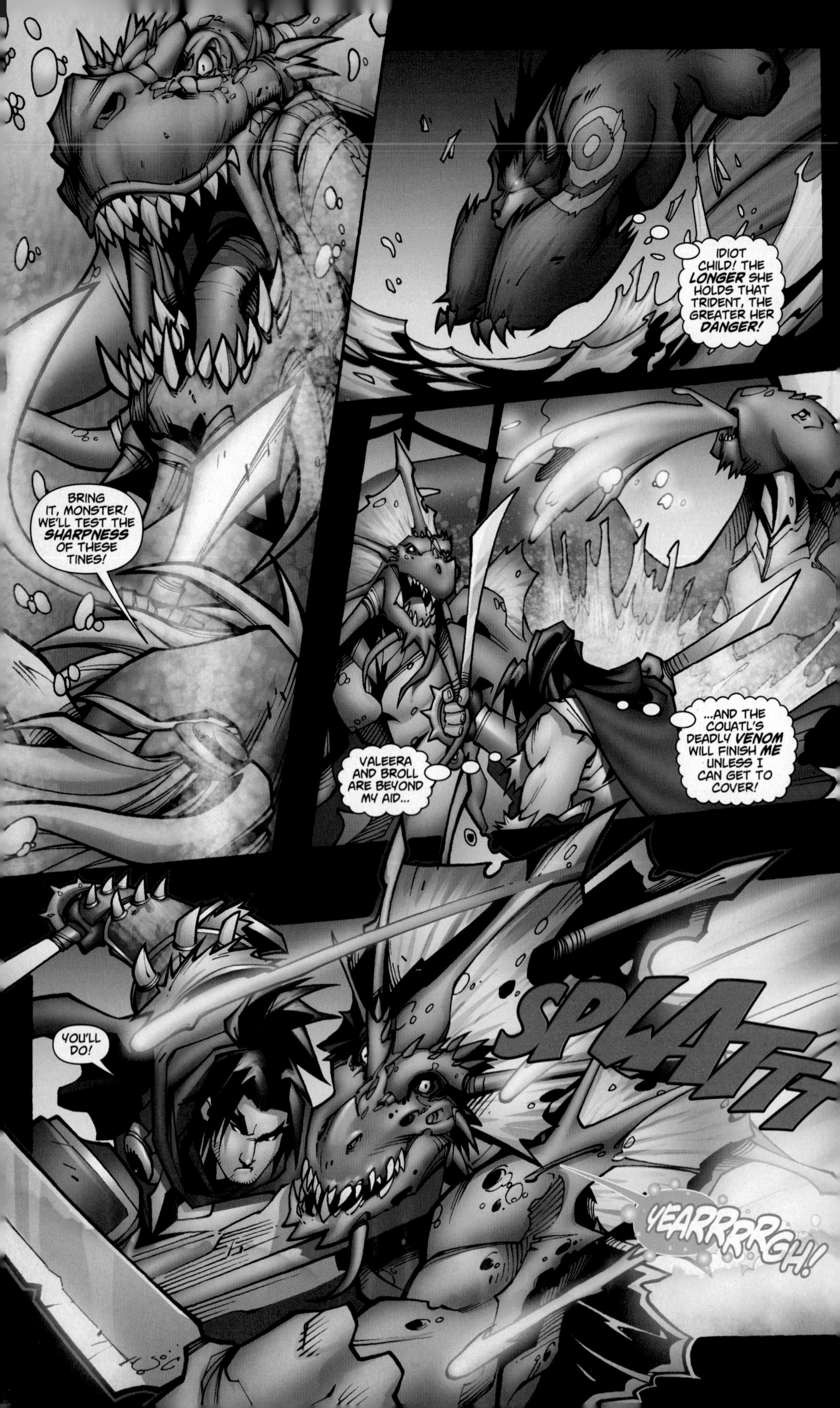
IDIOT CHILD! THE LONGER SHE HOLDS THAT TRIDENT, THE GREATER HER DANGER!
BRING IT, MONSTER! WE'LL TEST THE SHARPNESS OF THESE TINES!
VALEERA AND BROLL ARE BEYOND MY AID...
...AND THE COUATL'S DEADLY VENOM WILL FINISH ME UNLESS I CAN GET TO COVER!
YOU'LL DO!
SPLATTT
YEARRRRRGH!

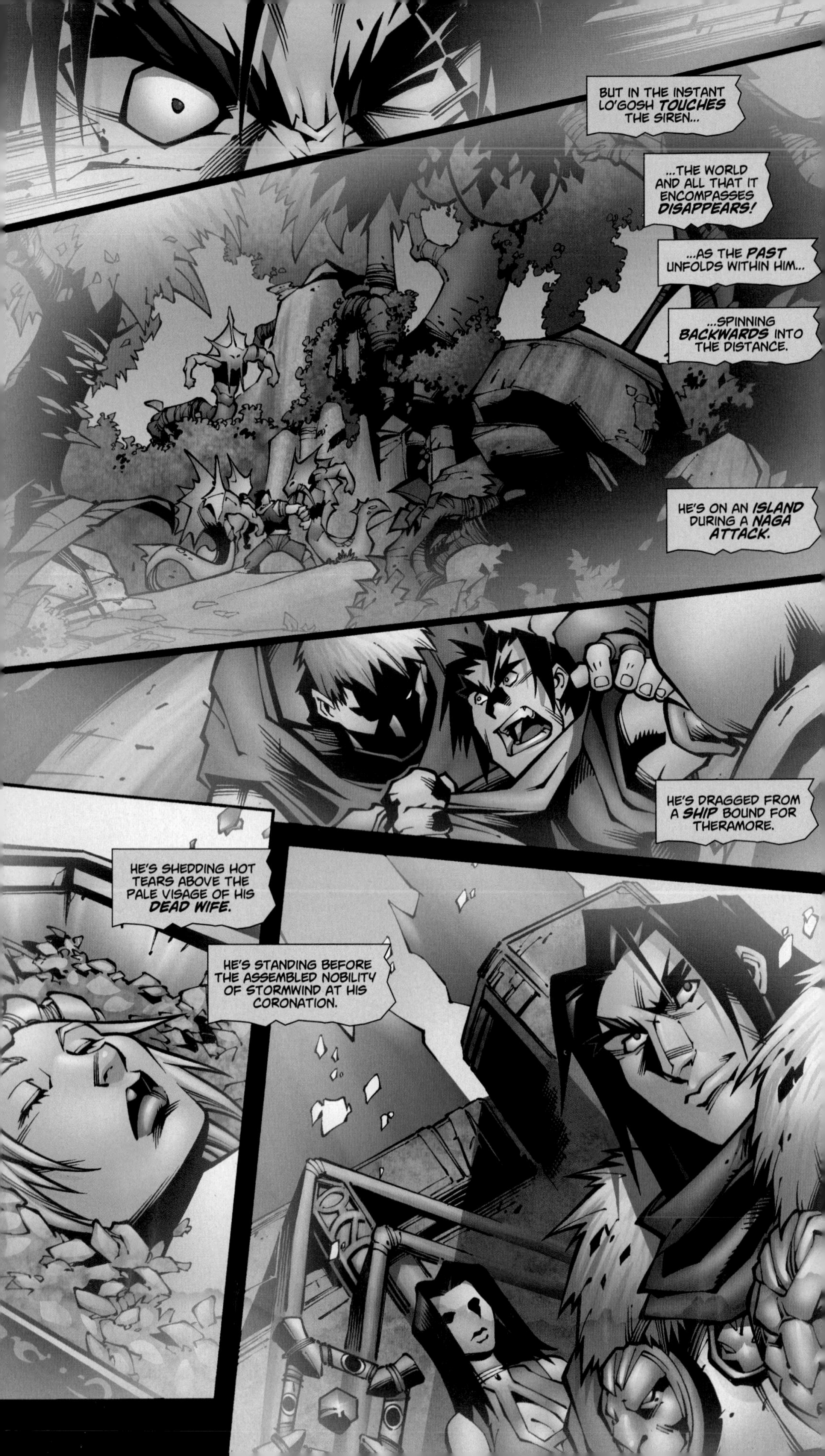

BUT IN THE INSTANT LO'GOSH TOUCHES THE SIREN...
...THE WORLD AND ALL THAT IT ENCOMPASSES DISAPPEARS!
...AS THE PAST UNFOLDS WITHIN HIM...
...SPINNING BACKWARDS INTO THE DISTANCE.
HE'S ON AN ISLAND DURING A NAGA ATTACK.
HE'S DRAGGED FROM A SHIP BOUND FOR THERAMORE.
HE'S SHEDDING HOT TEARS ABOVE THE PALE VISAGE OF HIS DEAD WIFE.
HE'S STANDING BEFORE THE ASSEMBLED NOBILITY OF STORMWIND AT HIS CORONATION.

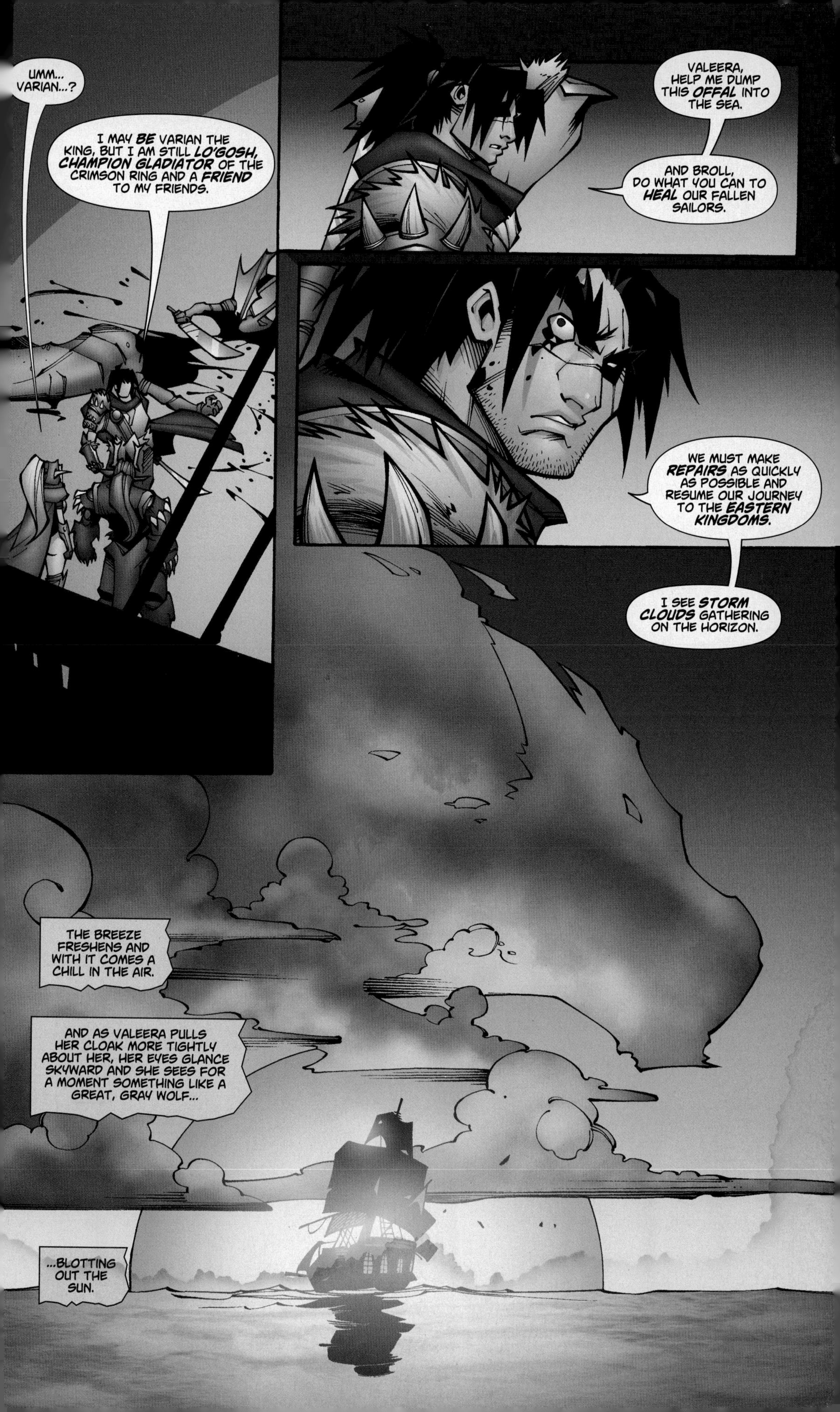
UMM... VARIAN...?
I MAY BE VARIAN THE KING, BUT I AM STILL LO'GOSH, CHAMPION GLADIATOR OF THE CRIMSON RING AND A FRIEND TO MY FRIENDS.
VALEERA, HELP ME DUMP THIS OFFAL INTO THE SEA.
AND BROLL, DO WHAT YOU CAN TO HEAL OUR FALLEN SAILORS.
WE MUST MAKE REPAIRS AS QUICKLY AS POSSIBLE AND RESUME OUR JOURNEY TO THE EASTERN KINGDOMS.
I SEE STORM CLOUDS GATHERING ON THE HORIZON.
THE BREEZE FRESHENS AND WITH IT COMES A CHILL IN THE AIR.
AND AS VALEERA PULLS HER CLOAK MORE TIGHTLY ABOUT HER, HER EYES GLANCE SKYWARD AND SHE SEES FOR A MOMENT SOMETHING LIKE A GREAT, GRAY WOLF...
...BLOTTING OUT THE SUN.

Sketches By
Ludo Lullabi

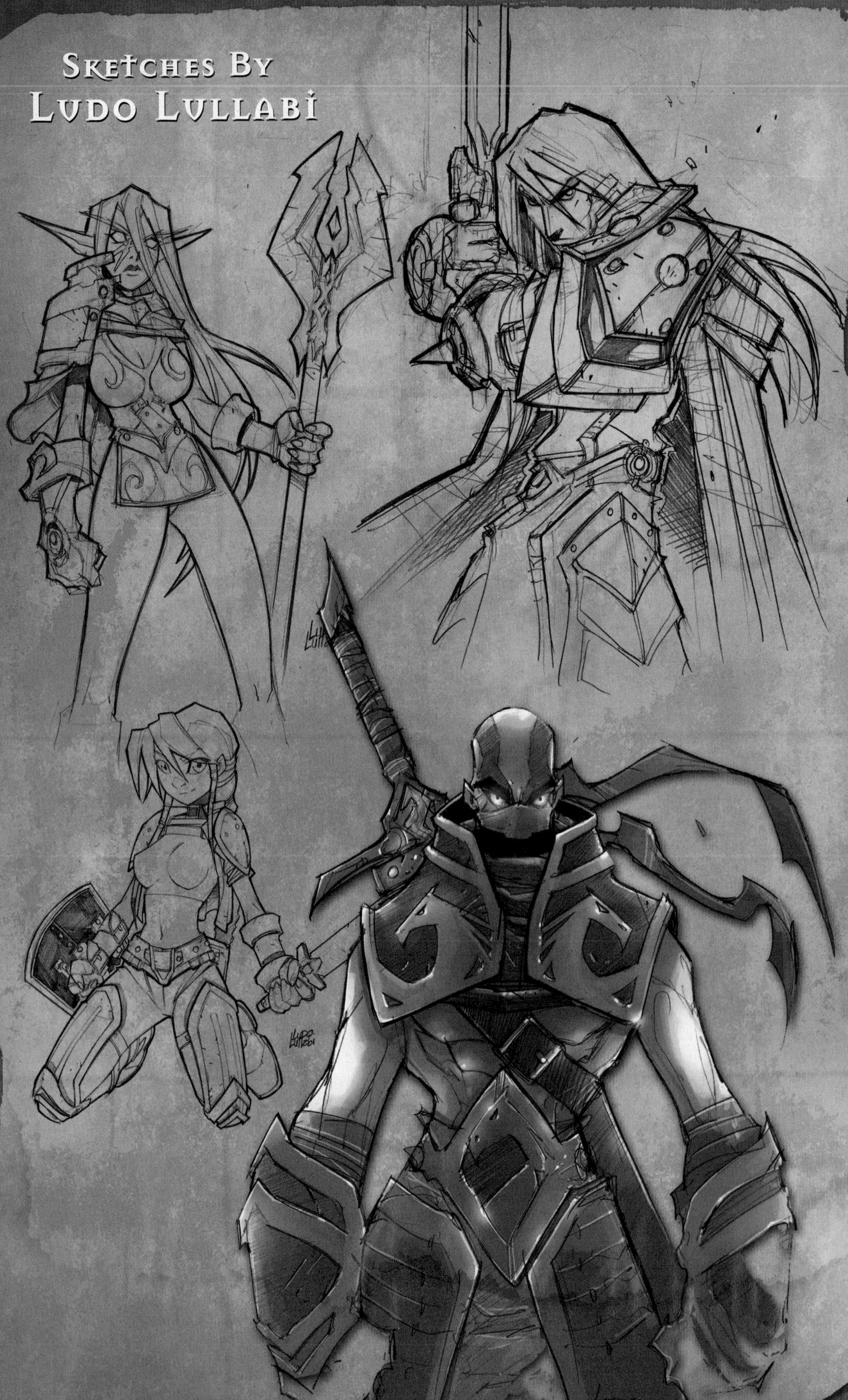

Stop Poking Me!

Lazy Peons

Quest

Orc Hero Required

Lazy Peons enters play exhausted.

Exhaust Lazy Peons to complete this quest.

Reward: Draw a card.

"Stop poking me!"

DARK PORTAL 303/319
©2007 UDC ©2007 Blizzard Entertainment, Inc.

Art by: Steve Ellis

- Each set contains new Loot™ cards to enhance your online character.
- Today's premier fantasy artists present an exciting new look at the World of Warcraft®.
- Compete in tournaments for exclusive World of Warcraft® prizes!

For more info and events, visit:

WOWTCG.COM/Peon

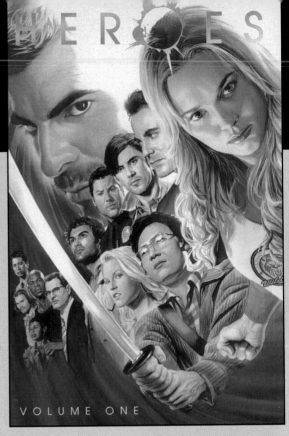